THE
PLOT

THE
PLOT

THE POLITICAL ASSASSINATION
OF BORIS JOHNSON

NADINE
DORRIES

HarperCollins*Publishers*

HarperCollins*Publishers*
1 London Bridge Street
London SE1 9GF

www.harpercollins.co.uk

HarperCollins*Publishers*
Macken House, 39/40 Mayor Street Upper
Dublin 1, D01 C9W8, Ireland

First published by HarperCollins*Publishers* 2023

1 3 5 7 9 10 8 6 4 2

A catalogue record of this book is
available from the British Library

HB ISBN 978-0-00-862342-5
TPB ISBN 978-0-00-862343-2

Printed and bound in the UK using 100%
renewable electricity at CPI Group (UK) Ltd

A nation can survive its fools, and even the ambitious.
But it cannot survive treason from within. An enemy at
the gates is less formidable, for he is known and carries
his banner openly, but the traitor moves amongst those
within the gate freely, his sly whispers rustling through
the alleys, heard in the very halls of government itself.
For the traitor appears not a traitor; he speaks in
accents familiar to his victims, and he wears their face
and their arguments, he appeals to the baseness that lies
deep in the hearts of all men. He rots the soul of a
nation, he works secretly and unknown in the night to
undermine the pillars of the city, he infects the body
politic so that it can no longer resist.

Marcus Tullius Cicero
Speaking to the Roman Senate during the Cataline War,
circa 40 BC

CONTENTS

FOREWORD

When I started to write this book, I thought that I would be telling the story of how Boris Johnson had been ousted from power. Instead, what I began to uncover were tales of a small group of men, most of them unelected and some totally unknown outside of a tight Westminster bubble, operating at the heart of the Conservative Party.

For twenty-five years or more they have set out to control the destiny of the Conservative Party. All too often it is their hand on the levers which rise ministers up and drop them back down and terminate their progress in the middle of a career-ending political storm – even if they are sitting prime ministers with an eighty-seat majority.

It is a story that has never been told. So not only is this book a shocking tale of corruption and unaccountable power, it is also a counter history of British political life in the twenty-first century.

We may not agree on which party or leader should be in power, but the point of democracy is that those disagreements are played out in public so that we as voters get to decide who we trust to keep us safe and free at the ballot box.

I was born in one of the poorest areas of Liverpool and was brought up to value my vote. It was drummed into me that in that vote lay hope and my individual power to contribute to change. Nothing in politics is as critical or as necessary as the defence of that principle.

Each person I interviewed during the process of writing this book, told me the same thing, that I was uncovering something dark and deeply undemocratic. And let me be very clear, I have talked to well over fifty people. From prime ministers and party leaders, through Cabinet ministers, to civil servants and back-benchers. From party grandees to special advisers. All of them had the same tale to tell and yet it is a tale you are entirely unaware of. Why is that?

THE HOUSE OF COMMONS

MONDAY 5 SEPTEMBER 2022

It is a political truth that opposition parties don't win General Elections, governments lose them. Every sensible Conservative MP knew that it would have taken more than a half-decent leader of the Labour Party to threaten our majority or to blow any individual MP off his or her perch in the heat and glare of a General Election campaign because, regardless of large parts of the media churning out negative coverage of the Prime Minister, who they would never forgive for delivering Brexit, we had the winner of an historic eighty-seat majority on our side. He was the person people in the street flocked to meet, to take their selfies with, and even when he met his most ardent adversaries, within moments they could not help softening their expression. A reluctant smile would hover as Boris enthusiastically shook an at-first-unwilling hand, looked them in the eye and asked with what was unmistakably genuine interest, 'How are you?' Despite themselves, they would tell him.

And now, he was gone.

On 12 December 2019, Boris Johnson won a landslide General Election victory that political analysts will use as a barometer for years to come. Was it really just down to Brexit? That is what many of the young and new MPs in the 2019 intake who voted to remove him would often tell me. Brexit is done, they would say in a manner that betrayed a worrying degree of naivety. 'That's what got Boris elected, Brexit. There's no big idea to vote for now, is there?'

'Who is it you want in his place, then?' I would ask and was invariably answered with a shrug of the shoulders.

My response was always that there was no Brexit on offer when Boris won the London Mayoral elections not once but twice in solidly Labour London, at a time when the Conservative Party was consistently seriously behind in the polls. We haven't won it back since he stood down, despite the party having been in power nationally since 2010.

In the General Election of 2019, Boris won a larger percentage of the vote than that secured by Tony Blair for the Labour land-slide in 1997. It was the biggest Conservative majority in forty years. At the time, the Labour Party had been the first opposition in living memory to be terrified of agreeing to a General Election and when they finally did, in the words of Boris, he sent a great big blue Tory ferret so far up Labour's left trouser leg that they were paralysed. We won seats that we could never have dreamt of winning and Labour had never imagined they could possibly lose. Fifty-four seats that had historically only ever wrapped an MP in a red ribbon to send him or her back to Westminster had dramatically turned from red to blue. Boris won an extraordin-ary once-in-a-generation victory, delivering a majority the likes of which we had not known since the days of Margaret Thatcher.

And all of this, on the day he was ousted from office, had been just two and a half short years earlier.

What each and every one of us was unaware of at the time was that behind the scenes, deep in the heart of the Conservative Party, a plot was afoot to remove him long before the polls had closed on that joyous election night and he first placed his foot across the No. 10 threshold as Prime Minister with a mandate in his own right. If a killer virus hadn't hit our shores in March 2020 four months after he was elected, his time in office would have been far shorter than it was.

CHAPTER 1

ON HER MAJESTY'S SECRET SERVICE

'What the actual fuck have we done?' was the first thing an MP said to me when I called out a greeting as I passed him in Portcullis House. It had been our very own summer recess of discontent, the end of the very acrimonious leadership election, and today we would officially know who had won, although we all suspected what the result would be. I had nipped across the road from my department in Whitehall, where I was the Secretary of State, into the unusually empty atrium, and passed through the tables and chairs that would normally have been heaving with MPs, visitors, journalists and staff. The sound of clattering cutlery on plates and gossipy chatter was yet to arrive and muffle the sound of my approach towards the lone MP slumped at a table.

He stared into his mug of cold tea when I struggled to answer. 'I'm totally and utterly fucked,' he said, more to himself as a statement of fact than as a comment inviting discussion. 'That's it for me.' He looked close to tears. I knew that he had bought a new house for his family the summer following his election in December 2019. The salary he earnt before he became an MP was less than half of what he was earning now. He also loved and had spoken out for his constituency with a passion that had brought more investment into his patch in his first twelve months than the previous Labour MP had managed in twelve years. I felt his despair keenly. He was right; that was it for him. He had given up his career to become an MP and now he was having to face up to the fact that he was going to be lucky if he survived even a single term. He knew it, the world knew it, but the Conservative Party had gone quite mad and appeared to be in the middle of a collective nervous breakdown. I slipped my green pass into my bag, which I hung over the back of a chair as I sat down next to him. 'You will be okay,' I said, and reached out to pat the back of his hand. He stared at the place where my hand had rested and looked utterly forlorn. 'I'll go and get us a nice cup of tea,' I said, his almost-empty mug giving me the excuse I needed. I could only guess: he had taken a bigger mortgage, promised his family that all his hard work, the price they had to pay, the abuse and threats that all MPs live with, would be worth it. That he would win the seat for a second term, that financially they would be secure and physically safe. But there comes a moment for every new MP when they are forced to stop believing their own PR and realise, in today's world, it's not policy or your personal hard work for your constituency that drives people to the polls, but the charismatic communication skills and the grav-itational pull of an individual party leader. It began with Thatcher, continued with Blair, and reached its peak with Boris. Major, May, Brown all lacked the necessary charisma and personality to be truly successful. Cameron pulled together a coalition govern-ment in 2010 and a workable majority by 2015 before he resigned in 2016. This forlorn MP was facing his own moment of truth: that it was Boris he had to thank for his seat, Boris who had unarguably won it for him – and as many will attest, there is nothing quite as ex as an ex-MP.

The Despatch Box café was empty; the barista, still under-occupied, was wiping the wine bottles on the shelves that had gathered dust over the summer recess. Wine that in term time,

MPs' staff could be seen hurrying to buy on a Thursday after-noon to take back as raffle prizes to constituency functions. I felt a heaviness in my own heart. There was nothing I could say to reassure this MP because the truth was, he had made the wrong call and followed the herd.

Just the day before, I had spoken to an MP who had told me that it was the summer holiday he had spent in his constituency that had brought him up sharp. He had been a cheerleader for Rishi; a vocal critic of Boris Johnson. He had WhatsApp'd me and asked, 'How do we turn this around and get the boss back?' He was consumed by seller's remorse. This MP was using the term 'boss' as a way of declaring his loyalty, letting me know, 'I'm onside again, you can trust me.' I wasn't sure that I could. I had called this particular MP rather than WhatsApp him back. He was confused and totally lacking in any self-awareness. People had walked up to him in Tesco and asked him what the hell was going on with the Conservative Party. The same people also told him they would never vote Conservative again. 'But you'll vote for me,' he had pleaded. 'Oh, no, mate. We voted for Boris,' had been the reply as they eased their trolleys past his.

He was a new MP who spent his time judging the public mood by reading Twitter and social media, and he had almost no understanding of how politics actually works in the real world. He found himself in the position of having to lie to his constitu-ents, faking disbelief at the terrible things he and his colleagues had done, agreeing that the parliamentary party had written a political suicide note, when, all along, he was as guilty as anyone. When the opinion of the public does not align with your opinion of yourself, when the person you think you are and the choices you have made are openly derided by the people who elected you, life becomes a struggle for any politician, and my colleague was definitely struggling. He lacked the inherent courage required to stand up for what he had done and the dawning realisation of that just added to his woes. He was a good man at heart, I suspected, but one who may have been better suited to a form of public service that did not involve playing the role of a foot-soldier in an army where words were the ammunition of battle, and the courage of your convictions, your shield. I paid for the tea and hurried back to my neglected colleague carrying a tray.

'It'll be Liz Truss,' he said as I returned. 'It's all over Twitter.' Once again I wanted to tell him that Twitter wasn't the real world, but in this instance, it might be. Liz had offered me my job back as Secretary of State in the Department for Digital, Culture, Media and Sport (DCMS) three times already during the leadership campaign and I was truly flattered, but not persuaded, even though she had been on course to win for weeks. 'I feel sorry for Rishi,' said the MP. 'He didn't want this you know, it was forced on him. He just had no choice.'

I would beg to differ. Rishi was very obviously up to something way before it became fashionable to plot against Boris. I had long since guessed Rishi didn't want to wait to become party leader until Boris stood down willingly. Who knew if the political cycle would then be in his favour? For Rishi, it appeared to be more about him being Prime Minister than putting the party or the country first. I had seen enough of his behaviour at first hand to know he didn't possess the essential personality to put him into the Thatcher, Blair, Boris camp. He was firmly in the category of Major, May and Brown. I had spoken at London Tech earlier in the year and took the stage straight after Rishi. His oratory was lacklustre, he had no presence, and frankly, his speech was hesitant, squeaky and disappointing. In a side room, his young social media team, photographers and officials flapped around telling him how amazing he had been. He truly hadn't. As I followed in his footsteps and took to the stage, looking down at my vast audience, bored expressions on their faces, I abandoned my prepared speech and freewheeled as best I could to try and liven things up. Taking the stage after Boris was a terrifying prospect for anyone; you could only disappoint. Following on from Rishi was a relief.

'I guessed it would be Liz,' I said.

'Can you imagine?' he asked me. 'Lifetime Labour supporters in my patch won't say, "I voted for Liz Truss" in the same way they would say, "I voted for Boris Johnson". It just wouldn't fucking ever happen.'

I mopped up the spilt tea from the table with the paper napkin. 'Would they do that with Rishi then?' I asked him. His eyes met mine. Whatever he was about to say, he changed his mind. His voice had dropped to a mere whisper and I only just caught the last words. 'It's a mess,' he said. He had got that much right at least.

He was in full-on self-pity mode now. 'Boris is like God in my patch, but he couldn't have led us to the next election; the polls.' They had been the whispered words of discontent in the corridors of power, infecting the body politic and he and others had believed them. Bewildered and confused, he gulped the tea, forgot to say thank you and stared at the notifications on his Twitter feed, which told him we were fifteen points behind in the polls.

'Is that what they told you?' I asked. We had been a mere four behind on the day he had cast his vote of no confidence in Boris and I sipped my tea and watched as he disappeared down the black hole of doomscrolling on his phone. A message popped onto the screen of my phone from my driver:

I'm parked in Speakers Court to take you back to the department. It's a circus out there and your next meeting is in four minutes.

The timing of meetings in my office is regimental; from my wonderful Principal Private Secretary down, I had spent the past year being herded and was never allowed to be late. Nor, for security reasons, was I ever allowed to walk. I sprang to my feet, cleared up the mugs, placed them back on the tray and, retrieving my handbag, I slipped the strap over my arm. 'I'll see you later then,' I said, but he wasn't listening. I returned the tray to the empties' rack and looked back over my shoulder; he hadn't even noticed I had left the table.

On my way down to Speakers Court, I passed a number of very glum-faced MPs reluctantly returning from recess, dragging their battered wheelie suitcases across the cobbles behind them into the members' cloakroom. There was none of the optimism that had hung in the air when we knew that Boris was to be our new Prime Minister. I felt the shock I had kept at bay for the previous weeks seeping into my bones. The day Boris had been elected, Conservative MPs were euphoric; we shared his vision that the UK is an amazing country that could be made even better with the right degree of optimism, energy and commitment, coupled with his own relentless can-do and can-do-it-right-now attitude. None of us thought Boris was perfect, far from it, but when it came to the big decisions that matter to people's lives, he had the crucial quality so essential in a leader of getting them right and getting them right fast. My private office staff were waiting for me to tell them the news: would I remain as Secretary of State under the new Prime Minister, or would I go? Had I accepted the offer to remain in the job I loved? A second notification popped onto my phone from my driver:

The office is asking for an ETA; we have to leave, now.

It was time for a decision I had spent the entire summer agonising over. Ever since that fateful Cabinet meeting, just two short months ago. It had all seemed so calm back then and it felt as though it had taken place just yesterday.

I had walked up Downing Street that Tuesday morning like any other Cabinet minister, clutching my red folder, serious face on, beaming inside. I had cherished every proud step I had taken in the year I had been attending Cabinet. Larry, the No. 10 cat, was lying prone across the front step and glared across the road at the photographers just as the iconic, glossy black door swung open. Once inside, I would typically grab a coffee from the table outside the Cabinet room; someone would even bring a plate of soggy bacon sandwiches and place them on a side table. The halls of Westminster are filled with the ghosts of MPs who expired long before their three-score years and ten, thanks to the notoriously bad dietary habits an MP can easily slip into. But on the occasional Tuesday mornings when it did happen, even this ritual of Cabinet I could not let pass.

I was one of the first to arrive, followed by Nadhim Zahawi and a very glum-looking Sajid Javid. The Chris Pincher affair had brought a fresh wave of opprobrium down upon us and the atmosphere was tense. It was Theresa May who had appointed Pincher following his first misdemeanour, but that didn't matter, it's not what the media were reporting, not what the public knew, and in the white heat of the moment, there was little interest in the back story or even in the detail or the facts. All the media required was an inflammatory headline to keep the newsfeed rolling.

I deposited my mobile phone into the pigeon-hole on the wall outside and entered the Cabinet room, where phones were not allowed, and wandered over to chat to Simon Case, the Cabinet Secretary, the highest civil servant in the land, who reported

directly to the Prime Minister and ran the entire No. 10 operation. I had often offended him by saying that the coffee in No. 10
was disgusting and that I hoped visitors weren't served it, knowing full well, they were. He looked his always-serious self. I could
never quite work him out. It was impossible to find a single civil
servant who had a good or kind word to say about him, and as
he was head of the civil service, I found that unusual. He had
been brought in by Dominic Cummings, a move that had raised
many eyebrows given how inexperienced he was. It was a mystery
to me how he had totally recused himself from running the
Partygate inquiry days before he was due to report. The majority
of young female civil servants working, ostensibly for him, in
No. 10 were fined, as were Boris Johnson and Rishi Sunak. Boris
for being sat at his desk. I once asked a senior civil servant in the
Cabinet Office why there was so much animosity towards Simon
Case and the answer I received was, 'a disastrous appointment,
it's totally impossible to understand how he got the job. It's an
absolutely baffling mystery to everyone.' The level of competi-
tiveness in Westminster means that gossip is rife and unpleasant
commentary about individuals is never far from anyone's lips. I
tried to make my own judgements and, despite being truthful
about the coffee, I think I got on with Simon fairly well, but then
I didn't really know him as others did. It did occur to me though
that if he wanted to give the appearance of being good at his job,
why didn't he just get someone to sort out the coffee?

We assembled around the Cabinet table as the Prime Minister
walked in and Cabinet began, as always on the second that the
vintage Dutton wooden clock on the mantlepiece reached nine
thirty, watched over by the portrait of Walpole above. I never
could quite feel like I belonged there surrounded by history and
grand paintings, that it was my rightful place or my destiny to be
sat at that table, and so I made sure I absorbed every tiny detail

and felt a thrill run down my spine as, during my time in that room, I began to understand exactly how it is that power, famously for some, eventually corrupts.

The Prime Minister and Simon Case arrived with a retinue of civil servants close behind. Boris was quite literally flanked throughout the day and marched from meeting to meeting. I once heard him ask a civil servant, 'Do you mind if I just pop to the bathroom?' I was slightly taken aback by the response: 'You can, but you only have about ninety seconds.' At the time I was leaving the room with a delegation of tech founders who were investing in the UK, and I saw the group of people waiting to enter the room for the next meeting hovering in the corridor. The Prime Minister's schedule ran from early in the mornings usually through to 10 p.m. at night. Even on the early nights, he finished at 7 p.m. after just eleven hours. His life was trapped in a diary controlled by others that would suffocate most people.

As I took my customary glance around the table, it amused me that no one ever noticed I was watching them. They were so intent on rehearsing over and over in their minds the speech they would make to impress. Interventions were usually taken when the Prime Minister had finished addressing Cabinet. There were those who almost always put their hand up, who couldn't wait to speak, who itched to demonstrate their brilliance to their colleagues. Oliver Dowden was invariably the first. I have never heard anyone talk for so long and say so little. Oliver used a hundred words when ten would do, and when he finished speaking I wasn't the only one left inwardly groaning and wondering at the greatest mystery of Cabinet: how a man of so little discernible talent had risen so far. And then there was Grant Shapps. Quick to raise his finger in the air to catch the Prime Minister's eye. So predictable. Boris almost knew where to look next as he scribbled people's names down in the order that they caught his attention. Grant's contributions always created an eye-roll from colleagues. He was overly voluble, but at least, unlike Oliver, his contribution could be described as interesting; the resentment from others stemmed from the fact that they wished they had made it.

The long, well-polished wooden table always gleamed and, as I sat down, placing my red folder onto the green-baize blotting pad in front of me along with the pencil from the carved wooden holder at the head of my blotter, Jacob Rees-Mogg, who sat to my left, and I would always exchange pleasantries. I liked Jacob, admired him, and though I often vehemently disagreed with him, I had grown really fond of him over the year in Cabinet. I had been raised in a house with an outside lavvie on Breck Road in Liverpool, he on a country estate with too many bathrooms to count. It was an unlikely but respectful and rock-solid friendship. To my right, Alister Jack, the Scottish Secretary, would fill my glass embossed with the crown and the initials ER from a silver thermos flask of water and place it in front of me before filling his own. He would then reach into his jacket and offer me an extra strong mint, following this up with an invariably very funny quip that would almost always make me laugh out loud. I sat between two of the most decent gentlemen in Cabinet. Our little rituals had become established in just a year and I loved every moment. I sat back in my chair and said to them both, 'Look at this, all three of us grew up on estates, but only mine was owned by the council.'

Today the Cabinet room was unusually quiet. There was none of the usual chatter that preceded a Cabinet meeting. I observed the goings-on surreptitiously from beneath my lashes as Michael Gove furtively took notes, his index finger rapidly flicking backwards and forwards, stroking across his top lip and beneath his nose. He peered across the top of his glasses down the Cabinet table and over to the Prime Minister, intent on his mission to record the Cabinet meeting, completely against protocol. Was he already anticipating the day when he might be ready to use his notes and sell his memoirs? I had often wondered why the Prime Minister allowed it. The Cabinet minister who sat opposite me would sometimes follow my eyes and, grinning, wink at me; he knew too. One morning he said to me after Cabinet had finished, 'I've been watching him; he writes all his notes in shorthand. Doesn't matter what meeting he is at, he notes everything down, even at COBR.'* There his finger goes again, flicking over and over his top lip as he looks down at the two notepads he always has on the table in front of him and flicks the pages back and forth, back and forth, mimicking the flight of his unsettled mind. He was a man I could only ever visualise as Brutus, the first person to stab Boris in the back in 2016, without warning on the morning he and Boris were due to run for the party leadership on a joint ticket. With Boris as Prime Minister, Michael as his running mate would have been Chancellor or at least been guaranteed the high office that still eluded him. His betrayal resulted in Theresa May becoming Prime Minister by default and the party almost losing power in the election of 2017. I had watched him then, too, and had sensed the day before his devious act of treachery that he was about to be disloyal, to create havoc and pull the rug out from under his supposed friend and ally. I had watched him in a meeting in Portcullis House as he stood to speak and had thought to myself, something is not quite right there. He looked uncomfortable, shifty and indeed, it transpired, all was not well at all.

As the Prime Minister addressed the Cabinet, I noticed Rishi Sunak rudely half turn his back on Boris and twitch in his seat.

* COBR: Cabinet Office Briefing Rooms where meetings are held in response to a national crisis.

This had become a familiar Rishi move. It was as if he could barely contain his irritation that it was the Prime Minister addressing Cabinet and not him. He saw me watching him and gave me a fixed and unnatural grin, the bleached dental white of his teeth almost blinding me in the reflected light. His face was set, his eyes steely. He was not happy.

Michael looked across, studied Rishi's face, and as Rishi met his gaze, I caught a knowing glance pass between the two men. My antennae tingled. Michael looked away and scribbled in his notepad. A meddler who just couldn't help himself was the common refrain among ministers by way of an excuse, and we did excuse him because whatever Michael did or ministers complained about, he always got away with it and that included admitting to taking cocaine. But I had noticed something had altered with Michael over the past year, and I don't mean the dancing in Aberdeen nightclubs with teenage revellers in the early hours of the morning, or his marriage break-up, or his admitting to taking class A drugs, or the fact that, because of his betrayal in 2016, very few MPs liked or trusted him. It was none of that. 'I've known him for well over thirty years,' someone said to me, 'but actually, I don't really know him at all.'

A Cabinet minister raised his hand and spoke. You could almost hear the suppressed groans from around the table as Michael laid down his pencil. It was Sajid Javid, who had styled himself as 'The Saj', only God knows why. He was a lovely man on a personal level, but had spectacularly failed to impress anyone around the Cabinet table in his role as Health Secretary. Weeks ago, when he had made a presentation to Cabinet, it was reported that he had been savaged by Cabinet members. The reports were exaggerated, but not by much. We were looking for answers to problems; he hadn't provided us with any but instead had reeled off a speech that sounded like it had been written by a junior civil servant. I'm not sure why we were disappointed; he had never shone in any department he had led and with each appointment the gloss had dimmed, he was now running on air. As he spoke this morning, his voice was monotone, reluctant, his contribution startlingly unimaginative. Since Boris had promoted him, he had requested meetings with the Prime Minister on a number of occasions. Boris had assumed he wanted to discuss ways to invigorate his department. 'All he ever wanted to talk to Boris about was sacking Liz and him being promoted to Foreign Secretary, not his actual brief,' an aide had told me, obviously frustrated. I knew this was true because one evening, just before a reshuffle, 'The Saj' had called me personally and told me the only jobs he would accept if the Prime Minister were to promote him, which he was sure he would be considering, were those of Foreign Secretary or Deputy Prime Minister. He had asked me to appeal to Boris on his behalf. I did, unaware that he had already asked for and half demanded those roles a number of times himself already.

When Sajid finished speaking, those who always spoke had their say. Alister Jack muttered his funny comments for my ears only when one or the other made a particularly tedious comment, and I would habitually glance up at the masterful paintings around the room, committing the whole scene to memory, telling myself: this may be your last time. *Was it different in your day, Walpole?* I would ask myself as I gazed up at his portrait.

As we left Cabinet, the atmosphere was heavier than usual. No Cabinet ministers were trying to catch a moment with the Prime Minister before the civil servants whisked him away. Simon Case was adept at turning his back on anyone bearing down on the PM's chair as he stood to leave. No one was approaching Boris today though, not even Nadhim Zahawi, who always managed to reach the PM's side before anyone else had even pushed their heavy oak chair back under the table. The thought crossed my mind, *What's happening here?*, as I noticed Sajid clasp an always-smiling and friendly Nadhim by the elbow and urge him into Rishi's Chancellor's office just off the main corridor. *Why were they going into Rishi's office?* I wondered. *Where was Rishi?*

Every person around the table knew full well that as soon as Cabinet was over, any controversial matters discussed or even just the business of the day would somehow appear in *The Times* newspaper, hence the Prime Minister's practice of beginning many Cabinet meetings with the warning, 'Colleagues, it doesn't help anyone if this meeting is leaked to the press before the ink on the record has had time to dry. We are, or we should be, all working together to deliver on the manifesto promises we made at the General Election. The opposition has one objective: to prevent us from doing so. And by leaking the contents of our discussion, whoever is doing so is assisting our opponents and damaging our efforts to help the British people and run an effective government.' Despite how often the Prime Minister said this, Steven Swinford, the political editor at *The Times*, knew what had been discussed before the last of our ministerial cars had glided back to its respective department and we were once more at our desks.

Later that day, Saj released his (yet another) resignation letter. He had always wanted to be Prime Minister and, like so many who hold that ambition, was singularly unable to accept that this role could never be his. What I didn't know then when I saw Sajid easing Nadhim into Rishi's office was that the office was empty and Sajid knew that. It had been cleared out. Rishi had already vacated his position as Chancellor the day before; he just hadn't told anyone yet other than his own confidants. The Treasury, unbeknown to the Prime Minister, was rudderless, and it remained that way until Rishi finally resigned. The final stage of the plot had been activated: failure was not an option, there was no turning back. Nadhim was promoted by Boris to take Rishi's place, and later that evening Nadhim took Alister Jack and I into Rishi's office in No. 10 and showed us the empty desk and shelves. 'Saj brought me in here straight after Cabinet this morning and tried to persuade me to resign,' he said. '"Come on Nadhim, you have to do this." He tried very hard to get me to agree. I said to him, "I can't do that to Boris; where is Rishi? Why are we in his office?" And Saj said, "Look around you, he's cleared out, he's already gone." "Gone where?" I said. I couldn't believe it.'

Alister and I took a second to absorb this information. I spoke our thoughts out loud. 'Hang on, Saj told you at 9.30 this morning that Rishi had cleared out already, but Rishi didn't resign until gone six this evening?'

Nadhim replied with a nod of the head and I sank down onto what was now Nadhim's plush blue velvet sofa. 'He who wields the knife never wears the crown. Rishi was never going to go first,' I said. 'He moved his family out of the flat upstairs a couple of weeks ago, didn't he? He's obviously been planning this for some time.'

I pondered Rishi's actions as the two men chatted about the economy. He'd obviously put off making his move until the latest he possibly could, just in time to catch the evening news and the following day's press, because surely, if the Chancellor went missing without leave for more than a day from the Treasury, it would be noticed. There was a whiff of meticulous, well-planned organisation about Rishi's exit. Why would Saj resign though? He was an ambitious man. Maybe he knew, with Rishi coming in, he would never reach the political heights he desired to achieve, as he had already discussed with me, of Foreign Secretary or Deputy Prime Minister. Had he done a deal with Rishi? *I'll resign and open the trapdoor for you to encourage others to follow me and resign, and if you are successful and become Prime Minister, when I stand down at the next general election you put me in the Lords.* I would never know if that conversation took place, but I could easily imagine it.

Now, after two months of a torrid leadership election, and trying not to think about it, I knew that the moment had come. I had to face what would be the hardest decision of my life: do I carry on or do I step down to write this book? Would I tell the story people don't know and do I expose what I suspected had taken place over the past three years? I knew that many would think the wisest thing to do in my situation would be to accept Liz's offer and get stuff done, finish the work I had started in my department over the past year, stick with the incomparable honour and privilege of being a Cabinet member and let sleeping dogs lie. The people I worked with in the department were among the best and I was fond of them all. They were courteous, professional, competent, a joy to be around. It would be so much easier to stay, to bask in the honour of being appointed to Cabinet by not one but two prime ministers and to leave all that should be said unspoken and unknown.

As I jumped into the black Range Rover parked on the cobbled courtyard of Speakers Court and rested my arm on the cream leather of the seat divider at the rear, my driver Louise handed me a tangerine and a tissue and smiled at me in the rear-view mirror. I smiled back and eased the peel from the fruit. Louise knew me well. She didn't only keep me safe, on time and in check; she kept me fed too.

I began to read my messages. *You're a writer, you should write the truth about this,* said one from an aide in No. 10 who had been in place since the beginning of time. She wasn't the first to say it. Almost daily it seemed, someone asked me, 'Are you going to write your political book soon?' I had always laughed and replied with the same line, 'No, because I write books about characters people are actually interested in.' I have read enough political books to know how it works. MPs and aides love to insert themselves into the footnotes of history and so the stories they repeat to journalists amazingly always have the version where they play a key and decisive role. The books are typically written by journalists, whose sources are the very people they are obliged to protect because they are a key conduit of leaked information. Sometimes, of course, those sources are entirely dishonourable and rather than insert themselves into the footnotes of history, maliciously they rewrite it and use it as an opportunity to attack those who have climbed higher up the greasy pole than they may have managed and often, to kick others back down, because why wouldn't they in exchange for a free lunch at Scott's?

'I can't,' I replied, 'no one will want their names put to anything, and I can't do it without first-hand witness accounts, and besides, I don't have all the facts.' The answer buzzed straight back: this person would never go on record, not in a million years. *If you promise me anonymity, I will tell you everything I know and so will everyone else. They can't go on like this.* I was doubtful. Who can't go on like this? MPs? People involved in politics are always fearful, terrified of offending someone who could impede their progress. I knew enough to know who some of the bullies were and that people were scared of them.

I called someone who worked at the heart of No. 10. He answered the phone immediately and I asked a direct question: 'If I were to write about all that has happened since the day Boris was elected, will you meet with me and tell me everything you saw?' The phone scratched and shuffled and went quiet. 'Sorry, I just moved out of the office. You don't mean policy stuff, you mean the games, the plot to remove him since long before he was elected, the dark arts, everything?' I was confused. 'What do you mean, long before he was elected? What, with an eighty-seat majority? How does that work? That's ridiculous.'

'Oh yes, they work as a group right at the centre and over the years have tarnished and ended many ministerial careers. Look, if I am going to speak to you, it would have to be totally anonymous, I'd lose my job otherwise.'

'Of course, of course, I'll get back to you soon,' I reassured him but my mind was whirring.

I clicked off the phone and took a deep breath. This was a dilemma. I would have to give up everything I loved, the job, possibly even my role as an MP. The people who I needed to speak to could lose their jobs too; it just wouldn't work.

'Right, back to the department?' said Louise. Our jovial Speaker, Lindsay Hoyle, strode past me, raising his hand. 'Secretary of State,' he began, as he always did when he saw me, and my heart lurched in response. If I did this, how many more times would anyone address me in a way that made me almost pinch myself each and every time it happened, but even as the thought crossed my mind, I knew what I had to do.

I texted back the first aide in No. 10 who had suggested the book. It was worth speaking to her just to gauge why she believed there would be enough that was interesting to form the basis of a book anyone would want to read.

'Can you meet tonight?' I asked.

The reply came within seconds of the two blue ticks appearing on my phone. We were at the traffic lights on the corner of Parliament Square and the anti-Brexit campaigner, the man known as Steve Bray, though it's much rumoured that isn't his real name, was blasting out 'Bye bye, Boris!' to the Bay City Rollers' tune from a ghetto blaster, as he had been doing every day for weeks. It was always a total mystery to me how he had managed to live in one of the most expensive houses in Westminster, next door to Jacob Rees-Mogg as it happened, and drive the 300 yards every day, parking in College Gate, where the police cars parked up, without ever being arrested or moved on. From his position outside, he blasted music so loud it made it impossible to work. 'There's Nadine Dorries, a Tory liar!' he shouted to the crowds waiting at the traffic lights. Louise's eyes scanned the throngs behind the barriers who were now staring into the car. We were silent as we both watched and waited, the only sound in the car, the repeated clicking of the indicator as we willed the lights to turn green. Since the day of the Westminster terror attack in 2017 when police officer Keith Palmer had been murdered in New Palace Yard, such moments were always anxious ones. The memory was all too vivid of being stood next to Grant Shapps on that day, frozen with fear, as the locked double oak doors leading to the members' lobby and the chamber shuddered backwards and forwards while two men in black balaclavas tried to gain entry. We had been locked and penned into the chamber for our own safety, with only our phones to tell us what was occurring. The stone arch above the oak doors, damaged in World War II when the Commons was bombed but retained in place during the rebuild under Churchill, who wanted MPs to always be reminded of how close our democracy had come to falling, was about to be ravaged again, this time by machine guns. 'We're dead,' Grant said in sotto voice. My throat had closed, I froze, I couldn't say anything. Apart from the sound of the shuddering oak doors, the members' lobby fell quiet. There was no panic, no screams, no running. If we were all about to meet our end, we were doing so stoically.

'Police!' the shout went out as the two men burst through the doors carrying machine guns. The fear of that moment was instilled and it has never left me.

The lights changed. We were safe. I breathed again.

Tonight at 7.30? I messaged back as the car glided into the stream of traffic. *The Two Chairmen pub?* I suggested, a favourite Westminster watering hole.

I looked out of the side window as we passed 'Steve Bray' and glared. 'Don't,' said Louise in her warning voice. I made a petulant grunting noise. I obviously wasn't going to say or do anything, it would be unseemly to make any kind of inappropriate gesture from the window of a ministerial car, but God, did I want to. I opened the red folder full of policy decisions I needed to address that Louise had left on the seat next to me, but I couldn't concentrate. My mind was buzzing.

CHAPTER 2

DIVER GIRL

I arrived at the pub just past 8 p.m., over thirty minutes late, and the moment I got there, I knew I had made a mistake. The night driver dropped me around the corner as I didn't want to be noticed.

'I'll get a cab home,' I said.

She looked at me in the rear-view mirror. 'You sure? I go past your door anyway on the way home; I don't mind waiting.'

'No, I'm fine, you go,' and before she could argue, I slammed the door of the car shut.

As I turned the corner, my head bent, hands thrust into my pockets, I could see the pavement was heaving with researchers and lobby journalists, seeking out young members of MPs' staff enjoying the new London high life of political intrigue, desperate to ply them with expense-account drinks and to loosen young keen-to-impress lips. The air was thick with smoke that hovered below the Victorian carriage lights on the wall and above the chatter, which subsided as I drew close. My name was whispered behind me as I moved through the crowd. 'Excuse me,' I muttered as hushed voices whispered, 'It's Nadine Dorries.' I bent my head. 'Secretary of State,' said one young man as I passed, and my head shot up. He stood to the side to let me pass and I recognised him as one of the officials from my department. I smiled. 'Glad to see they let you out every now and then,' I said as I moved in through the front door.

I had made a stupid mistake; this was way too public. If I was going to do this, it would be lesson number one learnt: don't meet people in the environs of Westminster.

The inside of the pub was empty apart from people at the bar ordering drinks; everyone else was outside enjoying the muggy September evening air. I glanced around and I couldn't see my secret assignation anywhere. Maybe I was too late and she had to leave. I cursed the unpredictable hours of my job as I took out my phone just as a notification dropped onto the home screen.

Keep on walking to the back, bottom right.

My footsteps echoed across the aged wooden floorboards until I reached the rear of the pub. Eventually, I turned and there she was, tucked into the corner, and I realised we were in a private place where no one would hear us.

'Phew,' I said as I slipped onto a stool and looked behind me. No one was watching, my arrival already old news. I shrugged my trench coat down from my shoulders and it fell over the back of the stool as I pushed my hair away from my face. She looked immaculate. Manicured, fresh French polish on her nails, her skin tanned. 'Have you been away?' I asked her. She folded her arms onto the table and leant forward. 'Yeah, South of France, but I kept connected to the shit-show back here while I was away, I had to.' She smiled and inclined her head towards the drink she had already bought for me. 'Champers. It might be warm by now and it's not the best here.' I sipped. She was right, it *was* warm and it wasn't the best. We exchanged holiday stories and embarked upon the same conversation everyone outside was having – Are we living in a bubble of insanity? What the hell has happened? – before we moved on to the purpose of our meeting.

'So, where do you think I should start?' I asked her. Her phone was on the table and vibrated as it buzzed.

'I'm sorry, do you have to be somewhere?' I asked.

She shook her head. 'I do, but I can be late.'

'That's one part of this job I won't miss if I do give it up,' I said. 'Back to normal-life hours.'

She unlocked her screen, took ten seconds to reply to a message and looked straight back up at me.

'Were you seen coming in?'

I put my glass on the table.

'I was.'

She looked over my shoulder. 'No one's looking now. You know what used to happen when Dominic Cummings arranged to meet the journalist Simon Walters, formerly at the *Daily Mail*?'

I frowned. 'No, why would I and why would he be doing that? Cummings had nothing to do with the media, did he? That was the head of No. 10 comms's job.'

She laughed. 'You are so, so going to have your eyes opened. He very much did meet journalists, big time. He and Simon used to meet in pubs in Fitzrovia and if either of them thought they had been recognised, they would call each other and dramatically hiss, "abort, abort", and arrange a new rendezvous.'

I was still confused. 'When was this? During Covid?'

She sipped at her own champagne. 'Oh no, always, he was briefing journos, right back to the days when Cummings first became involved in politics, back to the early 2000s, and obviously more so the whole time he was in No. 10 and the Cabinet Office. He created stories too – I mean, obviously, he didn't deliberately engineer Barnard Castle, that blew up in his face. If you do this, you will find out all the names of journalists Cummings leaked to and the stories they planted and how they used the media and weaponised those leaks. It will amaze you. But, of course, it wasn't just him.'

I was speechless and that is a rare event. I thought Cummings was all about policy, data, Brexit and, of course, the infamous Barnard Castle incident. She looked down at her watch.

Even though the champagne was warm, I sipped it and winced.

'Look, I can't tell you too much,' she continued, 'but it certainly isn't just Cummings. You need to speak to people – most of this stuff no one talks about – and if I were you, I'd make sure you meet with Iain Duncan Smith, I think he would be a good place to begin. Look at what happened to him, ask him to explain it to you, and that will help you to understand how these people operate and some of it will make sense, but not all of it. If you speak to Iain, it will give you context and help you to identify their pattern of behaviour. It's almost a rule book they operate now. They repeat the same acts of treachery over and over.'

'I was around at the time IDS was removed,' I said, trying to remember the events, but all I could remember was the term Betsygate, and something to do with his wife and her family finances. Expenses?

'I remember some of Betsygate,' I continued, 'but the most recent wife to be in the media concerning her expenses was Akshata, Rishi's wife; oh, and Carrie too.'

She looked up from her phone and held my gaze. I sensed the importance of the link.

'Who are these people, then?' I asked her as I opened Notes on my phone.

'I can't be the one to tell you that. You just need to start following the threads. Start with Cummings, he'll lead you to the rest, I promise.'

Her phone buzzed again. She picked it up and carried on speaking as she typed. 'Look, Boris has made mistakes, but what has just happened to him, it was unjust and wrong, it was a travesty and it must be the tipping point, the catalyst, the moment at which they have gone too far; they have to be stopped. Parties, my arse. He was never at any parties; if he was, that's what the police would have fined him for, not for being with a group of people, of which Rishi was one, that he worked and met with all day, unbeknown to him, walking into his office to sing "Happy Birthday" while he was sat at his desk. That's also the opinion of one of the highest KCs in the land. Whatever Boris knew about parties, Rishi knew too; they worked in the same building, cheek by jowl, and it was Rishi who lived in the flat above No. 10, not Boris. What Boris knew or didn't know, Rishi did or didn't know, it's as simple as that.'

She looked up at me, her eyes earnest. 'Look, I know Rishi didn't say at the despatch box that no parties took place or what-ever, which led to Boris being accused of misleading the house, but Boris couldn't know what he didn't know. He had no idea what was really going on and he still doesn't know all of it, but he had asked people questions and the answers he was given were, no boss, nothing to see here. Honestly, I'm not joking. To this day, the public have no clue what was happening inside No. 10. There are people who have a great deal to hide. And I can also tell you this: they won't be happy with Liz. They will panic her, they will get her out, she will make wrong moves, they will get Rishi in, and they won't be happy with him either because I can see what they are up to already. If it's Liz who's in, one or all of them who Rishi thinks right now are his new best friends, will be trying by any means possible to get a job in No. 10 and get close to Liz; they will already have decided who that is, probably Robbie Gibb. They will then work to get Liz out, and Rishi in.'

I couldn't type as fast as she was speaking. 'And they are already looking beyond Rishi, but right now they will want one of their group on the inside to start working towards bringing Liz down, and they will have plenty of connections on the outside to help.'

She continued, 'Boris would get rid of the lot of them if he ever got back in, so they know they have to work hard and fast to truly bury him. They are spinning out of control because of the threat of Boris returning. You need to find out who was hosting the regular secret parties in Downing Street when the Prime Minister was at Chequers. Why was what really took place at those parties never even mentioned by journalists, or by Sue Gray in her report, or by Simon Case even? But most of all, you need to put all the pieces in their right places on the board because they are all up in the air right now. People don't know who is connected to whom and how it all works. Listen, I have to go. I'm in trouble, I'm not a Secretary of State, I don't get forgiven for being late. I'll send you a list of names. People you have to talk to. But you will never be able to write a book big enough to fit it all in, there's too much. Speak to IDS, just to get a bit of perspective, and then I'll put you in contact with people whose identity you must protect at all costs.'

I locked my phone. 'Hang on, I haven't even decided if I'm doing it,' I said. The tone in her voice changed as she responded with an intensity that left me in no doubt.

'You have to, because no one else is going to and it's a story that absolutely has to be written. People have a right to know about the poison, the corruption and the cancer that lies at the heart of the party and the government when we are in power, and until that is cut out, the cycle will continue.'

I slipped my phone down into my trench pocket. 'But, no one will speak to me …' I wailed feebly. 'I'm not Tim Shipman;* it

---

* Tim Shipman, *Sunday Times* political editor and bestselling author of political memoirs.

will be hopeless. I like to write historical and romantic novels ...'
I sounded pathetic.

'Don't look for obstacles, you can go back to writing your
cosy Catherine Cookson-esque novels afterwards. Honestly, you
will not regret this. People will speak to you because you aren't a
journalist, and if you care about democracy and making sure that
nothing like this ever happens again, you will be driven to do it.
So, listen, on the anonymity, it's important; what about if you
give everyone a code name?' She had stood and was slipping her
jacket from the back of the stool and up the length of her arms.
'I think what you are embarking on here is a proper Bond-style
spy story. Call me diver girl from *You Only Live Twice*; it's my
favourite Bond theme tune.'

I pulled on my own coat. Bond references, that was a good
one: my literary agent was Piers Blofeld, whose father had been
at school with Ian Fleming. It was surely meant to be.

'I'll leave first,' she said. 'Give me a minute. Yeah, give everyone you speak to a Bond character, or tune name or something ...
I like that. Has an air of intrigue about it. Let's meet up again.
I'm sorry, I have to go.' She kissed me on the cheek and slipped
past me and out onto the noisy pavement. I looked down at the
last of the warm champagne and, picking up the glass, I gulped
the warm, flat, disgusting liquid down in one. I wished I hadn't
let the car go. I perched on the side of the stool for a few moments
as I checked my messages, wondering who I should speak to first.
There was one from Boris. *Can I come and see you soon?* I asked.
It seemed like a good place to start.

I looked out the pub door; the crowd had thinned, dragged
away by their empty stomachs.

As I left the pub, I heard a car horn beep; my driver was still
there.

'What are you doing?' I asked her.

'Well, I wasn't going to leave you, was I. Besides, I had to go back to the department, they've sent you a red box; it's in the boot.'

We both laughed, I with a hint of sadness as I knew that, from tomorrow, she would no longer be my driver. I knew all about her family and life, she about mine. We had become friends in the way you do when you share long journeys with once strangers. My phone was linked to the car's Bluetooth and I looked up Bond theme tunes and clicked on 'You Only Live Twice' as we pulled out along the embankment. The music filled the car and I looked down the river, its deep and inky water sparkling in the descending darkness as it reflected the lights from Westminster Bridge. 'Ah, I love a bit of Nancy,' she said, and began to sing along: '*Don't think of the danger ... You only live twice.*' She could drive, but she couldn't sing. I had so far refused Liz's offer to retain my position as Secretary of State and all that came with it. The long hours and red carpets and the seven-days-a-week workload, the prestige, the red boxes and the pride you felt at achieving a place in Cabinet, the driver and the car – I would give it all up to write this book. What I didn't know at that moment was what I would uncover and how much potential danger that might put me in. The very least that would happen would be that the entire establishment would pile in to destroy my reputation. MPs, the media, every political pundit who liked to secure a spot on Sky by saying something outrageously unpleasant, would fill the airwaves, out to get me. They would call me mad, say the book was a work of fiction, a conspiracy. I would have many battles to face; did I really want to do it? But what did I know? It would be the words of others, not mine. I would just be the holder of the pencil.

I replied to Boris, asking if we could meet after the weekend. I would give myself the time with my daughters and my family to think about it. If I had known then the secrets that had festered at the heart of the Conservative Party unspoken for many years and the Gordian Knot that I would begin to unravel, leading me to people and events that interlinked and draped across Westminster and No. 10 like a ghostly spider's web, I wouldn't have hesitated for a moment. The car dropped a gear as it turned up and away from the bridge and along the now-clear road home, the river to our right, Parliament nestled on the bank, the floodlit vista of the terrace across the water illuminating the Lowry-esque figures of MPs drinking in the warm evening. As was so often the case, they would be well refreshed. Lonely, away from home, hanging around for far longer than they should be. Nancy Sinatra's voice was seductive, filling the car, and I decided there and then, I would do it. I would give up the best job I had ever had in my life. 'Gawd, save us,' I said, laughing as my driver sang along.

'You're right,' she chuckled, 'even my angelic voice can't match Nancy's.' She stopped and giggled to herself.

I sat back in my seat as the haunting crescendo of strings washed over me. Then I texted the aide I had just shared the champagne with. *I'll do it, diver girl*, I typed. *After all, you only live twice …*

CHAPTER 3

BORIS: FACING OFF AGAINST ODDJOB

It is a bright sunny morning as I leave my flat and head out across the river to meet with Boris. My new trainers squeaked annoyingly, backpack slung across my shoulders. I was embarking upon a new phase in my life.

'You're mad,' my youngest had said as I caught the flying bread from the toaster and began to butter it ten minutes earlier. She loved my job as Secretary of State, or rather loved me doing it. She had the pleasure of being my plus-one to events. 'No more BAFTAs or Classic FM concerts,' she wailed.

'It's all right for you,' I said. 'It was work for me.' Even as I said it out loud, I knew I was far from convincing. But after twelve-hour days, such events were exhausting, and all I ever wanted to do was crawl home and into my bed, not dress up behind the office door for a film premiere and sit in the dark, fighting to keep my eyelids open, knowing that my red box was waiting to be attended to once I arrived back home.

It was only the third time I would have seen Boris since the day we were all stood outside Downing Street and he made the speech in which he quoted Lucius Quinctius Cincinnatus, the Roman statesman who left his plough when citizens called for him to lead them into battle. That had been a surreal morning. A small number of us had assembled in his No. 10 study. Most drank the dreadful coffee; I opted for tea as the obligatory cold, fatty bacon sandwiches appeared. The atmosphere was funereal. Simon Case gave me a hug, which was a bit weird, while Carrie, a total trooper, floated around looking like a supermodel in her hot pink Harmur dress and J Crew shoes, trying to cheer everyone up. 'She's older than her years,' someone said. She had remained dignified throughout and had been a rock for Boris, who gave me a hug just as someone took a photograph and the cup of tea wobbled precariously in my hand. There were no tears, there was no anger, just a sense of confusion, as though we were all playing a role in a drama where the scriptwriters had got the ending totally wrong. Carrie was serene, resigned, the rest of us were bereft. I half expected someone to walk in and shout, 'Only kidding!'

The following time I had met with both Boris and Carrie was at their house in London. The light had been eerie that day and the sky heavy, as though a storm was brewing. Boris had made a tray of Assam tea and brought it into the sitting room to Carrie and I. The children were taking a nap. Boris placed the tray down on the wide leather fender and, taking his cup, moved to the desk in the bay window that overlooked the garden. I was impressed with how he had laid the tray with delicate china and had apologised for there being no strainer. The phone on his desk rang. His silhouette was framed in the peculiar light and something made both Carrie and I look over. His response was sombre, his voice deep. He stood abruptly, pushing back the chair and, without saying a single word, hurried from the room, his phone in hand. Carrie and I exchanged looks, no words were spoken. I guessed that whatever Boris had been told, it related to our ailing Queen. As I left the house, the heavens wept, the dark sky over London parted and a huge rainbow spanned the Kings Road. I knew then in my heart that the call had been to tell Boris that our Queen had passed.

This morning, I was heading for his office and the room was flooded with sunshine. He poured us both coffee as we sat looking down over the silvery, snaking ribbon of the Thames below. As we chatted over events, Boris was his usual enthusiastic, ebullient self and demonstrated not even a hint of bitterness.

I wanted to talk to him about Michael Gove and, in particular, the relationship between Gove and Cummings. As indicated earlier, I had mistrusted Gove since the 2016 leadership election when, just at the point Boris was about to announce that he and Michael intended to run on a dual ticket, Michael pulled out and said he was going to run himself. A spectacular act of self-harm, as he didn't have the backing of MPs and earnt himself the dual sobriquets of Brutus and backstabber. As a result of his actions, by default Theresa May became Prime Minister and delivered three years of chaos, almost entirely losing our majority in the crash-and-burn General Election of 2017.

'So,' I began, 'I have been thinking and this is the first question I want to ask you. Dominic Cummings gets all the attention as your nemesis, but it seems to me that Cummings, he's more of an Oddjob to Michael Gove's Goldfinger. As in he does whatever Gove asks him to do, does the dirty work, that sort of thing.'

I had no idea then how spectacularly wrong I was. Cummings had worked with Michael Gove for over twenty years. There were the well-publicised stories we had all heard about how much David Cameron had disliked Cummings and banned him from No. 10, but if I'm honest, back in those early days, I hadn't the foggiest who Cummings really was. I had no idea that Gove had begged Cameron, pleaded with him to allow him to keep Cummings with him when Cameron made Gove Education Secretary, which is incredibly odd behaviour when you are being made a Cabinet minister and your Prime Minister is giving you an instruction to sack the aide you are refusing to be parted from. If Cameron had put his foot down and said, 'No, he has to go,' would Gove have refused the Cabinet job? Back then, I had only heard the disparaging murmurings about Cummings among the older MPs in the tearoom. I decided to set myself the task of reading Cameron's memoirs and was slightly stunned to discover that Cameron's opinion of the Gove and Cummings duo at the time aligns with that of many today.

Boris threw his head back when I described Cummings as Oddjob to Gove's Goldfinger and laughed out loud. 'Govefinger,' he blurted out.

I laughed too, slightly peeved that I hadn't thought of the joke myself, and ploughed on.

'Look, Cummings has worked with Gove since when? Two thousand and one? Two? He says he wasn't around when Gove stabbed you in the back in 2016; he's given interviews to that effect. People tell me he categorically *was* around and was seen the evening before. It's incongruous that you made Cummings your de facto Chief of Staff and Gove Chancellor of the Duchy of Lancaster as soon as you won the election. They had both betrayed you in the most public and cataclysmic manner. You gave them two of the most important positions in government. Why did you do that?'

Boris swivelled in his chair, turned, and looked down out onto the river, his hands clasped behind his head.

'So, look, the 2017 election [Theresa May's snap election] was totally stuffed up. We very narrowly missed losing power to a Corbyn-led Labour Party. If you remember, when I became leader in July 2019, Westminster was in gridlock. It was plain that following the election of 2017, Theresa had no way forward. Parliament was blocking her, she was going to have to step down at some point, and I thought, *I've got to get my act together and get ready to take over, if the party wants me to.* So, I'm casting around for votes and, as I discovered, sadly, I'm not loved in all quarters of the Conservative Party following Brexit and so I had to find support. Cummings had run Vote Leave during the Brexit campaign. He had stationed Lee Cain with me when Theresa won the 2016 leadership election because he had been removed from No. 10, he placed Lee with me and someone else he knew from Vote Leave with Dom Raab.'

This was interesting. Cummings appeared to be placing his people with those he thought stood a chance of becoming the next Conservative leader and he was getting a hold in every camp.

'I had been in intermittent contact with Cummings following Vote Leave, and as we got closer to the time of the leadership contest, it was Lee Cain who became very insistent: you have to get Cummings in, he has to be right on the inside, get the Dark Lord in. I mean … with Cummings, I'd known about him for a long time and I thought that he was probably a highly intelligent and able campaigner, and I broadly felt that he had a drive and an energy about him that I wanted to bring to No. 10 and into government. He's a classicist and a historian.'

I interrupted him there.

'Shall I tell you what others tell me he is?' I reeled off some of the descriptions I had been given, and at this point I had only held preliminary telephone conversations with some of the people that diver girl had put on her list. 'His personality has been described to me as dark triad coupled with everyday sadism. That is from an extremely successful individual who has been very adversely impacted by having to work with Cummings for a short period of time and had to seek professional help as a result. Almost everyone I have spoken to describes him as a narcissist and that's the nicest thing they say – his physical anger towards others has been witnessed and experienced, leading some to say he's a psychopath.' He was once described as a 'career psycho-path' by David Cameron, and civil servants complained of an 'us and them, aggressive, intimidating culture' when Cummings worked for Gove in education.

Boris exhaled. 'Well, there were plenty of people who said I was mad to take him on, lots of them. But I saw something in him that I thought could be channelled. Sane and rational wasn't working, hadn't worked, so we needed to roll the dice and find something that would work. Parliament was stalled, we were getting nowhere. He shared my kind of impatience with the way Britain was going, and my desire to see change. I got the impression that he was totally on board with the levelling-up agenda and that he was a patriot and wanted to deliver that, and in the early days, he was on board with all of that. And I thought that the 2016 referendum vote had been a colossal thing in the life of the country, because the people had voted for something different and better, and they wanted something radical to happen at the heart of government, and I felt that Cummings would help me deliver that in Whitehall. I didn't know very much about him, he was Michael's creature.'

'Or, Michael was his?' I interjected.

Boris frowned and continued. 'But what I knew about him suggested that he was a person who wasn't afraid of breaking the china, who would get things done, and who had an ear for where the public were at, who was good at diagnosing what people were thinking, and I could see the positioning and difficult place we had been in from 2016 to 2019, which had seen Parliament descend into stalemate. The country having basically become completely bogged down because of the failure to get Brexit done. And I could see that I was going to need a mailed fist or somebody, a kind of samurai robot, who would cut through and help to get things done. I think that that was my single biggest disappointment in the whole experience; he was good at digression, but not very good at campaigning.'

This was true. Cummings was not good at campaigning. It was all a sham, created by the aggressive, over-confident manner of a man who dressed like a student and walked around with an open laptop in his hands.

'He was very good at nihilism,' Boris continued. 'He was very good at breaking things down. But he was not so great at building things or repairing things, or making the whole ship of state sail on a calm and happy sea. He wasn't particularly good at delivering on instructions. There's just a sort of … there's a myth about him, you know, he used to make everybody read these books, about government and great projects and the systems and the Los Alamos project and all that sort of stuff. But actually we didn't make enough progress on anything; he didn't make things happen at all, he wasn't doing his job and then Covid hit.'

One of the Spads* who had been a regular attender at the weekly Spad school meetings which Cummings held every Friday in No. 10 had told me, 'It takes a while to realise this, months in fact, because at first it's all so plausible, but actually, Cummings just chats shit. He sounds good, reels off the name of books he tells you to go and read, but he does nothing, nothing happens, there is nothing there other than a man who creates bad feeling and trouble. And then you realise you're working with a narcissist and you start asking yourself, *What is the point of him? Why is he here?*'

I had been told a similar story by someone from inside No. 10 at the time Cummings had been there. He had said, 'It was all

* A Spad, or special adviser, is a temporary political adviser hired to support a Cabinet minister.

bullshit, the great Cummings con, all nuclear-grade fucking bullshit.'

I put my cup down on the table with a clatter and Boris swung around in the chair.

'But, surely,' I asked, 'by the time Covid had hit, there were already really serious signs that Dom was more of an anarchist than a strategist. He'd already been quite horrible to Carrie, not least when he found out she was pregnant with Wilf. We know that the reason why gold wallpaper was a story that zoomed around the world when it didn't even exist was because journalists had two sources, probably three, inside No. 10, claiming that it did, even though it didn't. I believe and so does everyone I've spoken to that the sources for the wallpaper stories were very likely Dominic Cummings, Lee Cain [his henchman, who was head of communications/the press office in No. 10 by that point], and possibly Cleo Watson, the person some people have referred to as "Dom's bit of posh". And maybe they had other leakers in No. 10 that I just don't yet know about. So, we knew he wasn't a team builder. We knew he was already at that point incredibly rude to you in meetings in No. 10. We already knew quite early on that something more serious was going on. Is that why you parted ways with him?'

'Yeah, I think that … I think that's absolutely true and that hairline fractures were appearing. I kept … I kept looking at all of these people with the eyes of faith, hoping and believing they were working as part of the team and would come good, and thinking they must put the good of the country first, but actually they weren't thinking like that at all. My instinct was that there were things I enjoyed about Dom's mind. And his outlook, you know, I liked; I like the sort of zap and energy and aggression, because that can be useful if it's channelled in the right way, and it was, to some degree. From when I became Prime Minister in

the July, until the General Election in December, we were dealing with issues like Brexit and the Supreme Court. It was really
very important to have focus and dedication like that. [This was
before the December 2019 General Election.] But when you
come to look back, when you know with hindsight how he
behaved, it's perfectly true that I should have, you know, we
should have moved on much earlier. We should have moved on
from him much, much earlier. If we had done so straight after
the election then things may have been very different, but we
had a Brexit strategy meeting at Chevening and it was so positive, there was much to be done, huge problems to be tackled.
We had to find a way around the huge legislative obstacles that
Remain MPs had put in our way. We had to, at all costs, deliver
on the referendum result because that was absolutely the right
thing to do.'

I moved back to Cummings. I was in the process in these early
days of identifying the roles of individuals, and who had done
what and when. I had only just begun and it felt like I was
mapping out the spread of a contagion that had infected both
No. 10 and the Conservative Party; I was contact tracing
everything backwards and I had learnt so far that all roads led
back to patient zero, and that was Michael Gove.

'What about the people Gove and Cummings brought with
them from Vote Leave and other places into No. 10? People like
Cleo Watson?' I asked. I had been given many opinions so far.

'Well, we needed a strong team and Vote Leave had been a
winning team. It was always a bit odd though,' Boris continued,
'how Lee Cain and many of the people working in No. 10 always
referred to Cummings as "the Dark Lord". I could never quite
get my head around that one. Most peculiar.'

Not for the first time I wondered why no journalist had ever
reported this bizarre fact about Cummings, that everyone

addressed him as the Dark Lord. It was used as a term of respectful acknowledgment, not banter.

'Was Gove really a Brexiteer?' I asked him. 'Because I'm increasingly convinced that Michael likes to take a big political decision and make his political gains on the back of public hysteria, but does he believe them? It's just that I remember the words of Gove's wife, Sarah Vine, following the referendum. Do you remember? She said, "You were only supposed to blow the bloody doors off." She was very clear. Was that it? Was it really just a big game to Michael?'

Boris drank his coffee and looked out of the window.

'Others have suggested they suspect it might be.'

I was amazed that there was not a trace of bitterness in his voice, sadness even. He hadn't answered half of my questions and I guessed that we were going to have lots of conversations like this. If Gove and Cummings were so closely aligned, given what Gove had done in 2016, why had Boris rewarded him with one of the most important jobs in government? My question had been answered, but not fully. I was in actual physical pain after having left my job. I wasn't sleeping properly. My family were still in shock at what I had done and given up. Being given the role of Secretary of State was the biggest honour of my life. To have walked away, the most painful. I had, however, resigned out of choice. Boris had been removed, against his will, from the greatest office in the land, and yet he was smiling.

'You don't appear to be even remotely bitter or angry,' I said, and without meaning it to, some of my own sadness had crept into my voice.

He didn't look up or answer me for a full minute. I could hear his staff chatting in the outer office. The whoosh of the main office doors as they opened and closed, the call of a cheery greeting as someone entered. Boats glided along the Thames far below us. I guessed the person in the outer office might be his next appointment. Sitting back in the chair, he said something to me that I have repeated often to myself since 'Never be bitter, no good will ever come from it. Right, come on, what's next?'

'Nothing,' I replied as I switched the transcribing Otter app off on my phone. 'That's enough for now. Can we talk about this every couple of weeks?'

'Sure thing.' He was already out of the chair and on his feet. The relief on his face that this was over was obvious.

I wanted to remind him that he was skirting over some of my questions, but I decided he wasn't ready for this yet. He was still trying to make sense of it all himself. We both knew he had been betrayed on a colossal level. There were things he'd definitely got wrong, but he freely admitted to those. I decided to take the advice I'd been given and speak to Iain Duncan Smith to give me a grounding, but first there was someone I had to contact in order to help me map out this book, how I was going to tell this complicated story. 'She will give you an understanding of how they work, she knows everything,' I had been told.

When I stepped out into the Millbank sunshine, I headed back up towards Chelsea and home. I was deep in thought when I decided that sooner rather than later would be the best time to make a strategic call. My contact answered immediately. 'I need your help,' I said. 'You wouldn't be free for lunch by any chance?'

The aqua glass building that is MI6 glistened in the sunshine and winked at me.

'I'm free if you're buying me lunch,' she said. 'Meet me in 5 Hertford Street. There is a private sitting room. I'll let them know you are coming. See you at 1 p.m.'

The secret watering holes of a spook, who knew? I thought, and put my arm out to flag down a passing black cab.

CHAPTER 4

MONEYPENNY

It was lucky I always carry a pair of flat shoes with me in my bag, just in case. Trainers it transpired aren't allowed in 5 Hertford Street, so I did a quick change in the cab. I was met as instructed and ushered into the small sitting room, and from the second I walked in, it was obvious I was expected. No words other than, 'Ah, this way', met me as I stepped through the door and was whisked up the grand staircase. I was guided to a room which was no more than 12 by 12 feet but was furnished in the most exquisite old-English country-house style. A sofa you sink into rested against the back wall below the window and two comfortable armchairs opposite were separated by a long wooden coffee table which was covered with a pure white linen cloth upon which sat a tea tray. A smokeless fire roared behind a burgundy club fender and a chain curtain as the flames filled the room with a warm and flickering glow. The room was so inviting, so comfortable, so something indistinguishably secure and rooted in Englishness and childhood that I could have sat there forever.

I glanced over at the manager, Christian. 'You don't have to worry,' my host said. 'No one will ever know you were here.' Christian smiled. 'It's him you should worry about,' he said, as he nodded towards the bust of a gorilla perched on the windowsill behind us. She laughed. 'I'll do a sweep for bugs before I start,' she said. The lamps in the room were as warm and comforting as the fire and, suddenly, I felt dangerously relaxed by the ambience.

We both ordered lunch, celeriac soup and Caesar salad, as she poured the tea and handed me mine, and she relaxed back into the sofa, the cup and saucer perched on what I am sure she won't mind me describing as a generous embonpoint. She hooked one finger through the cup handle as the other gripped the saucer. I wasn't sure where to begin and decided it was probably a good idea to talk about the actual book in more detail. I had given her the sketchiest details over the phone. 'Look, all I'm trying to do,' I said, 'is to present what was going on behind the scenes that the public were totally unaware of, the story the media never told because, for a variety of reasons, they were being fed a different tale on all levels.'

'Well, there's a lot of truth in that,' she said as she sipped her tea. A waiter joined us and laid out the cutlery. She conversed with him in Italian, he answered in French. I wasn't going to ask.

Instead, I dived straight in. 'Many people think Barnard Castle was the beginning of when things began to go seriously wrong. Others not so much. What do you think?' I saw the interest land in her eyes.

'Ah, Cummings, Gove's protégé. Of course, he would hate to hear me say that because actually, the reality is, Gove is his. Cummings, he's been around since the days of Iain Duncan Smith. Off the top of my head, he first started to work in and around the centre of the party at around 2002.

'So, it was a Saturday or the Sunday before Boris came in following the General Election, I think, although maybe not, there was a lot going on at the time. Cummings came in as basically a de facto Chief of Staff, he was never officially given the title. There was a bit of a do in Brown's, if you remember, and when he announced that Cummings was coming on board in that role, you could feel the air leave the room. Everyone felt a dread come upon them. You know, now that I look back and I can see Boris at that moment and Gove, with his team of acolytes, heading into No. 10 … of course, we were always going to be sat right here discussing Boris as a former prime minister not too long after that, weren't we?'

'But, if that's the case,' I said, 'why did Boris have these people working for him?'

'Good question; it's one people struggle with. It happened as a result of the pressure Boris was put under to employ Cummings. I can remember well the delegation of people working very hard together who pushed the Prime Minister to give Dom an official position in No. 10; they were absolutely unrelenting. WhatsApp messages, visits, phone calls. They never stopped.'

'Who were they?' I asked her.

'Lord David Frost, the former Brexit Minister. Munira Mirza, who had worked for Boris for years when he was London Mayor and followed him to No. 10 to become his head of policy. Dougie Smith, who is of course married to Munira. And when it comes to Cummings, always Michael Gove, also Lee Cain, a total puppet of Cummings. I assume it was the whole group of the Vote Leavers also – all of whom were uncomfortable with Eddie Lister being Chief of Staff – who wanted him out and Dom in the Chief of Staff chair.' She sat back and looked pensive. 'Dougie Smith is an interesting case. He's worked for Central Office for as long as anyone can remember, but he appears on no staff list. He always had a pass to No. 10. His roots go back to an organisation known as the Federation of Conservative Students, which was shut down for being too right wing, but they had reconvened into a group who gave themselves the informal moniker, "the movement". Not that they call themselves that today. You are going to learn a great deal about these people and how they operate.

'It doesn't matter who you talk to, no one has a bad word to say about Eddie Lister, who had also been with Boris for years.'

I interjected. 'Why on earth would they object to Eddie being Chief of Staff? He has huge experience in politics regardless of his loyalty to Boris; he's the silverback any Prime Minister would desperately want at his side.'

'Boris trusted Eddie implicitly, and they didn't want anyone around Boris who would give him advice that had influence, other than their own. It was about isolating Boris from the people he knew and trusted, so that he became vulnerable and dependent upon them. Boris would trust Eddie with his life and he doesn't trust many people. I see Liz has sacked everyone in No. 10; that was a big mistake, but understandable. However, in a crisis, having no one around you is no substitute for having people around you who you don't trust. Especially when the monarch dies.' She glanced at her phone. 'Are you going to view the coffin?' she asked.

I was utterly relieved that the funeral was being run by my own former department and my former Permanent Secretary, someone who I had total confidence in. She was an amazing person and I knew in my heart, without a doubt, that the Queen's funeral, just like the Platinum Jubilee, would begin and end without a hitch because she had been across it.

'It was me who took the decision to allow the public to turn up and walk past the coffin rather than an online ticketed affair,* so I hope so,' I said. 'Look, tell me about Barnard Castle, what happened there?' I wanted to keep on subject.

She laughed. 'Gosh, Barnard Castle and the eye test. Now there's a story. If you saw the interview in the rose garden at No. 10, there were a few raised eyebrows at that. Did he really think

---

* These plans had been drawn up before Her Majesty's death.

he was the Prime Minister setting up there? Sitting at a desk while journalists had to trot to a microphone and ask their questions standing, like they were naughty schoolchildren before the headmaster's desk. Cummings was supposed to have made an apology, but didn't, well thank God no one saw the rehearsal that went before, that was totally appalling. He had zero remorse or self-awareness. Zero regret. He just didn't get it. He thought he was in the right and it was as if he was testing that right, his authority, against the outrage of the political establishment and the people, and he definitely believed he could win. It was all most bizarre. I think Boris was flabbergasted by Dom's arrogance and simply couldn't understand his attitude. It was baffling to everyone, except Gove's people, who were behind almost every desk in No. 10. They knew what he was like, and to them it was more a case of, "Oh, it's just Dom, therefore it's acceptable behaviour."

'The first time serious alarm bells went off with Boris was over Dom's sacking of Sonia Khan, the Spad to Sajid Javid. Boris didn't know about the detail, but because it was Dom who did it, and because it happened in No. 10, Boris was blamed for it. Dom had told him there was a Spad working for Sajid who was leaking information and Boris said, "Oh, really, that's disappointing," but he had no idea how she was treated. There are other versions of that story that have been spun which are simply untrue and versions which were leaked with purpose as all the many leaks were. Dom had asked Boris for permission to take complete control of Spads, and as far as Boris was concerned, he couldn't understand why Dom wanted to do that, but if he did, he expected Dom to handle it in a professional manner. If a Spad was leaking, that was a very serious offence. It's both ironic and totally laughable that a Spad would be sacked by Cummings for leaking.'

The food arrived and the hot, creamy celeriac soup smelt delicious. We ate in the cosy room, the outer doors locked, and we were totally private. I wondered if I could bring other people here to interview. No one would open up to me like this over a restaurant table or anywhere they could be seen. The sharing of secrets can only ever be truly satisfying if told in private and without any possible witnesses.

She swapped the cup and saucer for her soup.

'When did you first know something was afoot, that they were trying to remove Boris?' I asked her.

'Well, for some time, but it was plainly obvious the day after the election victory in December 2019, that Friday morning. You know Dom always liked to be photographed or filmed holding a laptop open in front of him, as though he was studying the screen and his mysterious data intently, like he was controlling people with some sort of online games console to vote the right way? It's hysterically funny. Like he would press a few keys and ten thousand people would march like zombies down the street into a voting booth. There's that famous picture of the PM and Carrie on the night of the General Election win triumphantly punching the air, as they had every right to do, and there's Dom, in the background, his brow furrowed, staring at his laptop screen, as though he had some secret inside information and was MC-ing the entire show, this one man carefully controlling the minds of voters. It was an utter joke. It was just Twitter and WhatsApps he was viewing on his screen. Those who were closer around him than I will tell you. It was this act he liked to put on, the mad professor – it was all an illusion, so fake. He is really just a massive disruptor who put on this very clever act that took everyone in for a long time. And on that election night, they [the movement] were furious. Boris had won too big. They felt like the confidence that gave him would make it more difficult to control him and, in a way, they were right. Boris constantly pushed back against all of them; and that made them both determined and furious.'

'Why did no one cotton on to Dominic and the rest of them?' I asked her.

'Well, don't forget, Cummings wore a cloak of credibility that was provided by his protector, Michael Gove. People thought, *Well, if he's been with Gove all of these years, there must be something about him.* Dom can be very aggressive and bad-tempered, too, and most people will avoid confrontation at all costs.'

It was the best celeriac soup I had ever tasted, but, given what I was being told, I was distracted. She took my soup bowl from me and handed me a plate of Caesar salad. I think we probably both thought we were being good and healthy, but I'm not sure the cream in the soup would hold its nerve if questioned on that one.

'Thank you,' I said as I took the salad and balanced it on the snowy white linen napkin that the waiter had laid across my lap.

She put down her spoon. 'It was almost impossible for Boris, you know. The truth of the matter is that the behavioural changes I noticed in Dom on the very first day after the election, I mean within the first hours, it was startling. It was as if he had gone slightly mad. Something had turned in Dom's brain. It was as if he thought he was the person in charge, not Boris, that it was he and not Boris who had won the election, and yet he played almost no part whatsoever in the election campaign and that assumption could only have been on the basis of Brexit. I was about to discover: all was not as it seemed on that front either. It became clear that he began working aggressively against Boris very quickly; not *for* him, not *with* him, but without a shred of doubt, actively *against* him.

'If you are a trusted source from within No. 10 and you choose to secretly work with the media against the Prime Minister and undermine the Prime Minister from within No. 10, then that is a fairly toxic situation. During the 8 a.m. meetings with the Prime Minister, when Boris was going through the day he [Dom] would text people in the room: *What the fuck is this clown on about?* Dom acted like a thug. People were scared of him, and in sending those messages to staff, he knew what he was doing. And if you align the actions of Cummings inside No. 10 with the post-Brexit media on the outside, the BBC and the rest of them, you've got a very, very difficult situation. Add to that all the Remain MPs who obsessively hated Boris for Brexit, and there's a fair number of them, Conservatives in my opinion being the most vengeful. Those who were once ministers and believed they should be so forever, who think they are superior to their colleagues and too good for the backbenches – you know who I mean. And those who thought they should have been Prime Minister, who look at themselves in the mirror each and every morning and say to their reflection, *It should be you.* The One Nation group of Conservatives, who are mostly on the far left of the party, were a particular thorn in his side despite his electoral success and the boost he gave to their majorities. Despite all of that, with a strong No. 10 machine behind him, Boris would have got through to the next General Election and comfortably won it if those within No. 10, his closest advisers, had not worked so hard to bring him down, from day one. It would have been a bit like dragging a ball and chain around his ankle with that lot, but he would have survived because he was a colossal force of nature. Especially out in the country with the public, who totally got him in a way Westminster often didn't. And isn't that who we are supposed to be here for: the public? Aren't we supposed to be their servants?'

'Can you tell me how Dominic Cummings worked with journalists? Can you tell me more about that?' I asked her. She leant forward and placed her bowl on the table.

'So, Simon Walters was a political editor at the *Daily Mail* under the editorship of Geordie Greig; he and Simon, they both ran what was almost a campaign against Boris and Carrie. Simon's contact in No. 10 was Dominic Cummings, as Dom was for a number of political editors. Look at how many scoops found their way to ITV via Amber de Botton.* Where do you think they came from? There's no secret about this, certainly not among journalists anyway. There were other strategic leakers too, however; there are questions about who was leaking to the top of the Labour Party. There is someone we call "red throat" in No. 10 and we have to accept that it could be a civil servant and he or she was leaking directly into the heart of Keir Starmer's team, not to journalists.'

This shocked me.

'Well, it's been going on for some time. Some, a very few, were aware that something untoward was happening and that's when we code-named the situation "red throat". As in, it was reminiscent of Nixon and Watergate, and the leaker in the White House who was known as deep throat.'

'But, the leaking and the Walters thing, didn't Cummings just do everything Gove told him?' I asked.

She laughed and threw her head back. 'Oh no, it was the other way around. You should have heard Cummings on the phone to Gove; he barks orders at him and Gove obeys. He very definitely lived up to the name everyone gave him, the Dark Lord, and Gove became the rather pathetic puppy dog, doing exactly as Cummings demanded of him.

* Amber de Botton was ITN home editor at the time.

'The first objective was to get Sajid out and Rishi in his place as Chancellor. That was a stage in the plot, concocted by the group of men who have been at the centre of the party and, consequently, the government for over thirty years. That is why the sacking of Sonia Khan by Cummings was more significant than most people realise,' she continued. 'It was a strategic move on the chessboard. And what is as significant as the sacking itself is what came after, when she decided to take legal action. The harassment, the stalking, the filming, she was followed every-where, and she had to call the Met Police a number of times. So many times, she was given a named individual officer to call.'

I felt like this conversation was starting at the end.

'Can we start at the beginning?' I asked. 'As in, tell me who Sonia Khan is, who did she work for, why she was sacked, but most importantly, why is it relevant?'

'Sonia was one of Sajid Javid's Spads when he was Chancellor. She dealt with media enquiries into the Treasury. At the time, the Treasury was working on the education spending settlement for the Department of Education and there was also a science pack-age about to be announced, so it was very busy considering it was August. She had a very high-powered job working so close to the Chancellor. Before Sajid, she had worked for Philip Hammond, so she was professional and experienced in the ways of the Treasury. One evening, the diary manager of the Spads team came in to tell her she was wanted in No. 10. It was about six fifteen at night. Sonia had never met Dominic Cummings and couldn't imagine why he would want to see her, so she went with the diary secretary to her office to call Dom's office back. She asked why Dom wanted to see her, worried that she was going to be asked to duplicate conversations others were having about the complicated education spending settlement or on the science package. Her job was to deal with the media, not policy. Dom's assistant replied that she did not expect it to be about policy and told her to be in No. 10 at seven thirty, giving no detail as to why.'

'All very mysterious,' I interjected. 'Very unusual to be called to any meeting in No. 10 that way and not be given prior notice what it is you are going for so that you can prepare.'

'That's what Sonia thought. If Dominic wanted to discuss anything with someone from Sajid's office, he should have been calling Sam Coates, his senior Spad. Sonia went back to her desk in the Treasury Spads office feeling nervous and wary.'

'So, did Sonia go to No. 10 at seven thirty as asked?'

'She did. She went in via the back door and up the stairs to No. 11, to Dominic Cummings' office. But as soon as she got there, she was promptly walked back down the stairs and placed in what had once been the men's loo just off the main entrance to No. 10. Cleo Watson came in, stared at her, made a few remarks, grinned, and left. Cummings entered the room at 19.37 and shut the door so that there were just the two of them in that very small room. He asked her how she was enjoying things so far. She said that they were good, that she was busy. She said she had remained in place when the previous Chancellor had left so hadn't yet had a break in over a year.

'Cummings clearly wasn't interested and, out of the blue, he asked her, "When did you last see Philip Hammond?" Sonia replied that she had been with him when he had resigned, but that she hadn't seen him since. Cummings asked her a few more questions and then said, "Will you show me your phone?"

'Naturally Sonia was a bit taken aback by this, but she handed him her work phone and her personal phone. She unlocked the work phone first. He looked at it for a few seconds and then asked her to open her personal phone. He stared at this for a few moments, searching her messages, and then said, "You wait there." Tossing the phone casually onto a chair, he walked across the entrance lobby to open the door to the shared office opposite the waiting room. The room was filled with No. 10 aides. A number of them were now also standing directly outside the room she was in. Cummings did not go into the room, but shouted loudly across it at the top of his voice, "Clare! Clare!" Clare Brunton, who was kind of Dominic's PA or secretary appeared. "Can you get security? I want her escorted out immediately." Obviously, Sonia was shocked and at once asked him, "What is this regarding?" Cummings then told the entire room full of aides to shush, twice, to ensure they were all watching and listening to him, then said in a very loud voice as he pointed at Sonia, "You're fired. You aren't working in here for one more minute. You can get your phone, coat, and go out of the door, now."

'Sonia was stunned but had just enough presence of mind to ask him again what this was all about. Obviously, she had no idea what she was being accused of. "I don't know what I'm supposed to have done," she protested. He replied loudly: "You're lying." He turned to the room and shouted: "This lady used to work for the Prime Minister, she no longer works for the Prime Minister." An armed police officer appeared to escort her out of the building. Sonia was profoundly upset and pleaded, "I would like to know what I've done," but Cummings wouldn't answer. When Sonia looked at her phone on her way home, obviously upset and traumatised, she noticed that she had received a call at 19.59 from Paul Waugh, a Labour-friendly journalist, not known to be particularly generous to the Conservative Party. She didn't take the call. At 20.02, just three minutes later, Waugh tweeted:

"Exclusive: Chancellor's media adviser has just been escorted out of Downing Street after a meeting with Dominic Cummings. It appears she has been fired."

'Bear in mind, this is not a story that would ever ordinarily make the news or be of interest to anyone, so why was Paul Waugh posting it and why had it been leaked? Sonia was a media adviser, a staffer, not a household name. This was followed up at 22.48 with an exclusive story and a distorted description of the meeting between Sonia and Cummings, at which only the two of them had been present. An individual in No. 10 had been told to give the story to Waugh, to make it look like it hadn't come from within No. 10. But again, why? Stories aren't about media advisers, people the public don't know.

'At 21.30 Sonia received a message from a *Sunday Times* journalist:

"Hi Sonia, my phone has just exploded with people telling me that your employment has come to an end and that we [*Sunday Times* journalists] are to blame as they are fingering you for the Yellowhammer leak. As we both know, that's not the case – is there anything I can do to help? I feel horrible … how can they do this without proof?"

'Sonia was shell-shocked. This was news to her. At no time during her short discussion with Cummings had Yellowhammer been mentioned or discussed. [Operation Yellowhammer was the code name used by the Treasury for No Deal contingency planning.] She had no access whatsoever to the documents. The overall responsibility for cross-departmental contingency planning lay with Michael Gove should the UK have to leave the EU without a withdrawal agreement. And there had been serious leaks, frequently and far too many. It was becoming very hot for someone in the No. 10 kitchen as the calls from MPs for a leak inquiry began with ferocity. MPs were asking questions in the chamber and in the media of the Prime Minister. Who was leaking like a drain from within No. 10 something as important as Operation Yellowhammer plans?

'At 23.24, Sonia received a message from Simon Walters, formerly of the *Daily Mail*. His message read:

"Sonia, I heard what happened tonight, can you call me ASAP?"

'Sonia didn't reply, she did not want to be part of a media story. What she didn't know, of course, was that while she was being fired, Simon Walters was actually inside No. 10 in the corridor and witnessed the sacking as it took place.

'Sonia was in shock, reeling from what she had just experienced, stunned and embarrassed. Shortly after the call, Walters published a headline story in the *Mail Online* and on the front page of the *Daily Mail*, linking Sonia's exit to the major Yellowhammer leak, in effect, citing her as the leaker. But Yellowhammer was in Gove's portfolio which she had no access to, as she worked for Sajid.

'She felt like she had strayed into a parallel universe because so much of what was being said and written was entirely alien to her understanding of what the truth actually was.'

I jumped in here. 'Do you think they were using Sonia, sacking her in the way they did, meticulously briefing it out, making it such a high-profile and dramatic event, in order to provide enough cover to remove the need for a Yellowhammer leak inquiry, so it would look obvious that she was the leaker and so there you go, all sorted, leaker found and punished, no need for the inquiry that MPs were demanding. Was she a scapegoat for the leaker?'

She responded without hesitation. 'Of course, the demands from MPs for a leak inquiry stopped overnight. They had their culprit, or so they thought. Look, if they wanted to sack her, it could have been done without an audience, in an appropriate manner, without a full cast of witnesses, and definitely without the associated drama and inviting a journalist to observe, resulting in the ensuing media attention. The intention was to make her sacking as high profile as possible, to get it out there all over the internet and the media and, of course, they were killing two birds with one stone because they knew Sajid would resign in protest, as he was prone to do. They could push his buttons and get him to walk.'

'How did it all end for Sonia?' I asked.

'She took them to court. They played very hard ball and settled just two days before the court case. They knew they couldn't win, but it didn't matter because it was the beginning of the end for Sajid. The first step in getting Rishi installed as Chancellor. A price worth paying.

'Do you know about the "Order of the Phoenix" WhatsApp group?' she asked.

'I do,' I said, 'and always thought it was a pretty childish name. I knew it was the WhatsApp thread for the clan of Gove, but had no idea who was on it. There couldn't have been many MPs, if any, because Michael just wasn't that popular.'

'It has been in existence for a very long time,' she said. 'You had this Govite power base years ago, which was comprised of people on the periphery of Conservative politics, weak people who were drawn like moths to a flame, people who swam in the gossipy, game-playing, thrill-seeking student politics vein of Westminster, and over the years it just grew. That's how they got their jobs in No. 10. Gove had all his acolytes ready to go when Boris became Prime Minister and Boris would have seen this as an endorsement of Gove's effectiveness, that Gove had trusted people at hand, ready to serve, when really it was a WhatsApp thread managing a cult. I mean, everyone in No. 10 referred to Cummings as the Dark Lord.'

'But, why?' I asked her. 'It's a bit ...' I struggled to grasp the appropriate word, '... weird.'

'It was very odd and I know there were some people working in No. 10 who were not a part of the Gove clan who found it all seriously disturbing. But did they challenge it? Did they say anything? No, of course not, because although they found it very unprofessional, they worked in what had become a toxic atmosphere between Gove, Cummings, Cain, Dougie Smith and someone for whom we shall have to substitute the codename "Dr No", whose name was never mentioned and who everyone was scared of.'

'Dr No?' I must have looked incredulous. She laughed. 'I don't know why I'm laughing, it's not funny. If you're going to call me Moneypenny, then this man is my nemesis. He's a man who has been involved for forty years now and he is the key player in central office and No. 10 who very few people have ever met.'

'To your knowledge, how much of this did the Prime Minister know?' I asked her.

She sighed. 'None of it. Boris was like someone charging forward the minute he got through the door; it's the big picture for him, always. The energy. He wanted to get things done and he was obsessed about delivering on his manifesto promises; he's a bit old-fashioned like that. He thinks if the people vote for something, your job is to deliver it because that is what they will judge you on at the ballot box when you go back and ask them to vote again. Those commitments, they were the stick that he beat himself and everyone else with. Meeting them was non-negotiable. You will know this yourself. How many times, and at how many meetings, did he ask about the number of homes in the UK that had access to gigabit broadband?'

Gigabit rollout was in my portfolio and I had to keep a running total in my head because I never knew when the Prime Minister was going to spring that question on me, which he often did.

'They were so subtle, so organised, so strategic, there is no doubt that, from day one, when Boris wanted to get stuff done, these people pushed back against him. Gently at first, one by one they pushed and obfuscated until the move to oust him gathered momentum, and then they pushed harder. When you are working with them at close quarters, you pick up so many clues and the penny drops: it became obvious that they had wanted him out from before the moment Boris walked through the door after the election.

'Boris began to find it very hard to get things through. There was always a bottleneck and they would blame the civil service, but mostly it was Rishi in the Treasury. It became increasingly impossible as time moved on to get Rishi to agree to anything. This blind-sided Boris because, to his face, Rishi was charming and helpful and enthusiastic, even if he did keep on overtly hinting to Boris that he should be standing aside for Rishi; it was laughable really. Boris genuinely thought Rishi was a team player; he *was* a team player, but for Team Rishi, not for Team Boris or Team Government or party or country. None of that even came into it and it never came into the heads of those on the periphery who were supporting Rishi either.'

She had lost me here.

'Who do you mean when you say on the periphery?' I asked. 'You mean, not in No. 10?'

'Remember, Rishi is the MP in William Hague's old seat. How do you think Rishi, who had never been active on the political scene and had been living in America, got selected for a plum seat like that? The next question is, why was IDS removed from office? Remember that? It was decided by the great and good that for the sake of the stability and security of the party, Michael Howard would be put in place as a caretaker leader. No election, no votes. Caretaking what and for whom? Who decided that? The next phase in the history of the party tells you what that was about: caretaking for Cameron and Osborne, to be ready in time for 2005 when Cameron was elected as leader.

'It was all pre-determined. Nothing happens by accident for these people. It's a party of membership but the members have no say. Succession, it's no accident, it's all planned well in advance. No leader of the Conservative Party is left to chance, MPs think they have an important role to play and they do, to an extent, and that's why Boris being elected upset everyone so much. That was never supposed to happen. To these people, it's not about democracy, or the choice of the people, it's about decisions made by a powerful, privileged and controlling few.'

I remembered a meeting when I had been working for Oliver Letwin when we were in opposition and he was Shadow Chancellor. One particular day, Oliver and I were heading back into Westminster from a speech he had given when we got a call from Michael Howard's office to head straight there, for a meeting. It was 2004. Iain Duncan Smith had been ousted only months before. As we walked into the office, Rachel Whetstone, Michael's secretary, was on the telephone in Michael Howard's outer office complaining bitterly that someone was so terrified of flying that he was refusing to catch a flight to a stag-hunting weekend she was organising and would have to be driven. I later found out that someone was Michael Gove. Oliver sat at a large table in the inner office and at the table were Michael Howard, newly elected leader of the party following the ousting of Iain Duncan Smith, and a pair of young first-term MPs: David Cameron and George Osborne. My ears pricked up when I heard the mention of Boris Johnson's name. He was being talked about, and it was quite obvious to me that Cameron and Osborne were being lined up as the future of the party and that the way to guarantee this happening was to remove the vote from members and keep it to MPs only, as the most effective way to keep Boris out. I could see from where I was sitting how that would work for them. I was taking notes and began to feel angry. How dare a group of men sit around this huge polished-oak table and decide that they own the Conservative Party and can dictate who the future leadership belongs to?

'But in 2019, Gove and Cummings, all of them, they supported Boris,' I said to her.

'Yes, because they needed an election winner. Gove stabbing Boris in the back in 2016 got us Theresa May and had almost delivered Corbyn as Prime Minister. They thought they were clever but, in fact they behave like anarchists and they only ever created disharmony and trouble. In 2019 they needed Boris to save them from all the harm they had been responsible for. The person they had actually lined up to be PM, Rishi, just wasn't ready, but once Boris was in and had given them a big majority, it was time to get him out. He had served his purpose.'

'But they have failed,' I said. 'Rishi was beaten by Liz.'

She smiled. 'How long do you think they will allow Liz to remain in that job? Does she feel safe to you? Speak to IDS, familiarise yourself with what happened to him. The people who removed IDS are still there and they are now far more powerful and accomplished in the dark arts.'

'Tell me about the media, have you another example as to how it had so much impact?'

She looked back at me and smiled.

'Have you ever heard the expression, "a lie is halfway around the world before the truth has got its boots on"?'

'Obviously,' I laughed.

'Well, that happened so many times. Take Wallpapergate, only there was no gold wallpaper. It never existed. It wasn't quoted for; it was never hung. I mean, does such a thing even exist? What Boris and Carrie did was have the dining room wall painted red to celebrate the red wall victories in the election. There's a principle in the media that applies here called categorical denial. So, when a journalist calls and asks if a story is true, if it is categorically denied, where possible with evidence, they don't run the story. In this case, categorical denial did not apply, because not only was Simon Walters fed the story, but when journalists contacted No. 10 to confirm it, the existence of gold wallpaper was also confirmed by multiple sources.'

'How, if it didn't even exist?' I asked.

'Because the authenticity of the story was provided by a senior aide in 10 Downing Street and was backed up by two other senior aides from within the building, aides who were supposed to be Boris's Praetorian Guard. Who were supposed to be protecting him from adverse and, most certainly, untrue and harmful publicity. We know that this wasn't red throat leaking, because it didn't come through Labour HQ into the media.

'I believe it was Cummings who first planted the story with Walters. But this is all about the early days and setting the foundations, a narrative to place in the mind of the public that all was not well in No. 10, and that was important as all things would flow from it. Carrie was a pawn in their game to isolate Boris and that was easy for them, because Cummings is Gove and Gove is Cummings and Cain worked for Cummings and had contacts in the flat, with Carrie. Dom used this set-up to brief quite heavily against Carrie to Simon Walters and other political editors too. It was cruel; she had just had her baby, Wilf.

'Many suspected that his key allies had been calling Carrie "Princess Nut Nuts" for a long time. It was a nasty slur that went viral and caused immense hurt and harm, and the laddish culture they brought to Downing Street was apparent. They had ridiculous unprofessional names for each other – Caino, Sonic, Deccers, Roxstar – incredibly immature; and the worst of all: the Dark Lord.

'These guys made journalists' careers, they loved doing that; it was a power fix. Cummings and Cain, they made journalists dependent upon them to continue the momentum of receiving prized information from within No. 10, and then they would drop them, like a stone. If one became picky about ensuring what they were being told was truthful, when a newspaper editor became suspicious and pushed a journalist to ensure that a story stacked up, he or she was frozen out by Dom and Lee Cain; that was the pattern.

'Dom was so vain, he went nuts when media described him as a pit pony and Cleo Watson as a gazelle when the two of them had the audacity to stroll up Downing Street every day as though they were heads of state.'

I was intrigued. 'Who is the Labour darks art chap?' I asked her.

'He's very close to Starmer,' she said as she pressed the buzzer on the table to ring for more tea. It was already 2 p.m.

Christian answered. 'A nice cognac to finish?' he asked. I thought how much I loved this world of 5 Hertford Street.

'Paul Ovenden,' said Moneypenny. 'I'm not sure if he is still there. Whoever red throat is leaked stories to Paul Ovenden in Labour, who gave them to his favourite left-leaning journalists, and you don't need me to work out for you who they were.

Information was leaked from No. 10 right into the heart of the Labour Party.'

'But, why?' I asked. 'This all sounds so incredibly destructive and childish and harmful. Why, when we were in the middle of Covid? What was it all for?'

'Rishi,' she said. 'The antagonists, they were working to get Boris out and Rishi in. Red throat ... red throat was working to get Boris out and Starmer in, but they were aligned in removing Boris, which made it so much worse.'

'But, why?' I persisted. 'Who was it who wanted Rishi in at the cost of so much and so many? Why were they so aggressive?'

'One answer is that they were in a hurry because Rishi knew interest rates were going to rise. The Treasury officials, OBR, every think tank, the City, the Bank of England, they were warning him and he knew they had to move fast to get Boris out. Interest rates were beginning to rise globally. We were post-pandemic. In the middle of a very dangerous war. The truth is, it doesn't feel like it today, but rates will also decrease globally. It will take time; there's no quick fix though. We've been here before. But, in truth, Cummings and Dougie Smith, "Dr No" and all the others, they were united and had wanted Rishi in for a very long time. Inflation would rise and fall. Their timing was that they wanted Boris to cop it for the rise and Rishi take credit for the fall, but it doesn't work like that. It was so organised and coordinated; Lee Cain seconded one of his own team from within the press office to work in Rishi's office so that there were back channels of communication between the two offices, seamless. They were making sure that Rishi was presented to all journalists as the heir apparent, and did nothing to stop the perception that if something happened to Boris then everyone should turn to Rishi. And then of course, something did happen to Boris: he got

Covid and Dominic Raab took over when he was in hospital, and you watch this space, they won't forgive him for that; Raab won't last for long because, after Rishi, they have the next one lined up and they will want Raab out of the picture. They are like elephants; they never forget. Cross them and they will come after you eventually, no matter how long it takes. Raab at some point soon will be beset by negative leaking to the press until they fell him. He will suffer, of that I am sure; like many, many ministers who they wanted out of the way before him.'

'How did you first suspect they were so blatantly pro-Rishi?' I asked.

She sipped her cognac. 'An interesting observation about Cummings – we rarely saw Dougie and hardly anyone saw Dr No – was that he would criticise everyone, every single MP and Cabinet minister, be gratuitously rude about everyone and call them names. It was as though he didn't like anyone in the world at all; he was thuggish and unpleasant, but never, ever did he criticise Rishi – he was exempt from the verbal abuse that poured from Cummings' mouth. Rishi, he was Cummings' chosen one. Boris never was.'

'But, Rishi got fined in Partygate? There were stories in the press about Akshata's finances, her non-dom status. His green card. If they were so pro-Rishi, who did all of that then?'

'They did.'

I lifted the tea to my lips and for a second wished it was a cognac too, there was so much to take in.

'You are going to find out a lot about Partygate if you speak to the right people ... What I'm telling you here is the tip of the iceberg.'

'Cummings was involved in Partygate?' I asked.

'Actually, not so much. Dom didn't really drink. The big question is, who was leaking information about parties to the press. I think it was a Cummings leak initially, to cause harm, but it ran away with him. He couldn't hold that particular tiger by the tail once it was out. No one wanted the media on to the real Partygate stories. Who was holding the parties when the Prime Minister was on the road and on his way to Chequers? Did parties take place in the press office after the Prime Minister and Carrie had left? Boris and Carrie, they didn't have a clue. Knew nothing about them. Dom, he always rushed home to his wife and son. People holding parties in the press office didn't want to be discovered, so throwing journalists off the scent was the name of the game. So the fall guy was Boris. His head on a plate was handed to the media to protect others. I'm not sure it was ever their intention that Rishi should get caught up in the cross-hairs, as in he should be fined as well, but how could he not be? He and Boris were in the same space. The fact that Boris and Rishi got fined for what they did was bonkers when you think of what was happening on site every Friday night throughout lockdown when the PM was in hospital and then recovering in Chequers.

'If Boris was supposed to know what was going on, it was Rishi more so. I'm guessing that a decision was made that Rishi could survive the blow of the fine. To your question, it was someone at the heart of No. 10 who leaked everything about Akshata's non-dom status and Rishi's green card, but not necessarily the same person leaking both. If Rishi had been totally squeaky clean, what levers would they have had to control him? Bring him down a little, let the air out of his tyres and then they would be in the right place to pump him back up. I'm guessing that they leaked the stuff about his wife at the point when they thought they were losing their grip on him, as his star was rising. The trashing of the wife's reputation using her finances and her non-dom status – totally out of their playbook, they've done it before twice, with Betsy Duncan Smith and Carrie. It's their pattern and it won't stop. They hate wives. Wives have their husband's ear. What is remarkable is that no one has yet linked it all together.'

'But Samantha Cameron was fine; she had none of this and nor did Cameron,' I said.

'Yes, because Cameron, he was the project, and Osborne and Gove, they were at the centre of that project.'

She put down her drink and stood, smoothing the creases from her skirt.

'Just one last thing,' I pressed. 'When I said Rishi had lost and Liz had won the leadership, you answered, "for now". Why did you say that?'

She picked up her bag and pulled the strap up her arm with a yank and a shuffle of the shoulder.

'Because these people, they don't lose. They don't put all that effort in, for someone else to come along and take the spoils. For the first time ever, there is a man waiting in the wings who is connected to the money network of the world, and of course they hate it when the plan doesn't go to plan.'

We had yet to have the Queen's funeral; I couldn't see how Liz could be removed.

'Liz knows what these guys are up to. She knows who Rishi has on his side. She will be looking over her shoulder every day. One way or another, she will be gone. They are beginning to bellyache about the budget she will bring forward. I haven't yet seen anything mentioned that she didn't talk about during the leadership hustings all summer. I'll give her three months max. You stay here if you want to make calls or work; I'll let Christian know on my way out.'

* * *

I watched her retreating back as she turned under the archway. She had left half of the brandy in her glass and it glowed amber in the reflected flame from the fire. I picked up my phone, dialled, and waited only seconds until his voice boomed: 'Nadine.'

'Iain,' I said, 'can I come and talk to you?'

'Sure, what about?'

I stammered, 'Er … lots of things. I'm writing a book, I want to talk to you about your time as leader and how you were removed and the people who were involved.'

The line went quiet.

'Come to my office at four.'

CHAPTER 5

YOU KNOW MY NAME

Iain Duncan Smith, or IDS as he's known to almost everyone, has an office above the committee corridor, and no matter how often I visit, I can never find it. There are over a hundred staircases and three miles of corridors in Westminster, and every now and then, after seventeen years, I discover a new one.

I decide to take the stairs from the inner waiting hall just off the central lobby, and bump into a group of Conservative MPs leaving a committee. They look depressed. The Labour MPs from the same committee coming down the stairs behind them, in contrast, are laughing and joking. I haven't seen them look this joyous since the days when Tony Blair was Prime Minister; now they can smell it, they are back in the game. Some have let their guard down and have gleefully admitted during interviews that the only person they thought could stop them from winning the next General Election was Boris Johnson.

I skip up the steps past the marble statues of the former great and the good of Westminster and head off down a familiar corridor of plush carpet, fine artwork and carved oak doors. I had to call Iain on his phone. None of the rooms before me had Iain's name on. 'Through the double doors,' he said, and I realised he had said this half a dozen times to me down the years. He was waiting with his door open and that expression of weariness he assumes when he is in the presence of fools; he definitely has me in that category but I don't mind. In Iain's world, that is not a lonely place to be. He has been around a long time, and I imagine many of us, excepting the Pope, Betsy, his children and a few privileged others, live in his box marked fools.

His office is beautiful. A grand oak desk sits in front of a window overlooking the river, which runs directly below, albeit three floors down. Plush green leather sofas. An oak meeting table and chairs and lots of soft lighting. I far prefer the quintessential Englishness of these older offices to the modern ones in Portcullis House. When I arrived as a new MP, one older cad who only ever wanted to be Chief Whip (you have to question the motivation behind that) invited me into his office, whereupon he opened a pair of glass doors to reveal a vintage drinks cabinet and took out a crystal decanter full of whisky and two equally sparkling glasses. I looked behind me to the door I had left open to see whether he was expecting someone else. He told me to sit on the sofa. I sat on the chair, terrified of causing offence. He handed me the glass, and the smell of the liquor within almost made me reel. I pretended to sip at it while he very definitely drank his and told me how one day David Davis would be leader of the Conservative Party, and when he was, he would be his Chief Whip, so, if I wanted to play my cards right, I should bear that in mind. I seized upon the first excuse I could to escape from his office and flew up the narrow flight of stairs to the corridor that ran along the back of the chamber. It was empty and I was grateful for that as I headed to the wall phone to call my husband. I needed to hear his voice. It was 2005 and I felt as though I had morphed back into the 1950s. It was the first time I fully realised that this place is not normal.

'So, what's all this about then?' asked Iain. 'I've got an hour.'

I kicked off my shoes and perched myself in the middle of his sofa, cross-legged, the Otter app on my phone primed and ready to go. Iain took a chair, as I knew he would; he would never make you feel compromised by sitting next to you. He was a gentleman through and through. I knew he tolerated me, definitely didn't like me, although, despite his general demeanour of grumpiness, I had always very much liked and respected him.

I explained to him what I was doing and I could see he probably didn't think I could do it, but he was going to humour me anyway. Being underestimated is the story of my life but it has worked so often to my advantage, I really can't complain.

'Do you mind?' I asked, as I pointed to my discarded shoes on the floor. I felt as though I'd been in enough meetings in this office in the past to earn the right. He may not have liked me, but I was sure after all these years, he understood where I was coming from.

'Of course not.' He leant forward and clasped his hands together into a cat's cradle. Then, without any small talk, he began.

'So let's contextualise all of this. Thatcher gets brought down on the European issue. Okay. And then the government and the party collapses into a kind of meltdown.'

'A bit like now?' I asked. I realised he was about to give me a history lecture on the regicidal tendencies of Conservative MPs and maybe that wasn't relevant. He ignored me and carried on, the master educating the pupil. Iain is only three years older than me. I don't think he realised that. I sat back, prepared to listen. Iain was in charge.

'Major gets elected, he was a sort of stopgap figure; whatever else he had to deal with, the fact that he had Kinnock against him is what delivered him the '92 election. It wasn't a victory as such because he lost us our huge majority that had been won by Margaret Thatcher in '87. Everyone expected us to lose the '92 election.'

Iain was right, they did. Margaret Thatcher had been removed from office in the most appalling manner and you could still meet grown men today in the party who would recount the events with guilt and shame.

The morning following the '92 election was the only time I ever heard my mother-in-law angry when my husband and I called her gloating. She never missed a day when she didn't take the *Mirror* newspaper, and when we called, she became very cross and told us, 'You didn't deserve to win. Your party is full of turncoats and traitors.' She then put the phone down on us. 'Best leave her for a day or two before we call back,' my husband had said as I, listening at his shoulder, balancing the baby on my hip, suddenly felt a bit foolish. A wise woman, her words came back to me now.

'The polls consistently told us we were going to lose in '92,' Iain continued. 'But what actually happened was that the public weren't in love with Kinnock, they never got Kinnock. This is my point about not getting the right leader. So people were saying they would vote Labour but in the last forty-eight hours, intriguingly, there was a big swing and a lot of it was to do with that Sheffield rally where he made a bit of a fool of himself, which reinforced the view that this man, Kinnock, is not serious material to be Prime Minister. He turned to the audience and did that whole triumphant, "Oh, yeah", you know, like this, and he just got completely consumed by the whole publicity showman thing; it was his character, he had always been like that. So people took from that that he was flippant, unreliable, and then came the forty-eight hours of switchers that delivered the Tories the slimmest government majority at the last moment that none of the polls picked up because it was too late in those days. Major didn't win the '92 election, he didn't lose, the party was moribund. The loser was Kinnock in the last forty-eight hours. So

Major limps in, and then there is Maastricht [the foundation of the European Union].'

I knew that this was the time in politics when Iain earnt his stripes. He was one of the defining rebels.

'So, most of the men who have caused such problems within the Conservative Party and have removed leaders – I'm talking about me, and Boris – they were involved back then and were anti-Maastricht at the time. They were much younger people back then but they were everywhere. In and out of the anti-Maastricht groups and on the fringes, in political think tanks and the like, building up contacts as they went – when you look back, it was all very organised. The advisers to William Hague at the time, Michael Gove, Danny Finkelstein [journalist at *The Times*] and the like, who were all very strong with Hague – that's who they were.

'And their answer was that the reason we finally lost so over-whelmingly to Tony Blair in '97 was that really we should have lost in '92. Blair would have faced all the big challenges that we did. It was a big mistake to have won in '92, even though it was Kinnock who blew it.'

'How do you think they got rid of Boris?' I asked him, but he just ploughed on. I smiled to myself. This was the Iain I knew. He was on a roll.

'Anyway, we lose in '97 big time, and we're down to one hundred and sixty MPs. Okay. Then begins the story. So what happens is that the view among Gove and others is that the Tory Party is finished. That it is no longer a modern fit-for-purpose party. It's an old party. This may resonate with some of the conversations taking place today among some of our newer MPs – the party needs to be changed.

'When Hague fell, a group who were Michael Portillo fan boys, they thought Portillo wasn't capable any longer and some of them persuaded me to stand, and I took the point of view, somebody has to make the argument for the Conservative Party because most of them were throwing their hands in the air and claiming the end had come. They were just too young and immature. I knew it needed a grown-up. They wanted to destroy the party; I knew that to do that would be utter madness. But the view was, and I think it was Gove who actually said this to me, "Let it go." He said this to me once: "I believe the party needs to be burnt in the inferno and out of it should come a new party, which is modern, you know, right on everything right. We know what modern Britain looks like, you know, we don't bang on about Europe. What we want to do is get on and change our attitudes and views on the health service, everything else."

'You can see examples of that influence during Hague's time early on, when he cut his hair and wore baseball caps and did the whole "look at me, I'm the modern Britain bovver boy", until he realised that none of it was working and he suddenly shifted in the last year and a half and adopted the anti-Euro stance at the 2001 election.'

I remembered very clearly the images of Hague in the baseball cap.

'But these guys, "the movement" as they called themselves back then, they were very certain that this time we had to burn the party down. All young men, all still high on student political life. They came to see me at my home and treated my wife, Betsy, like she was a paid servant answering the door. Didn't acknowledge her and then came in and told me what it was I had to do, like they would know, and what I had to do was to manage the decline of the party into defeat.'

I stopped writing and wondered, was that what was happening today? Do these people want us to lose the next election? Is that why they removed Boris, so that we would lose? Let the

Labour Party undertake the mission creep to edge us closer to the EU and the single market and then use it as a weapon against Keir Starmer to beat him with at the following election?

'Is Michael Gove the Brexiteer he made himself out to be with Vote Leave?' I asked Iain.

'I never saw any evidence of that, as he was one of those telling me not to ever mention the EU, quite the contrary. So, it was a man called Dean Godson who introduced me to all of these people, Gove, and a chap called Mark MacGregor, and they wanted me to go in hard and be the person who would just destroy the Tory Party and rebuild it into the kind of party they thought it should be. I didn't agree with them.'

From what I already knew, the idea that they would let Iain stick around and rebuild the party, even had he wanted to, seemed highly unlikely.

'My theory was that the party needed to find a way to express what it believed in, and that had to be wider than just a few subjects. But actually, be on the side of the people. Anyway, so that was what I wanted my agenda as leader to be, and having been through Maastricht, I was never going to just drop Europe as an issue.

'It was Owen Paterson, who became my PPS, who was the first to raise the alarm that something was going badly wrong. He kept saying to me, "Iain, these people are going to bring you down. They have no interest in you. They just want to use you to basically take control with their own agenda to destroy the party." It was, quite frankly, a peculiar agenda. But they could never quite articulate it. It was as if that wasn't important to them, as though they were intellectually superior and it was beneath them to have to explain the evidence behind their beliefs – but I suppose what they did express was that they were against anything to do with removing ourselves from the EU. That was the only position they did and could articulate. They were very certain about that. It was an absolute anathema to them. All they would say at meetings was – and I'm talking Danny Finkelstein, Michael Gove and all the acolytes and hangers-on and underlings – that they didn't want to talk about Europe, we shouldn't talk about Europe at all, but it was all nonsense as the single currency was a massive issue and it was clear that was where Labour wanted to take the UK, into the Euro. So there was a big divide between the MPs who you would now call Brexiteers and all of these people who thought they were setting the agenda of the party, from the wings, the sidelines. Remember, Gove wasn't even an MP at the time, I think both he and Danny were working as journalists at *The Times*. I made a huge mistake. I thought the way to deal with them was to bring some of these people inside the tent.'

It occurred to me that Boris may also have made the same huge mistake.

I wanted to ask him, was this because he believed they had talent that could be harnessed, or because he was scared of them and the damage they could do on the outside of the tent? Both Gove and Finkelstein were influential journalists; they could do a lot of harm to someone's reputation if they so wished. I decided not to ask.

'But what was going on there right from the beginning was a lot of undermining of me once they realised they weren't going to get their way with me. That I had never been an opportunist on Maastricht, I was for real; that I was an early-day Brexiteer. That I would not bend to their edict of never mentioning the EU. And at that point, when they realised I was serious and they could not control me, just like a house of cards, it all began to tumble.

'They brought someone into the outer office and it turns out they took a ton of notes of everything that was going on in the office. That person was at the heart of the final coup that removed me.

'Anyway, I began to listen to Owen, and when I did, it became clear it was part of the plot. They were trying to insert all their people into key roles in my administration and it was becoming very obvious, I had simply been used.

'It seems like the reason they wanted me in place was to keep the seat warm until they could get Portillo back in, but they hadn't reckoned on how tough I could be or how clear my thinking was. I have principles and I stick to them, especially on the EU. They couldn't handle that.

'I began to be pressured by MPs who supported me to get some of these people out because it was becoming a nightmare. First one on the list was Mark MacGregor. He was CEO at Central Office, formerly of the Federation of Conservative Students, which was on the very right of the party. They were also known as Maggie's militant tendency and, latterly, "the movement". As soon as I removed MacGregor, the rest quite literally came out and began to openly attack me, straightaway. Portillo attacked. Then he pops up again and openly starts attacking a shadow minister.

'And that was the time of the big unite-or-die Commons speech where I said, you can either decide to unite or we're just going to die. They ran an attack line and thereafter, cut by cut, they were determined to kill my leadership. They were determined to get me out as fast as they possibly could and it all came tumbling down like a pack of cards. The thing that they tried to latch on to was that Betsy worked for me during that time; what they didn't realise was that she *did* work for me, very hard indeed. She did a huge amount of project chasing during the day. At night, I would load her up with tasks and calls to make the following day because I trusted her and it had to be done, and, like everyone, I had come to realise, you had to be careful who you did trust in politics. So they built a case based around a whole pack of lies about me. Astonishing really, and it famously became known as Betsygate, and it was my undoing. They were very clever.

'Of course, there was a full inquiry, which was exactly what they wanted. The inquiry found that the work Betsy did was right and proper and legitimate, but by that point, it was all too late, they had removed me. It was all so elaborate and fascinating and well-orchestrated. They picked their moments well, around my conference speech in 2002. Two days before it began, I heard that Robbie Gibb, who was working on *Newsnight* at the time, was about to run an entire programme on how I had been misusing government money. That accusation was utterly astonishing and of course timed to coincide with the opening of conference; it seems to me that it was intended to derail the whole thing. It felt like it was all a complete and total set-up.'

I was to discover that the name Robbie Gibb, brother of Nick Gibb MP, would pop up often during the course of my interviews. Formerly a member of the Federation of Conservative Students and a member of 'the movement', now he sat on the editorial board at the BBC. He had been at Theresa May's side throughout her time as Prime Minister as head of comms. It felt like Robbie had always been around and about Westminster. He was very close friends with Dougie Smith and Munira, and you didn't have to follow too many breadcrumbs to trace his path into No. 10. He had been there at the beginning of what became known as the Tory wars under Hague and Portillo, and had been in the mix in one way or another ever since.

Iain continued, 'We heard about it [the *Newsnight* programme] in time and we got an injunction out because it was totally untrue and damaging. They couldn't run it, so then what they did was begin a whispering campaign at the conference; I just say this to highlight how this group have certain tactics they deploy and the extent to which they will use them. There is a pattern. Their tricks are tried and tested. No social media in those days, otherwise they'd have got it out there more quickly. The whispering campaign on the fringes of conference eventually permeated and then a full complaint was made once it had broken through the lines of party gossip. The inquiry was called for and announced; they knew once an inquiry was started, bingo, they had me, because they had their hook, they could manipulate the media and all the headlines, and feed the hue and cry and frenzy they required in order to manipulate public opinion. And, indeed, to turn MPs themselves against me.'

Iain's phone rang. He seemed to struggle switching off the volume, so I said, 'Go ahead, answer it. Would you like me to leave?'

'Not at all,' he said. 'Just let me answer it.'

I was truly speechless at what he was telling me. What Iain was explaining was almost a blueprint for what had happened to Boris.

A message popped up on my phone from Moneypenny with a new name:

This person is a regular at Robbie Gibb's summer parties.

I had been aware that Robbie was closely linked to Dougie's wife, Munira. Indeed, I had been summoned to meet with them both in No. 10 when I was Secretary of State, without a set agenda or anyone taking minutes. Robbie spent the meeting trying to persuade me to appoint Lord Stephen Gilbert as head of Ofcom. Gilbert is a very long-standing party apparatchik who has worked from within Central Office for as long as I can remember. The interview process for the post had already begun under my predecessor, Oliver Dowden. Gilbert had somehow got himself into the mix in the interview process, which had surprised me somewhat. He was definitely not my choice to lead a huge and complex organisation such as Ofcom, which was preparing to regulate the online safety bill once it was passed. Since the day I had arrived in the department, under instructions to knock the bill into shape, my amazing officials had worked day and night to do just that, and whoever became the chair of Ofcom needed to be a man or woman with a serious degree of experience and ability. As I took over from Oliver Dowden, his advice to me about the online safety bill had been, 'It's a horrible bill, kick it into the long grass where it belongs.'

My opinion was the complete opposite. It was a bill that would save the lives of young people and vulnerable adults by keeping them safe online. My refusal to bend to the wishes of Munira and Robbie took me down a dark road.

Stephen Gilbert had been through the interview process for Ofcom and it was beyond me how he had scored equally with Lord Michael Grade. The two men were chalk and cheese in terms of knowledge of the sector, leadership, experience of chairing a large organisation ... the list went on. Michael Grade ticked every box, Gilbert didn't tick any. The first inkling I had that there was trouble afoot was when, on the evening after being summoned to meet Robbie Gibb in No. 10, I received a phone call from Munira. When she realised that even her second attempt was not going to change my mind, she informed me that I would shortly be receiving a phone call from Dougie Smith.

Was this supposed to alarm or scare me? I was simply perplexed.

The following night, the phone call from Dougie duly arrived. He was polite, but his strong Scottish accent was laced with irritation at my refusal to change my opinion from Grade to Gilbert. His manner was intimidating, bullying even. Despite feeling disconcerted and slightly vulnerable when I put the phone down,

I did not change my mind, which he had told me I most definitely had to. He was incredibly intense and formidable.

The following evening, I placed into the Prime Minister's red box an advice note recommending Michael Grade be appointed as the chair of Ofcom, for him to approve overnight.

It's worth pointing out here that Michael Grade had chaired ITV, the BBC and Channel 4. Stephen Gilbert had worked in Conservative Campaign Headquarters (CCHQ) almost his entire working life. He'd also worked for Stronger In, a pro-EU Remain organisation, and ran Theresa May's election campaign, meaning he was partly responsible for us almost losing the 2017 election and getting a Corbyn government. It was a complete mystery to me why Robbie Gibb, Munira and Dougie were working so hard to pressure me into selecting Gilbert and not Grade.

Astonishingly, during the course of the night, my advice note to the Prime Minister was changed in his red box and replaced with advice recommending Gilbert for the post.

I only became aware this had happened when I received a phone call extremely early the following morning from someone working in No. 10 whose identity I swore to protect. When I took the call, the enormity of what I was being told didn't hit me at first, because it was almost too scandalous to appreciate in those first few moments.

'You need to know, the advice note you put into the PM's red box to be signed off last night, it's been interfered with and someone else's name is in there.' I do not know for certain how and by whom the switch was made, and there appeared to be a number of candidates.

'How? The appointment is the Prime Minister's, based on my advice, based on an extensive interview process. It's my advice ultimately that's to be signed off by the Prime Minister. How can this happen?'

There was silence.

I put the phone down and telephoned the Prime Minister once there was a gap in my meetings. 'I'm on my way to Windsor, to see the Queen,' he said. 'I only have five minutes.'

'Boss, I need longer than that.'

I think he could tell by the tone in my voice, I was deadly serious, and I heard him put his hand on the phone and speak to whichever Private Secretary was working next to him in the car. What followed was a ten-minute intense conversation in which I knew I was fighting for my authority and that of every Secretary of State who served in his government against the influence of people in the shadows I barely knew anything about. I was fighting for the authority of the department, and for the credibility of the appointments process upon which every appointment rested.

I finished my pitch to the PM to salvage my authority.

'So, Prime Minister, will you back my choice?'

There was a long silence. I knew that by doing so, he would have to deal with a world of pain back in Downing Street.

'Of course I will. You are my chosen Secretary of State, and of course I back your decision; that's why I put you in the job, Nads. This is how it works.'

I went through the interview notes with him again, explaining the rationale behind my choice.

The appointment of Michael Grade was announced by No. 10 a few days later.

I took a closer look at the panel that had interviewed the candidates, which had bizarrely scored Gilbert equally with Grade. A panel member was Michael Simmonds, who is the husband of MP Nick Gibb and is Robbie Gibb's brother-in-law. Another was a lobbyist called Michael Prescott, described by the *Financial Times* as a 'friend of Robbie Gibb'. And Sue Gray, whose nickname in the civil service is 'Sue Gray area' – a very close ally of Michael Gove – was the chair. Back then, none of that made much sense to me. Oliver Dowden had been the Secretary of State at the time who had agreed to the panel, and was also a close friend of Dougie Smith and Robbie Gibb. I discovered that Michael Simmonds had been an early member of the FCS as far back as the Eighties, along with Smith and Gibb.

I was so impacted by the aggression of the previous forty-eight hours and the battle to ensure that the right person was appointed that a short time after putting the phone down to the Prime Minister, I was quite suddenly physically sick and the head of my private office called for the car to take me home.

Iain finished his call and placed the phone in his jacket pocket. 'So where were we? Right, yes, there was no way on earth I was going to survive an inquiry, regardless of how innocent I was. You know what it's like: the moment the inquiry is announced, you are presumed guilty until proven innocent.'

He was right. Since Boris announced the Covid inquiry, the whole world thought he had indeed attended frat house parties.

'Was this because that very phrase was planted with journalists in order to plant the image in the minds of readers, Iain?'

'Yes, because that's how they manipulate. I'll just point you again to the similarities in the way they have operated with Boris over Partygate, so you know who is at the bottom of all this. These people, they knew very well that once the notion that Boris had been attending illegal parties had taken hold in the mind of the public, even though he hadn't, he was done for. It was about perception.'

The weak and silvery lilac sun that had filled the room slipped behind a cloud. I could see the words 'frat house' and 'vomit on carpets' printed on news sheets, and other wholly untrue and damaging statements in relation to Boris, leaked and designed to conjure up lurid images and negative opinion in the mind of the reader. The man associated with and inextricably linked to No. 10 was Boris, not the hundreds of staff who worked in the building, and certainly not Simon Case, who was the Cabinet Secretary and responsible for civil servants in the building and the working environment in No. 10, and definitely not to Lee Cain and the press office staff.

'There was really no escape. Once all that was out there, all that stuff in the press, the inquiry had to—'

'Which, by the way, Boris launched himself,' I interrupted. 'All in good faith, to get to the bottom of the countless rumours beginning to circulate in the media and among the public. He wanted the truth to be out.

'What you're saying is, he got hoisted by his own petard by calling for the inquiry, but he would have done that in all innocence not knowing the same people would be pulling the media strings who were out to destroy him, confident he would never survive it. Boris was fined for people walking into his office while he was sat at his desk. He never went to a single party. The police had already decided that those very few gatherings which had been photographed, that were in his diary to thank someone who was leaving, were necessary for morale building in a crisis. Those tame actions are not what removed him as Prime Minister – and you're telling me, these people working against him, they would ensure that the inquiry killed his role as Prime Minister, with stories planted in the media in the same way they killed off you as party leader. It had worked once, it would work again.'

I thought about what Moneypenny had told me about red throat. Who needed a fifth column in No. 10 leaking directly to Labour when the people Boris felt he could trust were united and out to destroy him anyway? It made red throat irrelevant or, an even worse prospect, an accomplice.

'Cummings was a part of it all,' said Iain. 'He was working for me at the time; Gove brought him into my office to work. In the midst of all of this, just like Boris, I faced a confidence motion, which I lost and ceased being leader. All on the back of public hysteria, which MPs, being the cowards most of them are, quite frankly buckle under.'

I couldn't argue with this. 'Present company excepted, Iain.'

Having sat for the hour listening to him explain everything to me, my respect for him had grown further. He was right about MPs being mostly cowards. The vast majority would pee in their granny's handbag in order to avoid having to defend an honest position, if the eyes of the world were upon them. An MP's principles are, in many cases, as rare as unicorns.

Iain looked sad and I realised it wasn't much fun for him having to go through all of this again. He was looking down at his hands hanging between his knees, back into the cat's cradle. He looked up and smiled. How different it all could have been for him; and Iain is a good man.

'The thing is, what happened to Boris was a déjà vu event for some of us and I'm just surprised that he never saw it coming. The same scenarios and outcomes invented by the same people, who have done for Boris using the same tactics as they did with me, a Brexiteer long before Boris ever was. The parallels, the similarities. I suppose it was twenty years ago so maybe I'm being a bit harsh. But these people – they are a menace. They are addicts, addicted to power and politics.'

Some of them are addicted to far worse and that is something everyone I speak to comments on.

'Probably worth saying, one of them even had an affair with someone who worked for me until she was no longer useful, after which he callously dumped her. He had weaselled himself into her affections, and I've no doubt that has been a repeated scenario in No. 10 this time too; just a different woman, a new victim to groom. That is how seditious they were.'

I blinked. That was the most risqué thing I had ever heard Iain say.

'When Michael Howard became leader and I had been removed, I thought that was it, they had achieved what they wanted, but all the animosity towards me, it continued. They didn't want to just remove me, they wanted to make sure the coffin was nailed down tight. The inquiry was dragged out and therefore the media attention.'

It occurred to me that this was in the days before social media, so nowhere near as frenzied as it would have been now.

'They tried to have the vote removed from party members, in order to stitch it up for Cameron and Osborne and prevent any seller's remorse regarding me coming through from the members, so they thought they would get Cameron in without a vote, which was always going to be a complete nonsense, and interestingly, because of all I had been through, I knew exactly what they were up to and I was straight out of the blocks.

'It was myself and Tim Montgomerie, who had been my Chief of Staff in the last three months. Tim set up the website Conservative Home because we knew there had to be a grass-roots campaign to oppose what these people were trying to do, and I went straight out on the airwaves, and we won – they backed down – and that's where you see Osborne enter the field. Now, you may ask, was Osborne a part of all this? Who would know? He's a smart man and he makes sure his fingerprints aren't on anything, but he's still good friends with Michael Gove and, interestingly, Cameron and Osborne were left relatively alone by these people, until the referendum in 2016. Suddenly, Gove became a Brexiteer. The man who had been telling me I couldn't talk about the EU, and who was part of the pack that turned against me when I refused to renounce my Brexiteer credentials and beliefs, had suddenly become a Brexiteer himself. Work that one out, if you can?'

I could. 'Michael likes to take the big political decision and make his political gains on the back of public hysteria,' I said. 'Remember, Leave were never really supposed to win, just blow the bloody doors off.'

'Here's an interesting thing,' Iain added. 'When I had to defend myself against these totally malicious charges, at what would now be called the privileges committee, by which I was totally exonerated, they didn't stop their attacks. I ceased being leader in early 2003 and it dragged on, some say deliberately, all the way into the back end of 2004. It was a long grinding process before I could clear my name and it cost me personally three hundred and thirty thousand pounds in legal fees. The privileges committee is just a kangaroo court.'*

Listening to Iain talk about Betsygate and the expenses scandal, I remembered the fall-out Boris had with Lynton Crosby, his campaign guru in 2019. It happened at around the same time Boris brought Gove back inside the tent and, as always, with Gove along comes Cummings and then, lo and behold, without a single shred of evidence, it's all over the media that Carrie, who was not yet married to Boris at the time, was involved in an expenses issue.

I mentioned this to Iain.

'It's like a playbook, isn't it?' he said. 'The Carrie expenses story, I recognised it for what it was straightaway and I spoke to

---

* Interesting that Iain used this expression long before Boris's own trial by the committee.

Lynton Crosby. He got the measure of these guys, and Lynton's such a huge pro, he was out. He has better things to do than look over his shoulder to see what they are up to, because he knew they were trouble. From that moment onwards, it became quite difficult for those people who knew about how these guys operated to see Boris or to speak to him. I parted company with Cummings when I was leader. He was a disaster because all he ever did was brief to the bloody papers. Cummings then went for me along with the others. Just as Cummings has done with Boris. When Boris won the 2019 election, I said to him, "Do not employ Michael Gove or Dominic Cummings. If you do, I will give you less than two years. They will destroy you."'

Iain was wrong: Boris got three, courtesy of Covid. But as we sat there now in his office, Iain's comments still felt incredibly prescient. He's a wise man.

'Three days after Boris appointed his Cabinet in '19, he rang me up. He's feeling guilty. This is what Boris does: he's always conflicted by his own emotions. He wants to make everyone happy, to run a happy ship, and it's funny, because he has this public service thing, thinks everyone should be honoured to serve, and they aren't: most people are driven by personal ambition; they aren't motivated by any objective other than self-preferment. Boris is a bit unusual like that, but of course, he's always wanted to be Prime Minister himself.'

I wanted to say to him: don't you all, Iain? Isn't that why you stood as leader? I find it amusing when one male MP criticises the prime ministerial ambitions of another, as though it is something they themselves would never have dreamt of, when we all know that almost every male MP in Westminster catches their reflection in a mirror and whispers back, 'Prime Minister'.

When Boris had finished his eight-year run as Mayor of London, he was telephoned and offered a substantial gong. He has never said what it was but I assumed it was a knighthood or a peerage. He was almost confused at the offer. 'But I was just doing my job?' he had said and refused the gong. If he had accepted it, he would maybe have been Sir Boris Johnson for the past ten years, but he flatly refused whatever was on offer.

'Boris can't stop himself from feeling bad when he can't give something to someone who he knows badly wants it and that it's in his gift to give,' Iain continued. 'So he guiltily rings me up because he hadn't put me in Cabinet, even though he desperately wanted to because I am a straight-talking, effective communicator. I was watching a football match at home at the time and I said to him, "I'll give you one last warning about Gove and all the acolytes – these people, they will bring you down. It's the last time I'm going to say it, but they will." Remarkable isn't it? They have. We don't actually live in anything that even looks like a democracy at all.'

'Gove was very supportive of Cameron though,' I said. 'How did that work then?'

'Supportive? He was infatuated with him. His behaviour used to dramatically alter when he was with Cameron; it was pitiful to watch. It always seemed to me that Gove felt that, even though he was at the middle of all of this stuff, no one cottoned on that he actually was who he was and did what he did, and that we thought he was some innocent, and in a way, he's right.'

Maybe it's because I'm from Liverpool. Maybe it's because I was brought up on streets where you had to have your wits about you. Maybe it's just because I'm from up north where everything is far less complicated. But I have always thought it was a bit of a curse that I could very quickly have the true measure of most people in a very short space of time, and Gove was no exception. He was a man I suspected no one truly had the measure of. Charming, funny, a tragic man who is also a two-bit comedy actor. A smiling assassin. But most of all, a fake.

'I believe Cameron and his wife thought Gove was a traitor to them personally over Brexit,' Iain continued, 'and that really hurt Michael. He's a complex little character, you know, he's an intelligent bright guy who, in his early post-university days, meets this group of public-school boys. It was like a life that he dreamt of belonging to. The poor boy on a wet night in the cold outside looking through the brightly lit window into an opulent room with shining tableware and a roaring fire at this exotic, privileged life. He entered the Cameron court as the jester. That's what he was.

'And then he became a kind of young lackey of Cameron and Osborne. I watched him in Cabinet endlessly. And he played this little act out the whole time, it was really exasperating. Often, when Cameron used to come to him last in the middle of a discussion about something, he'd make some sort of overly intellectual jest in his bizarre accents or mimicking people, ridiculing them as you've seen him do with his ludicrous miming. Cameron would laugh. You could see the relationship between them revolved around the fact that Michael who was adopted and came from a background that he wasn't even certain of and suddenly, he's in the shining light of this glorious individual who was at Eton, who mixes with all the best people in all the best places. He wanted so desperately to be a part of this world. Osborne is not quite in the same league as Cameron, but there was this nexus, which Gove joined. And you could see it meant everything, it meant the world to him. He adored Cameron. It was almost like a love affair for him. He served David slavishly, and the biggest blow to him was when Cameron took Lynton's advice and took him out from education because he was deeply unpopular among teachers and parents, in no small part due to the influence of Dominic Cummings, who worked for him and who is fundamentally a disruptor by nature. Lynton told Cameron that the person who had to go was Gove. "That's the person the voters really don't like," he said. "You've got to get him out because he is going to disrupt you on everything else." So Cameron moved him, stupidly, to being Chief Whip. I mean, if ever somebody should never have been Chief Whip, it was him.'

The thought crossed my mind that because it was a parliamentary job, it meant that Cummings was totally unsuited as his Spad to join him, and so it was a sneaky way to remove Cummings.

'Cameron's demotion deeply hurt him. It was as if they broke him. And I think that played a part psychologically in his decision to go for Brexit; that's my personal view. That he and Cummings, who ran Vote Leave, just saw Brexit as a platform for power and massive disruption. Really, they are just anarchists. I may be completely wrong, but I don't think I am. Tactically, Cameron wanted the power of the government machine behind the Remain campaign and that meant collective responsibility kicking in and the Cabinet being as one, all backing Cameron to support Remain, but it didn't happen. Technically, that is one of the reasons Leave won, because he couldn't stop us going into purdah during the election and so couldn't get the government machine firing effectively; he didn't have the massive power of the engine of government to start blistering stuff all over the place. So that was a very critical moment in that process. Gove supporting Leave was a huge blow to Cameron. David thought that if he got Labour on board, he could ride roughshod over his own party. But he didn't get Labour on board, nothing went his way; that screwed him.

'And then, of course, they go through all the Brexit stuff and Cameron's not speaking to Gove at this point. And when they lose, Cameron decides selfishly to resign. He should never have resigned. He should have stabilised the government and taken this thing, and said, "Okay, I didn't vote for it, but we've got to get stuff through. Let's get it done."'

'Cameron cut Gove off completely. He just said, "That's it. You are no friend, you will never come back. You will never see us" – out into the outer darkness, in that cruel public-school boy way they can. I'm told Gove went off to Norfolk for a couple of weeks and cried his way through the days that he was staying there. He was bereft. Whatever he had thought would become of his relationship with Cameron after Brexit, it was never that. As I say, he's a very complex individual.'

I was almost feeling sorry for Gove by this point.

'What code name would you like, Iain?' I asked him as I finished off the interview. 'You will want all of this to be anonymous and off the record, won't you?'

He looked at me through narrowed bright-blue eyes. Not for the first time, I thought to myself, he was probably really quite good-looking in his day.

'Anonymous? Goodness, no. Happy for it all to be in my name.'

'Are you sure?' I asked. I'm surprised, but I shouldn't be.

This is typical Iain, putting a name to quotes. He is a rare bird in today's Westminster.

He is a good man, but not always right as even his closest allies will attest. When Iain wants something to go his way, he is stubborn to a fault. He served many years in Cabinet but that is never really enough for someone who once aspired to wear the crown, and he is rarely generous to others who have succeeded in doing so. It says something about Iain, though, that this is actually the worst thing anyone has to say about him, and that really comes with the turf; he was far more graceful towards Cameron than May has ever been to Boris.

Leaving Iain's office, I was so deep in thought as I headed to Westminster tube station that I tried to enter through the barrier using my House of Commons pass. It took me three attempts before I realised what I was doing. Safely on the tube, I stared at the adverts above the heads of the few commuters I was sharing with.

I was working as a Spad to Oliver Letwin when Iain was leader and I remember very clearly the moment Iain began to fall; when the whispering campaign during conference that he had described took hold. Oliver and I were stood in the middle of a street in Blackpool trying to work out where it was we needed to be for the next event when we were suddenly surrounded by photographers and flash bulbs exploding in our face. 'What's going on?' I asked Oliver, blinded by the light, quite literally. 'It's Iain,' he replied. 'That's it, he's gone.' Oliver was not comfortable saying this. I had got to know him quite well during the time I had worked for him. He was totally the eccentric mad professor, but he was also a very kind and thoughtful man, funny and far too brainy for his own earthly good. He was also a huge Remainer who did everything possible to thwart Brexit. At that moment in which we were both trapped, surrounded by cameras and the paps shouting, 'Is Iain going to go, Oliver? Are you going to run?', his eyes looked pained. If he had been a part of this, if he had known about it, it wasn't something he had been at ease with in his soul.

On the last day of conference in the Blackpool conference hall, I stood at the side and listened to Iain's 'quiet man' speech. The speech was fantastic. His delivery wasn't the best, he had a throat issue, but the speech itself was judged by the people sat in the hall. I looked around at delegates ... the Conservative members loved it.

Despite the delegates, who were lapping it up, there was a strange atmosphere in the hall. A disconnect from what was happening on the stage and in the auditorium. MPs and men I didn't then know or recognise were hovering around the edge looking disconcertedly at the members. As I left the hall I saw one MP give an excoriating comment to the waiting media, and I was shocked. Had he been at a different speech to the one I had just witnessed? At the time, there was a huge amount of self-right-eous commentary from certain MPs along the lines of, 'If IDS isn't replaced, we are all going to hell in a handcart.' MPs had fallen into the plot, which I now know had been laid by others. The herd mentality, by its very nature, is not difficult to control, and a stampede, well that only requires a little extra work from those who study the dark arts of politics and know which levers to pull, and when.

It wasn't long before Conservative MPs had been well spooked and had moved off the reservation. Iain received a call to visit Sir Michael Spicer, chair of the 1922 Committee, for the ubiquitous glass of whisky to be placed in one hand and the revolver in the other.

The deal made by the secretive few to replace Iain had already been done; he was replaced with Michael Howard. The removal of Iain was about clearing the decks ready for the arrival of David Cameron. The same Conservative forces who did for Boris had done for Iain, too.

Something Iain said had hit a chord with me: the Conservatives have spent far more years in office than Labour because we mostly had the charismatic leaders.

When a Churchill, Thatcher, Blair or Johnson come along, personality and charisma add extra weight to the way votes are cast. They were the prime ministers who energised voters who would normally stay at home and sit on their hands to put on their coats to turn out and vote. That was what the X factor did, it got voters out of the door and down to the polling stations. What I was learning in the short time I had been walking along this path was that, in my party, a very small group of men, some elected some not, acted as though democracy was a concept to be tolerated at best and at worst, ignored. The public voted for Boris Johnson and I was about to find out how this group of men used the qualities he possessed to win the majority they wanted and then, via the most duplicitous means, remove him.

Earlier, before leaving Westminster for the day, I had popped into my office to check the mail in my in-tray and read the ivory card edged in black. I had been invited as one of a small group of peers and MPs to receive our late Queen's coffin into Westminster Hall. On the wall-mounted monitor, it announced that Liz Truss was speaking at the despatch box, and it struck me that the death of the Queen had exposed Liz to too much too early. She hadn't had time to sleep even; of course she was going to be found wanting. It occurred to me, people most probably would look at the speech Boris gave in the chamber lamenting the passing of the Queen, a speech that was now leading the news, rather than the speech that Liz had given. This was not Liz's fault; like May, she found herself in a position where she would never have been elected if it hadn't been for duplicitous means and the sleight of hand of others.

It was time for me to meet Boris again. Despite the Queen's death, there were constant daily jabs about him in the media and, reflecting on what Iain had told me, it was clear that, despite having removed him, his enemies weren't going to stop, until they had nailed down the coffin lid. That was also in the playbook. Removing someone from office isn't enough; reputations had to be totally destroyed in order to prevent any kind of comeback and revenge from a position of power. The attacks, by necessity, had to be sustained.

CHAPTER 6

BORIS: THE SPECTRE OF DR NO

I'm back in Millbank and, true to his word, I'm scheduled to meet Boris again. The funeral is over. The future is marching on and Liz will shortly be making a budget announcement, or rather, Kwasi Kwarteng will, based on a tax-cutting pro-growth agenda. Something Boris could never have announced while Rishi was Chancellor. He would have had to sack him first and that would never have been an option. Rishi was opposed to all notion of tax cutting, he just wouldn't discuss it. His plan to raise corporation tax to 25 per cent was one Boris was most unhappy with, but Rishi had refused to budge. People have said to me: why didn't he just get rid of Rishi? The systemic alliances that were supporting Rishi would have made any such move terminal. Boris lasted three years; if at any time he had attempted to replace Rishi as Chancellor, the same scenario IDS faced when he removed Mark MacGregor, his CEO at Central Office, would have been replicated. It would have become all-out war virtually overnight.

I wanted to ask him again about his relationship with Michael Gove. I still don't understand why he forgave Michael for what he did back in 2016. I had a conversation with Michael in the early hours following the calamitous 2017 election that found its way into a number of books written after the event. In that call I implored Michael to behave, for the sake of the party; to make his peace with Boris. I told him he had to call Boris and the two of them had to work together, that Michael had to put petty meddling and game-playing aside. I had no idea at the time that to implore Michael to cease meddling and game-playing was akin to asking a leopard to change its spots.

The coffee arrived, and we spent five minutes chatting with his staff. I imagine they had had to put in a huge effort keeping themselves cheery over the past few weeks. He had been the positive one, buoyant even, but it didn't take a huge amount of emotional intelligence to sense that he was hurt.

'So come on Boris, what's the deal with Gove?' I asked him.

Boris furrowed his brow and adopted a pose. We both swivelled our chairs towards the window and looked down on the river, coffee mugs in hand.

A moment passed; then, composed, he propelled the chair to face me.

'So, I've known Michael since he was eighteen or nineteen years old and I was twenty-one, something like that. I literally met him in the Oxford Union when I was canvassing for votes. He said I tried to get his vote by telling him I was a green Tory.'

He laughed out loud as he obviously remembered a past conversation. 'Michael was an absolutely brilliant young guy. He was quite fogeyish, but such a natural debater who could go from twenty miles an hour to eighty miles an hour and make a compelling, passionate argument. Changing gear in his argument very, very fast; you couldn't see what he was doing and he would carry you with him. He was in LMH [Lady Margaret Hall; one of the Oxford colleges] and he was very amusing. I was in Balliol and there were a few Balliol people he knew. I think he read English. He was a part of my machine to get me elected as president of the Oxford Union. I drew support from a lot of places in those days; Simon Stevens was the person running the campaign.'

I looked incredulous. 'Simon Stevens, as in the former CEO of the NHS, Labour Simon Stevens?' We both laughed at the absurdity of how his reach across the political divide had stretched very far indeed.

'Yes, him. He was a good man, a friend. So, I had the Monday Club, the right-wing people, and the trades union college, and I had the hard greens and the SDP. I also had the body of the Conservative Party, but they were difficult, always difficult. A bit like what happened in July really.'

He winced. I commented that I was surprised he was still a Conservative after all that had happened. He came straight back at me: 'I will always be a Conservative because I absolutely believe in opportunity.'

I decided to move on to the substance of my prepared questions. I was getting better at this. I'd already spoken to people about Michael Gove before meeting with Boris today. People who don't want to be named in this book, even with a code name. They told me their stories, and said, 'It's for you to use, but not from me.' This is pretty normal in Westminster, the off-the-record briefings.

I thought I should share some of what people have said about Michael in relation to Boris.

'People tell me that Gove was in awe of you,' I said. 'That you had everything he didn't. Your charm, your personality, your confidence. You praise him for his oratory skills but he seems to have been blinded by your light. One person said to me, "Michael used to hang around Balliol like a love-sick schoolboy just waiting to be in the company of Boris. It was Boris's confidence, his eclectic background, Boris's own skills and huge intellect that were about to make him president of the Oxford Union – all of that, Michael wanted, but knew he could never have."'

Boris raised his eyebrows and looked very disbelieving of what I had said.

'Really?' he asked me with a quizzical edge to his voice.

'Yes,' I replied. 'You thought he was hanging around Balliol because he had friends there. People have told me, he was hanging around for you. That he was bedazzled by you because you were what he could never be, as he was with Cameron, only you were first. He went from being a boy of eighteen besotted with you to watching you cruise through life, through Westminster into positions of leadership, elected as Mayor of London, not once, but twice, when the Conservative Party wasn't actually doing very well in the polls. You defied political gravity.

'A host of people wanted to be in your company, wanted to listen to you and hear what you had to say. You were a shoo-in for the leadership contest in 2016, there was never any doubt that you were going to get there, whereas Michael would always struggle to get the support or backing. His friends weren't really among MPs but among the agitators on the outside, like Dougie Smith and Dominic Cummings. Cameron, who had a similarly gilded path to power, had ruthlessly cut him off. Michael stabbed you in the back to cut you down to size. Because he thought the crown of leadership should be his, not yours. Why should it be yours? He's clever and funny too.'

Michael, for all of his faults, is a clever and funny person. The sadness is, that is only one half of the person he is.

'The thing is, he had spent years working hard to get himself into the top of Cabinet, and the top job,' I continued, 'only for it to fall into your lap apparently effortlessly. He even helped to get you elected to be president of the Oxford Union; what had you ever done for him? He was, again, always the bridesmaid, never the bride. He was once more helping you to become elected as leader. He had supported and backed Cameron too, and look where that got him. Surely if he was that crucial, that indispensable to your campaign, it could also be him, no? He could bring you down a peg or two, deflate you in exactly the same way he had done for Cameron when he backed Brexit. Stabbing you in the back was just another act in the Michael show of tortured ambition, which is really all about Michael and his failings to be the man he fully expected to be and nothing to do with the party or the government; and to be fair to Michael, maybe he doesn't even see this for what it actually is. Or maybe he does. Isn't that just the thing about Michael? We will never know.'

Boris was thinking and nodding as he drank his coffee. If I was wrong and he did know something, surely he would correct me?

He didn't comment and so I carried on.

'People also say one should look to George Osborne. George always saw Michael's potential. Or rather, his usefulness. You know Michael's marriage has broken down and he's been dad-dancing in the early hours in nightclubs?'

Boris looked stunned. 'Really?' he asked me again, incredulously.

He turned back to the river and spoke, not facing me. This was obviously uncomfortable for him and I could almost see his brain working; taking in what I had said and processing it.

'Yeah, you may be on to something. I think there was always this simmering anger in Michael that he was subordinate to Cameron and Osborne when he was in Cameron's Cabinet.'

'You know, some people say that Osborne has some sort of hold over Gove,' I said.

'Really? Well, that's a bit rum if you ask me and very odd because George and Cameron loathe Cummings, did you know?'

I moved on to the EU referendum.

'Can we go back to the referendum, that his mission was never to win. That Vote Leave was meant to be "Vote Just About Lose" to make it look real? My own theory is that it had all been a clever ruse to strengthen the case for Cameron to return to Brussels and say, "Look, Remain only won by 1 per cent. If you don't give me more in the way of concessions, I won't be able to resist the calls for a second referendum and next time, I might lose."'

'Aha, well, I think Michael's mission was more complex than that,' said Boris. 'Cameron had already said that he wasn't going to fight the 2020 election.'

'So you think his role was to lead the Leave campaign in such an authoritative and convincing manner that when Cameron stood down and the leadership election came, he could put himself up as running mate, number two on the ticket to George, and become George's Chancellor then?' I asked.

He grimaced. 'I suppose that could have worked.'

'It sounds like a plan to me,' I said. 'George was a Remainer; the Brexit MPs would never vote for him, Michael could scoop up the Brexiteers; the hero who narrowly failed to deliver Vote Leave despite all of his best efforts, and he would thus be able to convince the right of the party to get behind George because it would feel safe to do so, given that Michael would be his running mate and number two, and Brexit would be safe in Michael's hands. Between them, they would cover and reassure both ends of the party. They would be seen as a unifying force for the party and for the country.'

Boris furrowed his brow. 'Well, there's no evidence for that, I suppose, but it's a good theory when you think about it. Remember, when Leave won in 2016, well I was there and Michael was very taken aback.' (I later discover that not only was Gove taken aback, but, in the words of another witness, 'Cummings looked positively sick.' Accounts given to journalists vary concerning the reaction of Boris, and reflect the many sources attempting to rewrite history.)

'So when it came to the leadership contest with me,' Boris continued, 'I think George was very influential with Gove and maybe he was saying, "Don't be subordinate again. You stand yourself; you do it. Go for it." It's well attested that there were a few people doing the same thing, saying the same thing to him.'

It's also reported that Osborne said that he was asked by a media mogul to persuade Gove to do the deed, with the persuasive help of Nick Boles, a close friend of George Osborne, who now works for Francis Maude and Baroness Simone Finn, who is Michael Gove's former girlfriend, with whom he is still good friends.

I couldn't help thinking, if true, it was a desperate and rare lack of political judgement for George, but then maybe Michael was George's way of getting back into Westminster. It's difficult to find anyone in the Conservative Party who thinks George left politics and intended to leave for good. He is a political addict who needed to wipe clean his Remain slate and be in place whenever the party might require him to step in after we had moved into a post-Brexit cycle. It was always the intention he would follow on from David Cameron; that ambition was thwarted by Brexit. If they were his intentions, Boris as Prime Minister, who had won an eighty-seat majority and would probably be good for three terms, would spoil any Osborne plan to return. His judgement may not have been having an off-day in 2016; it may have simply been the case that getting Michael to stab Boris in the back and stand himself was the only option available to George to stop Boris becoming Prime Minister for a prolonged period of time and to prevent Brexit becoming a reality.

'Why did you bring Michael into the Cabinet after what he had done to you then?' I asked.

'I thought he was capable, he knew how to run a department, or so I believed, and it would be better to have him on board, in Cabinet, working with us, than on the outside causing trouble and against us.' This is a political tactic that has been in force since the beginning of time.

I move on to Dougie Smith.

'Do you know him well?'

Boris shakes his head. 'Not really, we had him, with Munira, over to the flat one evening and it was all very jolly.' Munira had worked with Boris in City Hall when he was London mayor.

I could imagine that. The one thing I had learnt about Dougie Smith so far was that he could be a charmer. I've been told Boris was wary of him because of his fearsome reputation.

'Who brought him into the party?'

Boris frowned again. 'I'm not sure, it was years ago. He used to play poker with Michael Gove didn't he? I mean, I liked him and I loved Munira. In the beginning he was very much part of getting stuff done, making the country a better place. We were fired up, ready to deliver and change the landscape. The levelling-up agenda, getting Brexit done. And Nads …' His voice becomes enthused, he leans forward onto the desk and clasps his hands on top as he looks me straight in the eye.

'And bliss it was in that dawn to be alive. We knew we were doing something that was for the greater good and making this great country a better place. What got in the way was the flaws in the personalities. The fundamental mistake I made was this: in everything I've done that has gone well, whether it's in running City Hall or whatever, I've always had someone who was my alter ego. Someone intellectual I could bounce things off and argue the point with, and I think I thought that person could be Cummings. I thought he was clever enough but it just didn't work. He wasn't that man.'

'Can a narcissist play the role of an alter ego?' I asked him.

'Ah well now, aren't all politicians narcissists?'

I concurred, to a greater or lesser degree, but Cummings, he's surely out there miles ahead, on a far bigger scale than any politician I know. A scale where people tell me, 'It was like, in his head, he believed he *was* the Prime Minister.'

I told Boris a story that I garnered from inside No. 10 as part of this exercise. On the morning following the 2019 election, Boris was due to make the traditional speech from the lectern outside No. 10 to thank the voting public and to set out his stall. Logistics meant that he was scheduled to be elsewhere at the time he was due to give his speech.

Allegedly, Dominic Cummings had decided that this was not a problem, that he would deliver the speech to the nation from the lectern on Boris's behalf. He had been politely informed that that was not acceptable and wouldn't be happening. His few allies say it was just a joke, most say he was deadly serious. Cummings doesn't do jokes.

'Oh my God, really?' Boris spluttered in his coffee, as I finished the story. He clearly hadn't been told.

'The thing is,' I said, 'from what I'm being told, he arrived in No. 10 following the election win in a slightly odd frame of mind, as though something had happened to him almost overnight. The Dominic Cummings you had taken on to get stuff done had been replaced by a Dominic Cummings who actually thought he was the Prime Minister, and even if he wasn't, had the authority to act as though he was.'

Boris looked crestfallen. 'I know, I know,' he said. 'I sensed that change. It was all very sudden and very, very odd.

'There were elements of Amadeus and Salieri there, I saw that with my own eyes. He was like Dreyfus watching Clouseau, bumbling around and getting the acclaim. There was that rage at me, I could see it and feel it. One of Cummings' problems was, he would decide what he would want to happen before I had taken a decision; when I wanted to weigh up and consider all angles of what were big decisions, he would brief out to the media that the decision had been taken. Michael Gove told me he used to do that with him, too, when they were in education.'

I wanted to pause there, to explore when that conversation took place, because obviously Michael was confiding in Boris when he said that.

I didn't want to stop Boris now though.

'The thing is, I couldn't see the point of it, of Cummings' behaviour. It didn't make any sense. And don't forget the idealism of the early days. There was a huge vison. I needed that team of rare talents to deliver and to smash through – the mailed fist.

'You know that Partygate stuff, I was fined and deemed to have broken the rules by the Met Police for being sat at my desk … for working with people I had worked with all day long every day in the same building.'

'Dom Cummings briefed against you to journalists, you know that don't you?' I said to him.

His head swung up and Shelley came in with the obligatory second pot of coffee. I was grateful for the distraction.

'He did,' he said. He looked pained.

'Do you know that he briefed to the media that Carrie and you had split up?'

I couldn't believe it and had called Carrie at the time, stunned, and was relieved to discover it was far from true. I was told that it was Cummings who was spreading this rumour.

'There was deeply personal information leaked to journalists. It was all such utter lies and bollocks,' he said.

'It was part of the plan,' I told him. 'To destabilise you emotionally and to confuse you, to isolate you into only trusting a small number of people in No. 10 who, unbeknown to you, were the people doing the leaking.'

He was deep in thought. I told him the name of the MP who briefed a story to journalists that I had been told about; he worked once with Gove and Cummings and was friends with both men.

'All roads lead back to Michael Gove,' I said.

'Yeah, well, maybe.' He swerved the conversation away from Gove onto the leaky MP who planted stories on behalf of Cummings, 'I gave him a job.'

He then told me of a deeper connection the MP has to Cummings in terms of family connections, relatives by marriage.

'They are all buddies, aren't they?' he said. 'The trouble was, I was always busy trying to crack on with delivering on the manifesto, the reason people voted for us; that was what was important, it was what we were there to do.'

Boris doesn't do game-playing. He doesn't really do parties. He really isn't very good at small talk. He detests gossip. He prefers to read a book. The trouble is, his close-knit group of genuine friends around him with his best interests at heart would never speak to a journalist or an author, and so the public narrative is provided only by enemies and gossips and, as it transpired, those who needed a scapegoat to protect their own skins.

'Do you have specific situations you were aware of when Cummings leaked? Was he the Covid chatty rat?'

He avoided that question. I guessed he knew but wasn't going to give me a definitive answer, and besides, I could see he was still taking in the betrayal of an MP he had trusted and who had benefited under his patronage.

'All that kind of stuff, the leaking, it was all so meaningless,' said Boris. 'I woke up once in the middle of the night to discover that the *Sunday Times* had a splash by Tim Shipman, the political editor; it was way back in February 2020 I think, and things were beginning to filter through to me then. It turned out that Shipman had been at dinner with Dom Cummings and Lee Cain and they had told him some cock-and-bull story. I had to ring Shipman and contradict it; tell him what the true situation was. Cummings used to put me in difficult situations by briefing things in order to bounce me into a policy decision. That's when he started calling me "the trolley", because he would decide on a position he wanted to bounce me into, whereas I wanted to bounce around all angles of a policy and weigh it up, and he would hate that. He just wanted me to agree with every decision he took, fundamentally. I wasn't allowing him to call the shots and that was obviously what he was used to [with Gove I assumed] and this frustrated him. He would come into my office and catch me in the middle of something and try and bounce me into a decision, and I wouldn't allow that because it's not how you lead a government, and I think he just became angry.'

We talked about Wilf and Romy and he laughed, and as always when you mentioned the children, his face lit up.

If Michael Gove had told Boris that Cummings had leaked to the media to bounce Gove into doing what he wanted, thereby effectively controlling him, why had Gove kept Cummings at his side for so many years? Were people right with the scared wife analogy? Was Michael Gove some sort of victim of a man with a very unusual personality? Why did Gove keep supporting him, recommending him for jobs, promoting him, defending him, even refusing to take promotion into the Cabinet from Cameron unless Cummings was by his side? Why had he told various sources at the time, 'I can't take the job without Dom. I can't accept the job without Dom.'

* * *

Outside on the pavement, before I headed down Millbank towards Westminster, I took my phone out of the pocket of my trench coat and googled something Boris had just said: *and bliss it was to be in that dawn alive* ... Surely, he was quoting someone or something. The answer came straight back: Wordsworth. Boris is the only person I have met in my life who has the ability to effortlessly insert a great poet into daily conversation, without missing a beat.

CHAPTER 7

M

I've become a regular at 5 Hertford Street. There are worse places to base yourself when you are writing a book than in a secret nook in Mayfair where someone brings you food and drink all day long. I will often look up from the keyboard to discover that there are new logs on the fire, a fresh jug of cucumber water in front of me covered in a fresh crisp white linen napkin and I didn't even notice it happen. As the season changes to autumn and hints of what is to come in winter are carried in the air, I can't think of a better place to be.

My morning guest and I were sipping cappuccinos in front of the fire. I could see he felt relieved as he walked through the door marked private and found me tucked around the corner. Don't worry about Christian, I said to him as the coffees arrived; he forgets everything. Christian winked and my highly recognisable guest smiled. I made small talk. We discussed the state we found ourselves in. Michael Gove was cruising around the Conservative Party Conference attacking Liz Truss to any journalist with a camera who would listen. Telling journalists, he and Grant Shapps would have her out by Christmas. The markets were spooked and utter madness was unfolding before our eyes.

'Will she last?' I asked my guest.

He smiled. 'She has to, surely? I have no idea what it is with you MPs: her vanity was breathtaking, her campaign one of endless photoshoots recreating the imagery of Mrs Thatcher. How didn't you know? How didn't you all see through that?'

I wanted to point out to him that we have men who are far vainer, as Rishi's Instagram account came to mind. I wanted to get back to the days of Dominic Cummings and the plotters in Downing Street.

'How was it that so much was kept from Boris,' I asked him. 'How did he not know what people were up to?'

He smiled wistfully into his coffee cup. 'So the one thing I suppose I found surprising is just how good they were at keeping information to themselves. As time moved on, I suppose after Barnard Castle, people began to ask questions, in a quiet way, but it was clear there were many things being kept from the Prime Minister, and the fact that it was a number of people in key positions responsible for this, actually made it impossible to decipher what was going on, even for those of us who were trying to do so, and it was all so toxic and threatening. But, you know, given how there really is no such thing as a secret in No. 10, they were bloody good at it. Then again, as I think you are coming to realise, they've been at it for years.'

'When you say "they" were good at keeping secrets, who do you mean?' I asked. Secrets are the currency of Westminster. It takes MPs only a short while to work out that they have absolutely no power, not even when they become ministers. That always lies elsewhere. There is power in leaking though, immense power in secret whispers and the havoc they cause.

He looked down into his coffee cup as he summoned up memories, as if searching for a clue. The room was suddenly filled with the smell of cigar smoke; someone was smoking downstairs out on the pavement, and it had wafted in through the open window. He raised his gaze to the window. 'The usual crowd: Cummings, Dougie Smith, Lee Cain, "Dr No", Munira

Mirza – I mean, there's a group of them, isn't there, there's one behind every desk in No. 10. I don't know who they all are, we only know the key players. No one actually tried to bring all the ends together and make sense of it all. I'll be honest, I don't think anyone dared. I mean, No. 10, it's a warren of small offices, and really, nothing is private, everyone talks to each other, whether it's having a fag outside at the back, or at after-work drinks.

'They were the few, but they were the ones causing havoc. Having worked in No. 10 under a number of leaders and administrations, Boris had made it a happy, pumping place to work. With most of us having lost the will to live for three years in the May administration, suddenly there was a vision and a Prime Minister determined to deliver on his manifesto promises. People wanted to make things happen for him, but the Dark Lord made it all so hard, and the way Sonia Khan was sacked, I mean, people who work there have rent to pay, they were bloody terrified after that. Once Cummings had done that, he had everyone terrified. I remember a researcher once saying to me, "You're only ever two pay-packets away from homelessness," and I'll be honest, that scared me. I swear to God, on that first day after Boris won, you would have thought someone had died. Dom was not happy. He was rude and difficult with everyone, and used to treat a lot of people very badly. Like, it wasn't just that he had no manners or grace, it was that he went out of his way to be rude to people and to upset them.'

'Was he rude to people in public?' I asked.

'Oh yeah, at the Spads meeting on a Friday, particularly the Spads who didn't work in No. 10, he would go out of his way to embarrass them. He would ask them questions they couldn't possibly know the answer to and then humiliate them in front of everyone. Being a Spad is a vulnerable job to be in. You can lose your job at any moment and you have to work every day and long hours. No one does it for more than a couple of years if they've got anything about them, they just use it as a springboard into a better-paid job, but they all have London rents to pay and residential letting contracts they are locked into, so quite a lot began to get really anxious. They were mostly really uncomfortable with what was going on and what he was up to, they began to blame Boris for Dom, despite the fact that some of us knew that Dom and Gove were indivisible and it was Gove who had insisted that Dom was placed with Boris.'

I almost winced as I imagined what a bully like Dominic Cummings would say if he heard the person I was talking to say that.

'Another problem was that Boris was shielded from everyone and everything. They never let anyone near him, or talk to him. His diary was choreographed, his movements controlled, so like, former prime ministers would walk about the building and they would talk to people who worked in No. 10, even Theresa May did that, but they made sure Boris never got to do it, even when he wanted to. I saw a Secretary of State once; his Spad told me Boris had messaged him and asked him to call into a meeting that was being held in the Cabinet room. The SOS went over to No. 10 and, as he got to the door, Dom Cummings physically blocked his entry into the room and literally pushed him out into the corridor. And I know this because I saw it myself. When they came out of meetings with Boris, Dom would say to the waiting teams, the Prime Minister has decided this, and we knew it wasn't true, he hadn't. That hadn't been his decision at all, that was Cummings' decision.

'The thing was, Boris when he was Prime Minister was captured by what was a very organised web and network of control in No. 10, right down from when he got up and his first meeting, to who he spoke to and had access to, and they were really clever the way they did it. I mean, think about the relevance of the fact that via a process of being "unfairly smeared" according to the media "by Boris aides" they removed the professional Cabinet Secretary, Sir Mark Sedwill, right at the beginning. They had to because he wouldn't have allowed that to happen because he was a pro. Cummings and Gove insisted he was replaced by Simon Case. Ask yourself this: why?'

The appointment of Case, it sent a shockwave through Whitehall. He was inexperienced, mistrusted. He was rumoured to be a friend of journalists. At a later date when translating this interview it is believed that Prince Harry referenced Case as 'the fly' in his book, *Spare*. In the leaked Hancock WhatsApp messages about quarantine, Case quoted people being locked up and said, 'I just want to see some of the faces of people coming out of first class into a Premier Inn shoe box.' It is also reported that in Prince Harry's book, he talks about middle-aged white men who consolidated power through a series of bold Machiavellian manoeuvres. Also reported were Prince Harry's damning comments: 'The fly had spent much of his career adjacent to and indeed drawn to, s***. The offal of government and the media and wormy entrails, he loved it. Grew fat on it, rubbed his hands in glee all over it.' There is no place in a well-run civil service for someone who talks to journalists, nor in the royal household for that matter. Why Case? Everyone asked that question and it was Cummings who appointed him.

'A PM is so busy, going from meeting to meeting, reception to reception, talking to world leaders, trouble-shooting whining and whingeing MPs every five minutes – all that kind of thing; they work incredibly long hours – that a prime minister's priorities can slip unless they have someone there behind them, executing the detail, picking up the PM's words as they drop from his lips and putting them into action. Cummings had this reputation as a campaigner and a wizard, but you know, it didn't take very long for most people in No. 10 to work out that he was just a very rude man and an ignorant bully. Of course, Cummings and Gove were one, having worked together for twenty-odd years. Cummings had been the disruptor at education with Gove and Dougie Smith. Dougie would just walk into the middle of a meeting at the education department and nobody would know who he was, and then he would just walk out again. Obviously, he was there at the behest of Gove and Cummings, and they knew why he was there, but it made civil servants nervous and caused them to wonder what was going on. Dominic has a quality that came in useful during prorogation – sheer bloody-mindedness, probably his only real quality – but it gets morphed into other supposed qualities that just aren't there. He's not a strategist; others are.

'Then after the election, and my personal view, until I realised everyone else was feeling it too, was that there was this tension as to whose majority it was. It appeared that Dominic actually thought people had voted for him. Obviously it belonged to the Prime Minister, since he was the brilliant salesman, the man with the charisma and the vision and actually, a passionate belief that we were still a great nation. People in the north of England stopped voting Labour to vote for Boris Johnson, not to vote for Dominic Cummings or even Conservative. He seemed to think that everyone had voted for Brexit, but it was pretty clear, they voted for Boris. You can see that now; as soon as Boris was thrown out of the building, so was our chance of being in power. Look at the polls today, thirty-six points behind. That's wipe-out for the party. We are a party system but Boris breaks that rule and he showed that with the mayoral elections in London.

'It was weird the way Dominic began strolling up Downing Street with Cleo Watson. He loved his posh blonde acolytes at his side posing for the press pen as though he was the Prime Minister and, what's more, acting as though he was. If I'm honest, it became very difficult for everyone working here and it became a bit of a joke in the building. He became a much more remote figure to me, but the massive tensions never went away in the building and it was obvious they were between Boris, Dominic and Lee Cain, and this is where there is a massive fault-line: Lee Cain was Cummings' creature, he was loyal to Dominic, answered to him, but he was employed by the Prime Minister. I think there were a number of people working in No. 10 who suspected that many of the reports in the media that were negative and caused problems for Boris and Carrie came from Cummings. Dominic hated Carrie, he couldn't hide it, and I honestly think they saw her as a barrier to some plan they had to have total control of the Prime Minister. They wanted to place so much strain on the relationship that Carrie would walk. I think it was a very disappointing day for Cummings, the day he found out that Carrie was pregnant.' He shook his head. 'There were massive tensions, it was ugly.'

'So are you saying that the things in the press about Carrie weren't true?' I asked him.

He laughed. 'Well, Dilyn definitely did hump legs and pissed on a handbag, that is true, but no one minded, unless you wanted to go out of your way to harm Boris and Carrie and make something out of it and place it in the Sunday papers, which of course, they did. I never felt Gove was someone I could trust, not in the way that I trusted the Prime Minister. I never felt that way with him, but on the pandemic, you know, again we didn't see it at first but Dom, Gove and Lee were totally aligned on the hard end of lockdown, but not one person backed the Prime Minister. They bounced the Prime Minister on numerous occasions into doing things that he obviously didn't want to do and that history tells us probably weren't necessary. The one that will always stick with me is the 30 October meeting to do with that November lockdown. I remember Dominic very much wanted to do it based on the graphs he was producing via a couple of bods he had working on data modelling. Matt Hancock, Michael Gove, all on the same page. They all wanted to lock down but the Prime Minister didn't; he was trying to work from the position of "How do we keep everything open?" They were the very hard-line end of "How much can we lock down?" and there was no one the Prime Minister turned to, whether it was the scientists or the epidemiologists or his closest advisers, who would tell him anything other than that he had to lock down and now, but still the Prime Minister resisted. When they weren't getting their way, Gove turned on him and said, "You do understand, don't you, that if we don't do this, there will be tanks parked outside hospitals with soldiers turning away ambulances?" And it was, I mean, an incredibly extreme thing to say, but he's saying it to the Prime Minister in a formal meeting where minutes are taken and logged for a future inquiry we all knew would be coming, and Gove kept on and on, with Cummings by his side.

'It was as if it was all planned and well-rehearsed beforehand. Cummings: "I'll present the evidence, such as it is!" and Gove: "And then, if he's still wavering, I'll cosh him over the head with the emotional hammer!" That creates amazing, intense pressure, because if Gove was right, where would that leave the Prime Minister if he stuck to his guns? Could he have one day been looking at calls to appear in a court of law? If you consider how people have lost their minds over the pandemic, it wasn't an unimaginable scenario to me. And then, obviously, as soon as that meeting was over – I don't know what happened, who briefed who, which one of them was the chatty rat, I think we can all guess, but it was a very determined attempt to bump the

Prime Minister and to go ahead with that lockdown and not let it be unpicked in the way that the previous attempts at a lockdown had been when the Prime Minister had resisted. Boris was happy to lock down when he was reassured the evidence required it. The news that we were locking down was whizzing along the wires before the PM knew it had been leaked, and I think it is the only time I personally ever heard him really angry. The Prime Minister was always about proportion, but they were certainly all aligned on the very hard end of delivering lockdown. It was Gove who made it happen, but as with all things associated with Gove, few actually knew that, and those who did were on Gove's side. I just wish I'd said more, but it wasn't my place, I wasn't at that level. I wish I'd found a way.'

I switched the tape off, pressed the buzzer button on the coffee table and ordered more coffees. The lady who kept the fires burning came in at just that moment too and threw two more logs onto the fire. I was beginning to feel like a therapist. There were people who were genuinely deeply upset about what had happened to Boris Johnson and were lamenting their lack of ability to do anything to prevent it from happening. There was a common theme: they all cottoned on to what was happening too late. By the time they were aware, the work had been done and the Prime Minister was in the hands of his parliamentary party, and that is the one power an MP really does have: to remove a sitting Prime Minister. I decided to return to prorogation (the formal ending of a session of Parliament) and the Supreme Court.

My source spooned sugar into his coffee and stirred as the spoon clattered against the side of his cup, and I wanted to reach out and take the spoon from his hand.

'Well, it was all an awful time,' he said, 'and I don't know what I don't know, but I'm quite honest about that. Prorogation was the only card left in the pack; it was either that or No Deal, and the Surrender Act, and all the game-playing by Remain MPs who had the majority in Westminster and who were making life incredibly hard to deliver on the referendum result ... It was more, let's do this, it's all we have, and it will deny everybody the time to try and find a way to block out a No Deal Brexit, which was what we were basically heading towards at that point in time. I sensed the Prime Minister took a lot of persuading to do it and that he was told things that turned out obviously not to be true, such as the likelihood of a successful legal challenge. You know, the idea that we would end up where we ended up with the Supreme Court, finding he effectively hadn't been straight with the Queen. He was so enamoured of the Queen, so respectful towards her, I think if anyone had said to him, if you do this, if you prorogue, you will be accused of lying to the Queen, he would have recoiled in horror and run a mile. Nobody at any point said to him that was a possibility because, of course, he hadn't. The civil service lawyers started off in the way they do, indicating that the chance of this legal challenge being successful was highly unlikely, and it went on and on, and every meeting they kept adjusting downwards back to a fifty/fifty likelihood of a legal challenge at the end, but I don't think the PM was well advised when it came to the government lawyers; they let him down badly. He was quite entitled to prorogue, a new Prime Minister setting his own legislative agenda, but I don't think he was well served by any of us in No. 10 really or by anyone in the civil service or the civil service lawyers.

'It had to happen, because if it didn't Boris couldn't deliver on the referendum result. The question then becomes: do we have a democracy or not? Do people's voices matter, do votes matter? But the cost to the Prime Minister's personal reputation was huge. Boris knew what the alternative was if we didn't prorogue and it wasn't something he was really comfortable with because he knew the risk to himself coming up against the establishment and the media. Not getting Brexit done was not an option; there were no easy answers.

'I don't know how he remembers it, but it was … you know … it was grim for him personally. I mean, really, really grim. In passing the judgment that she did, Baroness Hale politicised the judiciary, possibly for the first time in a century or longer even; it was a shocking and outrageous ruling and the ridiculous symbolism with that grotesque spider badge she wore. I remember thinking at the time it was all so surreal, like the ground was shifting beneath me but then MPs were behaving so badly over in Westminster, the Commons was in gridlock, the party imploding, how could we complain about the judiciary when every day on our televisions the disgraceful behaviour of MPs was beamed into people's homes?'

He nursed his cup between two hands and looked down into it as though he was remembering something that was painful to recall.

'It was a grim time for Boris. I don't think any of us can imagine the strain something like that would put on you. If you're being presented to the world in your role as Prime Minister as not having been straight with the Queen, the humiliation of that was pretty awful, it's a pretty awful thing for you to have to carry as a new Prime Minister. He was in New York when the Supreme Court verdict came during UNGA, the United Nations conference, and he had this brilliant speech he was going to give. It was about AI and way ahead of his time; I mean, everyone's talking about AI now. He was so different from every other Prime Minister, who all have speechwriters; for him, his speeches were a personal thing and he would write most of them himself. He had a meeting with the President and had just travelled to the USA. We had to get them to get him up – I think it was five in the morning, New York time – to hear the Supreme Court verdict and it was pretty shattering when it came through. No one had prepared him for that because the legal advice had never been that Brenda Hale [Supreme Court President] would possibly reach that judgment. His civil service legal advisers had never indicated that, they had totally failed him, and if the term "the blob" was ever attributed to anyone, it should be to them. And then he had to do this breakfast for investors at Hudson Yards, people investing in Britain. And he was being chased around by journalists and camera crews shouting, "You lied to the Queen! Are you going to resign?" The comms people who were with him said it was grim, dire old stuff, and I don't think he ever expected to ... to end up there. So yeah, grim. And then we had to get him to the airport and fly him back in the middle of the night, and he got hauled back into Parliament, which was recalled. It all hit him so hard, so personally, that he had been found guilty, but what hit him harder was the narrative that people would say he had lied to the Queen. She really mattered to him.'

He sat back and laid his head on the back of the sofa and I drank my coffee.

'You know, Boris has extraordinarily good instincts most of the time. There were times when I could see the doubt in his mind over prorogation and I wish now he had gone with his instincts.'

'Well, he wouldn't have got Brexit done,' I said.

He nodded his head. 'Yeah, but he would have been stronger for all the other battles that came his way; he would have lost a powerful army of enemies. Brexit and what he had to do to deliver it, it's destroyed him and I'm not sure how many people appreciate that and the personal price he has had to pay and he had all that to deliver, with his own enemies within. Dominic Cummings tried to make him agree at the beginning, "If you are bringing me in, you will do exactly as I say," which was ridiculous because Boris was never going to allow that to happen, but by his having said that, even though he got no response from Boris, who I think laughed out loud because he thought Dominic must be joking, Cummings exerted this intense pressure. You could see the Prime Minister struggled with a lot of the things he was advised to do. His instincts were right as the pandemic progressed and Dominic left the scene. You saw things begin to change for the better once Dominic left. The air inside No. 10 felt lighter. The really big calls – not closing the country down again at Christmas, reopening when Boris did – they were huge decisions, and he made them in the face of some very cautious official advice and intense pressure from people like Michael Gove and Matt Hancock. Boris was vindicated for lifting restrictions when he did and the anarchists, the MPs – they've pissed it away now, but the economic head-start that gave us was great. And that was all his instinct alone.'

'What about Matt Hancock and Sajid Javid in Health?' I asked him.

'So, they were the two most hardcore proponents of lockdowns. Hancock, I think, because that's just what came with sitting in the Department of Health. As for Saj, he went into health writing opinions in the press, saying, "I'll be different," and within two weeks he was out banging the drum for another lockdown or whatever. Gove was so seriously hard-line lockdown. I don't know why he was so, so hard on it, never veered. He served the Prime Minister very badly throughout Covid with such uncompromising advice.

'There were tough decisions, near impossible ones. I mean, I remember sitting in the PM's office back in March 2020, with Whitty and Vallance, and they actually had the conversation, the one about the potential worst outcome where doctors would have to choose who to save, and the outcome of saying to some-one, "You'll have to die because we don't have the infrastructure to cope with every case." It was grim for us to hear that, but we're not having to make the decisions. The Prime Minister, he's the one deciding and that's a massive burden. Never seemed that he felt sorry for himself either. He just … I remember he said, this is not what I imagined it would be, but this is what I've signed up for. Listen, this is what I've got and I have to deal with it.'

'Were you around when Boris was admitted into hospital?' I asked.

'Yep. I mean, I certainly didn't know how ill he was at any point. I think very few people in the building did. Some would see him every morning on Zoom, because he insisted on doing all the meetings. You know, those Covid dashboard ones, and every-one would say he looked rubbish, his rugby shirt on and his collar up. But it genuinely shocked me when Sunday rolled around and he said he was going into hospital. I had not seen that coming. I mean, I knew a doctor had come in on the Thursday and things were taking a dramatic turn for the worse.'

I had spoken to Boris on a number of days when he was ill, and it was obvious he was deteriorating. When I discovered he didn't have a GP, and couldn't remember the last time he visited one, I knew we had a problem; and in trying to find help I began to wonder if No. 10 had become a ghost ship as we witnessed the scene of Dominic Cummings fleeing the building when the Prime Minister's diagnosis was made public. By the Thursday, it was apparent that his blood oxygen levels were heading very much in the wrong direction and, despite us hoping desperately that things would turn around, he reached a critical tipping point which necessitated his urgent admission to St Thomas' Hospital's ICU.

I decided to move on to Partygate. 'Were you at any of the events?' I asked.

He answered without hesitation. 'There was the investigated one, the one which received notoriety, but I wasn't at that and, frankly, the Prime Minister wasn't even in the building. Whatever you think of him, Boris had absolutely no knowledge that they were taking place. Nobody, but nobody, would have mentioned to him that they were happening.'

'What about the culture of drinking Sue Gray alluded to?' I asked him.

'Well, I mean, that's not right for 90 per cent of the people in the building. We were ... we were just working, but we were operating in different teams. What our team did do is, at the end of some days, usually after twelve hours or so of work, we would sit at our desks and we would have drinks on the desk as we worked, but the parties got their name from the events held in the press office on a Friday night which have never been reported on. In their defence, and I'm not comfortable saying that, the press office held similar events right back to Cameron's days and I dare say further back. It was a long-embedded culture and not one that came about because Boris had arrived; it was there long before him. These young people often lived alone, in flats, or in rented rooms. The working hours were so unsocial and always have been in Downing Street. No one gets away with less than sixty, and that's on a good week. It's necessarily intense; that's why people rarely last longer than two years. But the Prime Minister, he was just never there on a Friday; he was often in Uxbridge or up at one of the red wall seats, and he went straight from wherever he was to his office at Chequers.

'The thing that is undoubtedly true, and which *we* were at fault for, not the Prime Minister, is we thought it was okay. We weren't in the press office, but we knew the Friday night parties were happening and we didn't say anything. But then, frankly, I wasn't the Cabinet Secretary. I wasn't the one running No. 10, that was Simon Case. The whole point of all the rules was to make sure that you were not giving each other Covid and to break chains of transmission. And when we understood that, we got into a mindset, which was as long as we're here in the same room all day long, all the time with each other anyway, pretty much working cheek by jowl, we were in our own bubble – social distancing was not great; we tried our best but the building's not made for it. Not possible to do it – if we stay here for an extra hour, and we have a drink at our desks, we're not affecting the chain of transmission. We're not increasing anyone's risk. And that was the mindset that we got ourselves into. What we didn't do is stop and think, but I know there are other people who can't do this, who aren't going to work, who are just sat at home, not seeing anybody, working from home. That's what we got wrong. And I think we – each man and woman – put our hands up to that. Did we do what we did because we were bad people? No. But was it a mistake? Yes. We should have stopped and taken a look at ourselves. The press office, that was a whole different ball game, and it's quite ironic really that they were the people dealing with the journalists. I expected to see some of that highlighted in Sue Gray's report, but we didn't, did we, which I thought was a bit strange to be honest, because she surely must have known about them?'

His voice tailed off before he resumed.

'I think no one in No. 10 felt there was a sense of one rule for them and one for us. No one was thinking like that. Outside of the press office and the comms teams, which were in their own little Friday night club world, there weren't "parties". The Prime Minister coming into a room of people he had been with on and off all day, to wish people who were leaving well, it was all about morale boosting and fostering a sense of team, because we were asking some very junior people in difficult environments far away from home to keep the place going. It will have been in his diary, ten minutes marked out, I'm sure; something like, X is leaving, say a few words etc.'

'Did you feel the pressure? Did you ever feel like it was a stressful environment inside No. 10 before it all blew up?' I asked him.

'There was never a point from March to the vaccines when we weren't under intense pressure every single day with something going wrong. At the start, it was all about: what the hell is this? We'd never experienced anything like it before. There was no plan; we were making it up as we went along. And there were really crucial things that we needed. Things we didn't have, and every day you felt like some new disaster was going to hit you, meetings where we were told by the NHS, we're down to the last twenty aprons for people working in hospitals, and then the desperate sort of scramble to buy them off the tarmac in Turkey or wherever it was. I mean, it was at one hundred miles an hour every day all day long and then the next day; we'd find out we didn't have the rubber bungs we needed for intravenous blood-giving sets, and it was real. You felt as though every day it was like having to make sort of life-or-death decisions to try and get hold of this equipment, because, you know, plainly while the NHS was supposed to be putting in place a pandemic plan, there wasn't one; it was useless. Or we had a load of PPE stuck in warehouses that nobody could access, and God, that was our massive crisis that day.'

I asked him who was to blame for that.

'Well, questions have to be asked of the NHS and previous secretaries of state. Jeremy Hunt was there for seven years, but I think he dodged all the bullets by firing his own straight into No. 10, didn't he? That was obviously his method of deflection and preventing too many questions being asked of him. He must have thought he had got off scot-free because I don't remember anyone holding him to account for his failures. And of course, there was the NHS leadership of Simon Stevens, who we virtually had to force to stand on the podiums for press conferences, and then we only got him twice. The most politically adept bureaucrat you will ever meet. The Prime Minister got very tough with him when it came to vaccines. Simon resisted the PM's targets when Boris wanted to set numbers for how many people were vaccinated each week; the NHS delivery plan was very modest and the PM was like, no, you will go faster than that, and when they resisted further and told him it couldn't be done, the PM called in the army, and it was when he actually did that, the NHS got its act together. At the end, the Prime Minister had to bang a lot of heads. Simon Stevens hated that, the army being brought in, and you didn't see very much about that in the media, which, as it's all about perception, would have given the government a huge boost in the public eye. But because it upset Simon Stevens so much, the Prime Minister played it down, it was barely reported. He wasn't looking for plaudits, he was looking to get out of lock-downs as fast as was safely possible. I'm sure others will tell you that we wouldn't have been first with the vaccines if it hadn't been for Boris, he personally drove the whole thing like a Prime Minister obsessed. He wanted to get out of lockdowns as fast as possible and in his mind, he was clear, vaccines were the only way to achieve this.'

I had been a minister in health throughout Covid. I had once been called by Boris very late at night when he became aware that two million vaccines from the Serum Institute of India had been made available to buy on the market. He wanted to know, had we bought them? We had. I thanked him for his call, switched off the phone and tried to get back to sleep.

'I'm hoping that history will be kind to Boris because the judgements that actually, really, really matter – he got them all absolutely right. I think you can forget the criticism that was thrown at him over lockdown one; he took the decision to implement it, he hated it, it was horrible, but he had no choice. From my point of view, it worked, it was a huge achievement which I hope one day people will probably understand. And then, throwing everything he had at the vaccines was brilliant. He … he didn't do that because the machine told him to; he did it because he has a vision that we can still do amazing things in this country, and you have to give him massive, massive credit for that because he personally made that happen.

'He fought to get Kate Bingham in place [as Chair of the UK government's Vaccines Taskforce] and for her to have the power to do what needed to be done with the vaccines. He fought for her, despite a lot of resistance from within the machine. The pressure was huge and when the briefings against her began in the media, he got on the phone and personally hosed all of that down himself.

'The next big call was how he responded to the subsequent waves of Covid he faced down; you know, screaming and screeching from the health establishment, from Labour, from the BBC, and from just about every broadcast media, calling for the country to be closed down again, which would have been a disaster; the easiest thing in the world would have been to lock us all up that Christmas when Omicron infection rates were rising. He didn't and he was vindicated. And again, massive credit is due for his deciding to open up in 2022 when other countries were locking down, again. Honestly, I was there and I was flabbergasted when I heard Rishi during the leadership debates telling everyone that he flew home from a work meeting in the USA to save us from an Omicron lockdown. He flew home

M

because he had gone on a three-week holiday to California at a time when the country needed a Chancellor and the media were demanding to know where he was.

'And then, lastly, Ukraine, when I think the West probably was edging itself towards saying, we're going to have to let Russia have this one, because the cost of trying to take Russia on and take on Putin is too great. And Boris said, "You know, I'm not having that because it isn't right." His historical knowledge of the region is immense and the G8 leaders got a sense of that pretty quickly; he dragged the West with him after that first phone call with the G8, when again he knocked heads together. He was also the one who stood up to the establishment and took the decision that we should send anti-tank missiles and lethal aid to Ukraine as fast as was possible. As Ben Wallace confirmed when he praised Boris for doing so, we were the first and that is an act which thwarted Putin and allowed Ukraine the time it needed to push back and not be overwhelmed. And that was Boris with the encouragement and support of Ben, the best Defence Secretary this country has known in my lifetime who was appointed by Boris. For none of that has he been given any credit and there is so, so much more.

'But I can assure you, most other prime ministers would have gone with the official advice being given. When it came to it, Boris knew it was wrong; he called the West out and said to the leaders, you are mistaken to appease Putin, here is why, and he gave them all a history lesson, they listened in stunned silence and he left them with no place to go. He dragged them to take a stand and, if you ask me, that's why the bond between him and Zelensky is so close. It was Boris who, when the mandarins were telling him not to go there, to back off from taking a stand against Putin, said, "No, I'm not doing that, we stand with Ukraine." His knowledge of the region and its history was far greater than any mandarin walking into the room to give him advice and you don't witness that very often in a Prime Minister's study.

'When Zelensky did his address to Parliament over the screen, were you there?'

I was. I had been sat on the front bench a few down from Boris and I think it was one of the most powerful and emotional experiences I had ever sat through in the chamber. We had all stared up at the screen to listen to the address, silent, none of us knowing if Zelensky would even be alive the following day. During his speech to Parliament from a bunker, he was effusive and emotional in his personal thanks to Boris for what he had done for Ukraine and the Ukrainian people.

The media barely mentioned it, but reporting favourably on the man who delivered Brexit didn't come easily.

'So yeah, that's the big things. Got them all right. Now, there's a lot of little things we got wrong, he got wrong. But by comparison, the magnitude of those things ... I mean ... I think ... I believe there were forces arranged against him that were so determined, and so powerful, that I don't think there would have been any let-up for him; so much happened which was totally unexplainable inside No. 10 and outside. Including those who will simply never forgive him for being the bloke that took us out of the EU. They decided, we're gonna get him, and I include the BBC in that. But also plenty of others. There are a lot of former ministers knocking about the party who will never be ministers again, and they were bitter towards him, as were the people who were never going to be given a job. And then there was the 2019 intake, which lacked spine and like children panicked every time they got an adverse comment on their Twitter feed. There was all of that, and something else I could never put my finger on, like how every time he was out of contact on his mobile phone, like on a visit to another country or in a plane, something totally unexpected would blow up in his face in the media back home. At first we thought it was a coincidence and then we realised it wasn't, but if you tried to work out what was happening, it could make you dizzy, and I realised one day, I was being lied to, to my face, by someone incredibly senior in No. 10, and that comment, "You're only ever two pay-packets away from homelessness", sprung to mind, and I think, like almost everyone in No. 10 and Westminster, I put myself first. I'm sorry about that because I think I could have done more to work out what was going on at the time, but I suppose like some of those panicky MPs, I was a bit spineless too.'

We said our goodbyes and I had to usher him out so that he didn't bump into the next person I was speaking to in five minutes. Two sets of staircases came in handy.

I now had a sense of how controlled was the physical space Boris operated in within No. 10. My next meeting with a Downing Street passholder confirmed this.

New coffees ordered, he got straight to the point.

'I passed Boris in the main entrance one day,' he said. 'He remembered me from City Hall and he called out to me, "Come into my study, let's have a chat." He told the officials to disappear so it was just the two of us, and by the time he had removed his jacket and placed it on the back of the chair, and we had finished the small talk, one of the little gang burst into the room and said, "You, out!" to me. Boris looked shocked and said, "Hang on, hang on," but they talked over him and said, "You don't have time for this Prime Minister, your meeting is on ..." or whatever. And that had been the point at which I was going to tell him what I realised I knew and he didn't. As I followed him to his study I thought, "I'm going to do it, now", because I loved the guy. He made you want to do your best for him and it was painful to see how he was being manipulated in this way. I wanted to tell him about the parties in the press office on a Friday night.'

'Did you go to the parties?' I asked him. 'Don't worry, this is anonymous; no one will know from me.'

'No, I wasn't in the inner comms circle, but I saw the prep often enough. All the glasses and the wine bottles being laid out in the vestibule outside the press office on a Friday night, when Boris was out of the building and in Chequers. Our offices and our staff didn't go, only press people and the odd journalist who popped in on a Friday night, who would then report on Partygate. Sue Gray wrote in her report that, concerning the party in the garden that was reported on, Lee Cain said he had only popped outside to see how many were there and then he came back indoors. Not true. And the reason I know it isn't true is, I looked out of my office window, and the reason I remember this is because he was sat on a chair with a drink in his hands, surrounded by young women sat on the grass in front of him with wine glasses in their hands looking up at him. And I thought to myself that it was such an odd sight to see in this day and age.'

'Did you ever see first hand how those who were working against the Prime Minister operated?' I asked him.

'Kind of, but not really. It was more a sense of it, because they were secretive. There seemed to be two power bases, which fought each other and then came together again. Power base number one was Dom, Lee, Cleo and Gove and all the Vote Leave crew, and power base two was Munira and Dougie, the shadowy "Dr No" with Robbie Gibb as an appendage and a few of the policy Spads. The most uncomfortable aspect of all of it was that none of them were fighting Boris's battles. Boris had been an amazing Mayor of London, probably the best it has ever had or ever will know again. Do you remember the killing of the little boy, Damilola Taylor?'

I did. I could recall his smiling image in a flash. An image that had dominated the news cycles. I was a young mother at the time and it had been heart-breaking.

'Well, Richard Taylor once told me that Boris Johnson was his friend. Like literally, Boris was the kind of guy that people in London loved regardless of their background because they could see that he was a genuinely nice, happy guy who genuinely cared about them. There is no politician's side to Boris and that is why the media slaughter him. He doesn't fit the mould.

'So people like me who already knew how Boris worked, we knew the aggression and the intimidating atmosphere in No. 10 was not from Boris. None of it was how Boris would have done it. Both factions were trying to wage war with people who, on a normal day, would say, "I met Boris and I loved him." It was like they wanted to make anyone who would be a natural ally of Boris, hate him. By proxy, they turned people against him by dripping poison and telling lies. It was very clear that they were doing things Boris would never have wanted them to do. Both power bases were acting as though they were the Prime Minister, making decisions and claiming that these were the Prime Minister's decisions, when people knew they weren't. The audacity was breathtaking. And the odd thing is, although these two factions were separate, they were also co-dependent; it was parasitic. Dysfunctional beyond my ability to explain, and you could see it was becoming confusing to the Prime Minister, but the person who faced him was Gove, and he was the glue, the bridge between the two camps. Smooth, plausible, confident, he was such an operator, but I think the most unusual thing that I noticed – and honestly, that's saying something – was how inbred they all were. Like how at some point they have all worked at *The*

Spectator or they've all been to the same universities. I mean, it's really horrible. And someone like me, I was an outsider from the minute they all walked through the door, despite how long I've been doing my job.*

'Look at James Forsyth, political editor at the *Speccie*, now Sunak's Political Secretary, Sunak's best man, married to Allegra Stratton who was caught in the video sting talking about parties. Wasn't that a Friday night press office party she was talking about? That video could only have been leaked by someone on the inside wanting to take down others, but the more interesting thing is why did Allegra resign? Some say she had to because she was damaging Rishi's brand and the success of the plot, for when they were ready for Sunak to replace Boris because James was so close to Sunak. Did she have to resign as damage limitation? Dom Cummings' wife, Mary Wakefield, had been at the *Speccie* for years and worked there with Cleo's sister. The Conservative Home website was edited by Paul Goodman who is a long time and close friend of Dougie Smith from the days of the Federation of Conservative Students. He was Chairman in '83 and '84. Paul Staines, who founded the powerful political blogsite, Guido Fawkes, and was known as the worm of Westminster and a man who said himself he hates politicians, also goes back to the FCS, although it would be wrong to suggest that anyone tells Paul Staines what to do. But it may not be too difficult to trace who their sources for leaks are in No. 10. It's all so incestuous.

'Dom, Munira and Dougie genuinely clashed in No. 10, particularly Lee and Dougie – they never got along, until they needed to. Yet they were all very pro-Rishi and anti-Boris, and that I never got. I'm not sure the country will ever see such an

* Boris had been editor at *The Spectator*.

M

unconservative Chancellor again and I suppose the thing I'd finish on is that very few senior advisers in No. 10, very few were in there to work for Boris Johnson; they were all working for someone else. I could just never work out who that was because that person was so lacking in political vision or depth or gravitas. I never in a million years would have guessed it was Rishi.'

CHAPTER 8

SKYFALL

Liz has gone. The budget was a disaster. Rishi is in.

It is Monday morning, 31 October 2022. My phone is ringing. It is Rishi Sunak, who I know is making calls and appointing jobs, on his personal phone. They are being announced on the radio in the car as I am driving.

I pull the car over onto a grass verge and stare at the phone, and Rishi's name on my screen, and I will admit, I am tempted to answer. He would be the third prime minister to offer me a place in Cabinet and that is a legacy I shall leave for my grandchildren with some degree of pride.

It's a clever move on Rishi's part. I am known as Boris Johnson's most loyal supporter and it would be a major coup, should I accept. It would be the ultimate olive branch, a message across Westminster to everyone: no hard feelings.

I screenshot my phone, press the decline button and, slipping into first gear, head back onto the main road. He didn't call back.

I'm really curious to know what happened inside No. 10 while Liz was there and decide to meet with someone who was along-side her and to ask, did the darker forces of Conservativism have any influence in her decision making when she was Prime Minister?

There was another figure few were talking about, the ever more mysterious 'Dr No', the man who wasn't there. I'd done a bit of

googling and was astonished to discover how little available there
was on such an important figure and influence in No. 10. A man
who had been first at the fringes of the party forty years ago and
is now right at the heart of No. 10. The same was true for Dougie
Smith, also at the heart of No. 10 and a Conservative lifer, who
used to run the 'Fever'-branded sex parties and he also has almost
no internet footprint. He is now a key adviser to Rishi and has
been his friend for many years. Dougie had been a speechwriter
under David Cameron and is reported as once having said of his
own sex parties, 'It's more action than any man can dream of' and
described his party-goers as 'the SAS of sex'.

Dr No was a regular attendee at the parties and I had heard
extraordinary accounts of how he liked to watch sex taking place
among the partygoers, prowling around the periphery, just
watching, and no one really cared because everyone in attendance had their own fantasies to live out. If ever there was someone
you'd think was perfect journalistic fodder he surely was it, given
that he is paid by Central Office, has a pass to No. 10 and, some
say, Rishi doesn't move without first seeking his advice; and yet
people can spend years working in No. 10 and never hear his
name mentioned. 'Dr No' was once on remand in prison for
alleged arson. When a girlfriend ended their relationship, it is
rumoured that he had her little brother's pet rabbit chopped into
four and nailed to the front door of the family home to greet him
when he got home from school, in true Mafia style. I heard stories
of how he liked to hint that he had once been a spook. What
really made my ears prick up was the story I was hearing from
senior figures within the party, people with responsibility for the
party's finances.

'Each time a new party chairman or a treasurer came along
and looked at the books in Central Office, they asked, "Who are
these people we are paying an extraordinary amount of money to

as employees of CCHQ? Who is this one, Dr No? He never comes in and why has no one ever met him? I've never met him. Has anyone ever met him?" No answer would be forthcoming. No one knew who Dr No was or even what he did, other than Michael Gove and a select few, and of course prime ministers. This would always make the person asking the questions more curious to find out more, quite obviously. This scenario has been played out over decades with a repeated number of party treasurers and financial directors with responsibility for the financial governance of the party.'

I interviewed a number of high-profile figures and they all tell me the same story. Dr No was never in the CCHQ building, rarely seen in No. 10 by the civil servants. 'He was this invisible figure and every party chairman would conclude when poring over the accounts, "Well, sack him then. We don't pay people who don't earn their money. We are a political party, not a charity."

'Within no time at all of that decision being taken, the phone would ring and it would be Michael Gove, who would very robustly make it clear that Dr No was going nowhere and would remain on the CCHQ payroll. He would spin stories about how he was the employee who dealt in the dark arts, and would cast this cloak of secrecy, like, you can't go there or know who he is, you just have to accept it and keep paying the money. It was very clear, there was no way Gove was letting him go. It was utterly bizarre. Dr No is the strategist who the Prime Minister will speak to often, daily sometimes. He was said to have seen the inside of a cell in Brixton jail on remand for alleged harassment. For a man with a secretive past, he appears to have trouble keeping clear of the authorities. Dr No loves violence too. If ever there is a demonstration in Downing Street and he's in there, he will slip out of the back door into the street and he seeks out the violent clashes. He doesn't take part, he just cruises around and watches.

It really is quite remarkable, over forty years, only a handful of people who have been in No. 10 could point him out to you. If a staffer ever asked, "Who is that man?" as he shuffled past, there would be no answer forthcoming. Someone who I managed to speak to who has had the misfortune to run up against him said to me, "He's just a very bad man with an evil mind, and in politics every Prime Minister needs a man just like him by his side." He's spent time with Rishi and Akshata. He has facilitated Rishi's journey all the way into No. 10. Without Dr No, Rishi Sunak would never have been Prime Minister; Rishi's a Goldman Sachs banker, he didn't have a clue but because he was a banker, he wasn't averse to or any stranger to Machiavellian tactics at work.'

As one person I interviewed said to me, 'What with Dougie Smith and Cummings and everyone in No. 10 calling Cummings the Dark Lord, and we've got this other master of the dark arts who controls everything, Dr No: it's all a bit fucking weird if you ask me. It's a good job the members or the voters don't know. They would think we were a political cult, not a legitimate party.'

I was reminded of the Govite 'Order of the Phoenix' WhatsApp group and my immediate thought was, did Gove think he was Voldemort, his own little Dark Lord?

Of course, the Dark Lord was also Sauron in *The Lord of the Rings*. I was reminded of my late husband when, on our honeymoon, he read out loud to me *The Lord of the Rings*. He undertook this arduous task because I refused to read it and it was one of his favourite books. He wanted me to share in his joy. So in African airports – in steaming hot, corrugated tin-roofed terminals that were mere shacks precariously erected on the red dust of the African bush, while we waited for interminable hours for an unpredictable biplane to take us to our next destination, with my head resting on his lap, half asleep – he read out loud to me *The Lord of the Rings*, until, his mission accomplished, just like him, I loved it.

I remembered him now. Sauron, the Dark Lord. The ruler of Mordor with the ambition of ruling the whole of Middle-earth. Sauron appears in *The Lord of the Rings* as 'the Eye'. Cummings made the most bizarre claim when he was caught driving in Barnard Castle that no one could understand: that he had to test his eyesight. Which was always totally, utterly baffling and bonkers. No one drives forty miles after a virus to check their eyesight.

My first conversation with someone who was at the heart of No. 10 during Liz Truss's time takes place in an Italian-run café in Mayfair. She looks damaged. We both ordered a full English with cappuccinos.

'Has it been tough?' I asked her.

She shook her head. 'Worse than that, terrible,' she replied. Despite a weekend break following the resignation of Liz, she had dark bags under her eyes and she looked drained.

'Can you tell me what happened? I mean, I don't need to know everything, but there are certain people who gave Boris a hard time and I'm writing this book ...'

She nodded her head and folded her arms across her chest. 'I know who you mean,' she said.

The weather was dreadful and raindrops the size of pebbles were hitting the window with force. It occurred to me that the weather aptly matched her mood as she removed a grab-clip from the back of her hair and, scooping wet tendrils from her cheek, smoothed them backwards with the palm of her hand and returned the clip. She folded her arms on the table, picked up a packet of brown sugar from the bowl and turned it idly over and over in her fingers. The sound of steam leaving the coffee machine, which was close to our table, provided a space for her to pause and think as the waiter headed towards us with two steaming cappuccinos.

'Do you know people in "the movement"?' I asked her. She nodded, ripping off the top of the brown sugar, pouring it in and letting it sink into the froth in her cup.

'Years ago, they all got together when they were the Federation of Conservative Students. Dougie Smith kind of led them and then stood for chairman, until someone pointed out that he wasn't actually a student and was, in fact, much older than the rest of them. The federation was way over on the very right of the party; it was actually funded by the party back then but they caused a lot of trouble. I mean, it was putting forward the total liberalisation of drug laws, incest, paedophilia, hanging Nelson Mandela. Not everyone agreed with the extreme positions, but the core members, those who did, they were more like anarchists. They were kind of, "Oh, we're libertarians, true Conservatives, it's all about freedom," when actually, they were just weird and hedonistic. I suppose they were sex, drugs and rock and roll, but if you replace the rock and roll with politics for that lot, that was kind of it.

'They were shut down by Norman Tebbit for a while, caused thousands of pounds of damage to accommodation during conference. Tebbit sensed the danger way back; he was a wise man. And Liz, even before she got in, she was scared of them. She saw what they did to others in the leadership elections, what they had done to anyone they thought looked like a rising star in the party. In Cabinet and in No. 10, she watched Gove at work and she thought he was a bad apple. She was saying back then, Gove is advising Theresa May and he's driving her off a cliff; I think he's deliberately sabotaging her. He's the one telling her to do a deal with Corbyn. It's like he's strongly advising her to do all the things he knows will anger Tory MPs, who will vote to remove her. It was a Gove/Robbie Gibb thing. It's always one of them, close to the centre, that's how they work it. It's like they take turns.

'Have you heard of "Dr No"?'

'Yes. His name has cropped up but just general background information, nothing specific,' I told her.

'I'm not surprised. He keeps a very low profile. I've heard he's been a mentor to Rishi Sunak for many years along with Dougie. They keep their heads down; that's how they have remained so active and why no one ever draws the dots together – they are secretive. It's all about power and control to them, not publicity. Controlling the lives of others is where they get their kicks, and if you control a Prime Minister, well, by proxy, you are actually controlling everyone in one way or another. They have been right at the heart of Rishi's operation, long before he became PM. Have you spoken to Iain? Someone said they saw Mark MacGregor deep in conversation with Rishi at Wembley during the final leadership debates, not long before Rishi went on stage. I don't know if it's true, I didn't see him myself, it could have been someone else but they are so very clever, so covert and strategic in the way they operate, they think no one will pick up the threads.'

'Did Liz have any direct interactions with any of them?' I asked.

My source wrinkled her nose and sat back in her seat, cappuccino warming her hands.

'Well, Liz didn't get on with Gove and she had run-ins with Robbie Gibb in the past under May, because she could see right through them.

'You know the reputation of Gove can never be impugned in the media right, the biggest leaker in Cabinet as in, *never*? In the end, the letter Simon Case sent to her was what ended it all but of course, as these guys do, he sent a letter to Liz but it was leaked to the media and by the time she read it, she knew she had been bounced. If anyone thinks Liz wasn't done over, they are delusional. She is a lesson in how they operate, if you aren't part of their network, you will not survive. In the letter he repeated the Bank of England view you cannot cancel the increase in corporation tax from 20 to 25 per cent and you cannot reduce the upper tax band and of course, it was too late, the narrative of a U-turn on the substance of her budget was already running riot down Fleet Street. It was over. Look, she failed because she panicked, but you would have to understand what she was put through during the leadership debates to know the state of mind she was in once she got into No. 10.

'In another life, did you notice, by the way, how Robbie's brother, Nick, called for Boris to stand down at a strategic time and quite viciously? A pathetic little statement and totally approved by those inside No. 10 working against Boris. You only have to join the dots, don't you? You also have to look at the number of times Nick Gibb has been a minister, and on whose advice he has been appointed. Hardly a man of overwhelming talent, but then, his husband is Michael Simmonds, one of the original members of the group from their FCS days.

'I suppose it's a question of whether you think it is a coincidence Michael Simmonds found himself sat on the appointments committee for the Ofcom chair given his links to Robbie Gibb, who himself is on a committee at the BBC? You had the barefaced audacity to choose Michael Grade and reject their man. Grade was an excellent choice by the way. But they went to all of that trouble to get their man in place and you defeated them by choosing your own, and I know you won't like this, but I think that when you did that, you made them so angry that this was when they upped the ante on Boris. You poked the hornets' nest with a big stick when you took them on over the Ofcom chair role. Boris backed you and I bet they gave him hell for it, I mean absolute hell. The thing is though, you can't do that and get away with it. You rocked the boat.'

Our food order arrived and I was grateful to move on.

I wanted to ask her why no one else had ever made the connections, but I supposed it was obvious. The average life of an MP's career is eight years. You would have to be around for a long time to join the dots and, like me, she had been.

'What do you think the point of it all is?' I asked her. 'Why bring down and remove our most electorally successful Prime Minister since Maggie?'

'I don't suppose I've ever thought about it long enough to work that one out,' she replied honestly. 'Too busy looking over Liz's shoulder.' She buttered her toast as she moved on, with pace. The arrival of hot food appeared to have revived her.

'So, you know, when we get to the leadership campaign and Liz can see that the entire crew are all lined up behind Rishi, I strongly got the sense that Cummings was involved too.'

'How did you get that?' I asked her. Cummings and Cain had gone, Boris having ousted them from No. 10 ages ago.

'Well, you get to know the people working on the opposite team quite well really, and although no one ever said it out loud, like, "Hey, guess what, Dom's back", because they knew the media would pick up on that and it would have a totally negative kick-back, we knew. They have got Rishi in now, that was the plan all along, but they will already have plan B in place. They work through a variety of scenarios. They have no personal loyalty to Rishi, not a shred. Poor Rishi, he will be thinking that these are his people, that they will fight for him, they are his friends and will have his back. The poor sod doesn't have a clue. If he doesn't listen to them and let them make the decisions, if he pushes back as Boris did, they will get him out and someone else in.'

'Do you think they control the party, totally oblivious to the fact that they create the crisis in the first place?' I asked her.

'Of course, they all have this messiah complex writ large. They are all oblivious. A lot of it stems from hatred of the party membership and MPs. I mean, I imagine the idea of democracy meaning that we are a party of grassroots members who have powers, that must be a total anathema to them. Liz said to me once, "That lot, they are the thirty-year fault-line of the Conservative Party." They started the Tory wars and they are still fighting them and have never given up, other than when we had Cameron and Osborne in place. Over the summer, as we moved into each leadership hustings, I could see they were beginning to have an effect on Liz. She was becoming more and more paranoid, and when I asked her why, saying to her, "Liz, they can't hurt you," she said to me, "You have no idea what those people can do. I warned Boris about Gove, I warned him so many times, but he wouldn't believe me; no one ever does," and I got that.'

'Did they show their ankle?' I asked. 'Did they do anything to frighten Liz?'

'You must know about that dirty dossier about Liz with seriously made-up nasty stuff that was sent around to newspaper editors about her? We all guessed it was produced by Team Rishi. It's classic Dr No modus operandi. He used to do it to ministers he didn't want to see rising up the ranks, or to those he wanted sacked or forced to resign so that he could get someone else in, so that they would be grateful to him and owe him. He used to write them in the style of a CCHQ research document. The thing is, a journalist once showed me one of these supposed research documents on his phone and at the top was the name of the sender and, it was him, Dr No. The stuff they put out about Liz: it was mostly sexual, disgusting and untrue.'

I did know about the dossier. Jacob Rees-Mogg and I had both heard what was in it, and before we publicly backed Liz in the leadership race, we both went to see her in her office to ask her about it and verify that none of it was true. Liz was very adamant and obviously aware that she was in for a dirty and rough ride.

'So, what did you do about the dossier?' I asked as I shovelled scrambled egg into my mouth.

'Liz got some help and advice from IDS, who of course recognised all of them and all the tactics. It was like she was looking over her shoulder, and when we said anything about them, urging her to ignore them and focus on moving forward, she would say, "Look, you don't understand. These guys who are with Rishi, they brought IDS down, they created havoc for May and they did for Boris; they were never going to give up if Rishi lost the leadership election." They also manipulated Rishi, but he couldn't see that. Look at the newspaper that broke the story about Akshata's non-dom status. Look at the reporting in the *Independent*, where Simon Walters now works, a key Cummings contact. They didn't want Rishi to be too confident, they wanted him to need them, to keep them close by his side, and it's typical of them: use the wife to create the furore and make the principal emotionally vulnerable.

'But then, Rishi's green card stuff crept in; that wasn't supposed to happen. It was only the wife who was supposed to get it. That confused them and then someone said to me, "They leaked the wife, red throat leaked the Rishi green card because red throat had another agenda that overarched their own. Whoever red throat is, that's not his or her style. They would never go for family. It would be strictly politics, hence it being Rishi and his green card."'

If my mouth hadn't been full, I might have let out a whistle.

'They also like to cause trouble in the home in order to destabilise things; tension, arguments, they tried that on, big time, with Boris and Carrie, but really what they do is make whoever it is feel vulnerable and scared and dependent upon them. It's mind games and they are quite good at it, but it never actually really worked with Boris because he kept pushing back and they hated that.'

What she was saying actually made sense. It echoed completely with what Iain had told me and I could see the pattern. It's not like the *Independent* is a major newspaper, but other journalists pick up from it. It's also their pattern for things to leak via Labour-friendly papers like the *Indy*, the *Mirror* or the *Guardian*, to keep it at arm's length from No. 10 and stop anyone suspecting that it came from within the centre.

'Lee Cain and Cummings, they leaked lots to Amber de Botton at ITV which was where all the Paul Brand reporting came from; and the scoop of the party video of Allegra Stratton, the wife of James Forsyth at the *Specci* who is Rishi's best friend, she broke all of that. Which is ironic when you think that the only gatherings which could be called parties, were held in the press office on Friday nights.'

'Do you have any idea who red throat is?' I asked her.

She shrugged her shoulders. 'Look, there has been talk of a red throat in No. 10 for a while. I think it is possibly a civil servant who maybe has connections to Labour? But it may also be a politician. I don't know. You can go mad in that place trying to trace the sources of leaks.'

She clearly had nothing further to add so I changed the subject.

'Tell me about Partygate.'

'Where do I start?' She took a sip of her drink. 'Why don't I tell you about Sue Gray instead?'

I wasn't sure what she meant so I stayed silent.

'So, the first thing to say about Sue Gray is that she plays a very deep game. She was head of Propriety and Ethics and that meant there was almost nothing about any government minister she didn't know about.'

'What's the second thing?' I asked as I gulped my coffee.

'The second is that everywhere Michael Gove goes, she goes too. She was also working with Oliver Dowden at the Cabinet Office; he is very close to Gove and is a total puppet of Dougie Smith. Oliver Dowden is a part of the extended group. Baroness Simone Finn is an ex-girlfriend and now a close friend of Gove; she was a big fan of Sue Gray and along with Gove, pushed Boris to appoint Gray to write the Partygate report. I say pushed; I mean, insisted. They are all there. Robbie Gibb has never gone away, he's always there, hovering around No. 10, and all the main players. Just follow the links, they are all connected. Sue Gray is very happy to swim in those waters. Gove leaps to defend her every time she comes up with a whacky idea in No. 10. Just like he has leapt to protect Cummings and Dougie Smith many, many times and "Dr No", too. Look at how long she has worked with and followed Gove around various departments or jobs, or Dowden. She was a senior civil servant and part of the gang.

'I can tell you this: Michael Gove leaks to political editors and journalists every single week. He is a copper-bottomed source for stories they can print, because of the credibility of his position. That's why you will rarely see a negative story about Gove in the press; he is too valuable to journalists. They know in No. 10 that he's kind of out of control, very like his creature, Cummings, but no one dares to fire him. Look at the way he went out in front of the cameras at conference to attack Liz. If anyone sacked him again, he would do it again, and because he's a familiar face, and because they know he's quite mad and not always with it, the journalists and the cameras lap him up.'

We carried on eating for a few moments, both in silence.

'He binds all the dark arts people together. I should tell you, what Liz doesn't know is what was in the Team Rishi sex dossier circulated about Liz to journalists. It was complete and utter bullshit, just ridiculous. One of the claims in it was that she made civil servants deliver papers to her while she was lying in her bath at home. Find a civil servant who will confirm that. It would be front-page news, not a dirty dossier. I was told that Dr No showed the dossier to Rishi first and, to his credit, Rishi told him not to use it. He was worried that the source would be discovered and it would reflect badly on him. Not that he didn't think it was an appalling thing to do to Liz, just that it might damage him. But Dr No ignored him, because Rishi wasn't in charge, they were. The dossier was so appalling that when the press didn't use it, it was texted to a journalist that "we're keeping this ammunition for use at a later date". He meant after she had won the leadership election.

'Another journalist was sent a text message. This one was discussed on a journalists' WhatsApp thread. It said, *The Queen is dead, long live the King*, and it was some kind of cryptic message about how they would get Liz, even though she had won.

'She was in the job only a week, and then another dirty dossier was released about her husband, Hugh, who is one of the most ordinary, nicest people you could meet, I mean, lovely. He's an accountant and a family man, but he's just a lovely man and I mean ordinary in the sense of the people we have to put up with in politics. The dirty dossier on Hugh went around the Westminster WhatsApps like wildfire. Do you think Hugh married Liz knowing that would happen to him one day? Can you imagine the stress? No prizes for guessing who sent that around. This is what Dr No does. He promulgates these dirty dossiers in order to undermine and destabilise people; even if they aren't used, he likes the victim to know they are out there attacking their family and that someone might just print something and upset their children, and that thought, that worry, they know, keeps them awake at night and sinks down deep into their psyche. Even when you know it's not true, but someone is sending this stuff out about you and your family to all and sundry, it not only hurts you, it makes you panic because you worry about your children and the impact it will have on them. It's one thing having your own reputation harmed, but when your family are drawn in, it is on a different level. That people are reading this stuff and judging you. That people are thinking that there's no smoke without fire, all that crap. It's totally destabilising, distracting and, of course, that was exactly what Dr No wanted. Dr No sent that around a week after Liz won the leadership contest. He fired a rocket deep into the heart of her family and it floored her because, as fictitious as it was, she knew it was out there.'

'What do you know about Robbie Gibb?' I asked her.

'Only that he's very close to Dougie Smith and Munira; as I said, he's part of the gang. I think it was Dougie and Gove who put him into Theresa May's office when she became Prime Minister.

'He's a manipulator. If you look back over his time as a political editor at the BBC, he went hard on leaders he didn't like and soft on Cameron, who was the dream – that's my belief anyway. Their unofficial leader today is Gove, which is odd as Dougie Smith once told someone Gove was a total pussy, that he didn't have it in him to ever be a prime minister. Smith is always there and behind him there is the faceless, silent Dr No. The thing about Dr No is he's at Rishi's right hand, but you can also find him on the yachts of anti-Corbyn Labour Party supporting men who are as secretive as him. What's that about? They are like a spider's web, strong. They have people behind desks in No. 10. People alongside secretaries of state in departments. People in the media, people on yachts. They mix with the money men of the globe and they hated Liz. She was a total outsider. She had never bent to their will, they had zero control over her and Boris, he was a life force of his own.

'You ask me about Robbie; he was constantly contacting people on Team Liz and trying to get into the team and on the inside via a job with Liz. When he was challenged and someone said to him, "But, Robbie, you're on Team Rishi though," he didn't deny it but said, "No, I'm on Team Conservative Party." He was double dealing and we just laughed and made sure he got nowhere near Liz. Mark Fullbrook, Liz's Chief of Staff, cancelled various passes on the day she was made Prime Minister. They were back in No. 10 on the day Rishi took office. Robbie kept trying to get on board when Boris was elected too, Dougie was pushing hard for Robbie to be head of comms and to run the press office, and not Lee Cain. That was a source of tension in No. 10 between Robbie, Munira and Smith on one side and Gove, Cummings and Cain on the other. None of them, though, can live without each other for long. Robbie, like the rest of them, is like a recurring rash that sticks around – constantly meddling. It was all about getting their people into positions with the help of Dougie.'

She scooped up the last of her egg with the remains of her toast. She looked drawn after her months of hell. What she really needed was a good pan of scouse to stick to her ribs.

'Look, no one is surprised that Jacob Rees-Mogg is a Tory, are they? But they are surprised at the likes of you and Liz, from working-class backgrounds. You are instinctively ideologically wedded to Conservative values and that's why Liz burns with the intensity of a hundred thousand suns on small government, low taxes, but what she inherited was an economic orthodoxy about wealth preservation, not wealth creation. And that wealth preservation is most brilliantly exemplified in the European Union. We've got it, but we won't let you have it. Better to let Africa have handouts rather than trade with Africa, because we need to preserve our farming subsidies. So we basically create a wealth-preservation climate, and that's what the West has become. We know that India is growing, that China is growing, Africa too. The rest of the world is playing catch-up as the percentage of our global wealth in the West is getting smaller and smaller – the UK is getting smaller and smaller and so, let's preserve it – and Liz saw that: that's why it was about growth and not preservation.

'And this says something: that the Conservative Party went for her and went for Kwasi with such animosity and such fervour when all she was doing was following a classic Conservative economic ideology. She's a wealth creator not a wealth preserver, and I thought that's what we were all here for. Look at Rishi, May, Cameron: all the same, ultra-cautious wealth preservers, and it's a ticking time bomb you know, and when the music stops, someone will be left holding that bomb. Liz was a Lawson mark two, but the party has changed, and remarkably so. Honestly, I'm still getting my head around it. Look at corporation tax in Abu Dhabi: 6 per cent. If they have any sense, they will give up on investing in the UK – they all will. Nine per cent in Singapore and Rishi wants to go up to 25 per cent. The Conservative Party is on a path of self-destruction and it's hard to know how or why it got here. We are a lost cause now and it almost feels like it's deliberate, like the plan is to lose.'

We moved on to lighter topics, and when we stood up to leave, I was deep in thought as I took my umbrella out of the stand and shook the drips onto the carpet. It was a lot to take in. She made one last comment.

'The thing about Gove is this: there are four people in No. 10 who over many years he has stuck his neck out to protect and defend and who he would put his head on the block for – Dr No, Cummings, Smith and Sue Gray – and I have often asked myself, "Why?" I hope you can answer that question.'

We walked out onto the street. It was still raining. She put her hand out to summon her driver. I scanned the road for the warm welcoming glow of an orange light on a black cab.

We hugged and, in seconds, her car had pulled out and I was alone with my thoughts. Michael Gove has brought down IDS, Cameron, May and Boris, and tormented Liz. What part of his life does he think is successful? Where does he find his peace and joy? Surely not dad-dancing in Aberdeen nightclubs? I had asked someone about Gove's lifestyle recently.

'He's out drinking until all hours. He embarrassed himself so often by getting drunk at the poker nights, he had to stop going. You know he lives in an official residence in Carlton Gardens and has done for years now. Why? Why does he have that privilege? He doesn't hold a high office and never has done.'

My phone pinged as the reply to my text message came through. The message I had sent to someone involved in the Sue Gray report was this:

When Gray was writing the Partygate report, did she show any special favours or consideration to anyone in No. 10? Did she try to cover for anyone?

The reply was as I expected:

155

Nothing Lee Cain told her was challenged. What he said was simply placed into the report, whereas everyone else was challenged. Nothing they said was taken at face value. Everyone was put through the wringer, but not Lee. Lee worked for Cummings, who was the other half of Gove.

I sent back some times and dates to meet, and missed a number of cabs as they sailed past me as I messaged. When I finally flagged a cab down and settled into the back, despite the warm breakfast, I felt strangely cold.

CHAPTER 9

ALL TIME HIGH

I'm back in 5 Hertford Street and I'm drinking jasmine tea with someone who Boris trusts implicitly. I've never really properly met him before, but I've heard his name mentioned a number of times by both Boris and Carrie. I wanted to speak to this person because he was there at the end in the final days and he is also well connected across Whitehall and the media world.

I have spent the past week meeting and lunching with journalists who confirmed a number of scenarios I put before them, but obviously wouldn't say so on the record. I was bemused by one who even seem scared when I asked him about Dr No.

'I don't want to talk about him,' he whispered and laid his hand over my phone, which was recording our conversation.

'Why not?' I asked him.

He narrowed his eyes and shook his head vehemently, his hand hovering over my phone as if he were about to confiscate it. I received the message loud and clear and moved straight on past Dr No.

By the end of the week and a kilo heavier – journalists love nice lunches and they don't give you their time for free – I was very aware that they all knew something, but no one knew everything; also, that the ecosystem of journalists and political consultants, comms, public affairs and Spads was pretty incestuous. The people I was writing about had made and created award-winning journalistic careers.

I know that the man I'm sharing a submerged, unfolding, fragrant flower with this evening has a perspective on Partygate, but he begins by talking about Boris the person.

'The key point about Boris is he is a terribly, terribly nice person. And I mean nice not in as my mother would say, nice; I mean he is a nice, trusting, loyal, kind person who is a big softie really and I particularly enjoy his company. His brilliance is a combination of his academic intelligence and his creativity, and the two don't often go together. It confuses people. It's a highly unusual combination.'

I had never considered this aspect to Boris's personality before, but he's right. He loves the arts and loves to paint and draw. Carrie proudly showed me a painting once where I was one of his subjects. I tried not to wince as the image of myself in oil on canvas came back to haunt me, but had to agree, he was good.

'How do you think the civil service adapted to that combination of creativity and academia?' I asked.

'They didn't. I thought the civil service was complicit and found wanting, if I'm honest. The failings of the government, infrastructure, and in particular, the civil service to structure decision making around the peculiarities of the Prime Minister was one of the most significant issues. For me, he is a man of unique brilliance, and with that level of exceptionality, you don't get normal. I have met every Prime Minister since Major. Tony Blair would be sat in a little room about the size of this with a sofa and a coffee table. Papers on the little table, there was never a computer anywhere. Outside was Jonathan Powell. It was just a very orderly, quiet environment where Tony did his thinking and his reading and decision making. It was set up to lean into his own uniqueness and manner. And Tony had obviously got this room set up in a way that suited him and his personality and his manner and style of working, which was orderly and quiet. The press found out and slaughtered him. I think he was described as running a sofa government, when, in fact, it was a very successful government. With Gordon Brown, it was bonkers. Papers everywhere, people lined up, an air of panic and confusion always. But Gordon wanted it in that mad-professor kind of style, even though it was quite obviously a mistake. It was chaotic and he blew his stack when mistakes happened as a result of his chaoticness.

'Look, I could go on, but my point is, because the Remain machinery was fundamentally against Boris, it never leant into his way of decision making, it made life as difficult as it possibly could for him. I'm talking about the establishment here. Forget the political anarchists like Cummings, Gove, Cain and Smith, and the man even I didn't get to meet, and Boris had never met him either, Dr No, and all the rest of their cult-like minions. The absolute narcissistic egotists who make up the Conservative parliamentary party. Your own MPs, I'm sorry, but they are the most self-serving unpleasant bunch of individuals I have known to serve in a government in my lifetime. They are such an appalling lot. But no, I'm talking about the civil service here; it was disrespectful to the Prime Minister and it just refused to make life efficient for him. The miracle is that he survived as long as he did. How did he get Brexit over the line? The anarchists knew they had the civil service working against him too; they knew their life was made easier by this. Brexit was at the root of it, and when you get people criticising Boris, it makes my blood boil because the establishment is punishing Boris for Brexit and it will continue to do so. These guys, they have all bases covered. They have their link into every part of government and the worst of them is the one who operates out of the House of Commons.'

'I'm guessing you mean Gove?' I said.

He took a sip of his tea and nodded his head in affirmation.

'Gove's people were like mice, they were everywhere. And that's on him, that's on Boris for not seeing through Gove and allowing it to happen. It was on him to stop and think, *Hang on, there is something not right here*; to stop and reflect; but really, almost from the first moment he was through the door, it was too late anyway. What compounded the problem was how fast the door was opened by Gove and Cummings for other people to walk in. I worked it out one day that in the key morning meetings, you know the ones Boris called at 8 a.m. every morning, 95 per cent of the people present in that room were put into their jobs by Gove or had some sort of fawning personal relationship with him; and while Boris was speaking in the meeting, they were sending shitty little messages to one another about him on their weird little cult WhatsApp group. It was fucking out of order and when you and I were there, in No. 10, you kind of shook your head in disbelief and thought, *Hang on, Boris is the Prime Minister. What the fuck are you doing here?*

'The ghost of Gove was in every meeting, his spies were everywhere. And I don't know Cummings right, I don't really know Gove, but all I see are people who have not lived up to the trust that has been invested in them at the highest level in the land. And that's unforgivable, from my point of view. Cummings, he was given this incredible opportunity. He was at the centre of power and, you know, he was obviously one of the men at the forefront of efforts to undermine Boris from the very, very beginning, I mean on day one, and people saw it, but they sort of shook their heads and thought, *No, this can't be right*. I just find it bizarre that we didn't deal with that much earlier on or connect the relationships that everyone around Boris had with Michael Gove; even one of the women in the morning meetings was Gove's ex-girlfriend. I mean, what the actual fuck? His Political

Secretary, one of the closest people to him, the guy who told him he absolutely had to go out to the despatch box and back Owen Paterson at all costs, was a Gove appointment. Why did no one put it all in one basket and say, *Hang on*? I'll tell you why: because they knew what they were doing and they populated the place before Boris could hang his hat up, and Boris trusted Michael and that was one huge fucking mistake.

'Entering your world is a bit of a mindfuck, if I'm honest, because it's so badass. The people, the facilities, and by that I mean No. 10. I know I come from this with a corporate perspective, but if I had been Boris, I would have been embarrassed to entertain world leaders in that place. It's a shambles. The whole place is set up for mediocre performance, the whole thing. So I'm sorry if all of this is not going to sound political at all. Because it's not, it's just how a sort of corporate person coming into your world sees it and goes, *What?* I mean, even the bacon rolls: who eats that shit, it's so bad. They serve stale white rolls and slices of cold yellow fat to people?' He shook his head, and sipped his drink, as if repulsed by the memory and needing to clear his palate.

He then began to laugh and put his hands over his eyes, then wiped them.

'I mean, Jesus, it was like it was 1945. I thought they would be serving fish-paste sandwiches to Macron for lunch! Anyway, the absolute most bizarre moment of those last days was when Gove phoned up to say, "I'm coming in to be supportive, to shore Boris up, you know." This was half believable to some. There had been a handful of resignations, but there was no oomph behind it, they were watery resignations that were more a damp squib than a thunderclap, and it was very possible at that point that things could be turned around. I knew though, in my heart of hearts, what their intention would be, and from the second

Simone Finn came into the room and said, "Michael wants to pop in," alarm bells rang. It was July, right? We could have turned it around to get Boris safely into the recess. You lot went on your school holidays from, when, 20 July until September, and then you have a couple of weeks back when nothing really happens, and then you all fuck off for the conference season, so I was thinking, what's the plan here? What are they up to? And I chatted to the likes of you and a few of the others and it was as plain as day, the vote of no confidence, all of that stuff, the timing of it, the leaks and everything – it was all to get Boris down in July, fast, hold a leadership election over the summer and get Rishi in place before the conference in October. They were basically running out of time because they knew they had to get someone in to give them time to bed in before an election in May of '24. It was all about the timing.

'By this point, Boris had finally begun to be suspicious of Michael, but even then, he gave him the benefit of the doubt. We weren't expecting the message that Michael was coming over and we said to Boris, "But are you sure? Are you absolutely sure that's what Michael is going to do? He's coming to support you?" Because I was at that point trying to ensure that no one got to walk in through the door to his office and say, "I want to be the first to say, Prime Minister, you should go." There's always someone who wants to be the famous one, isn't there? Right? Written into the history books, to write themselves into the story? To be the person who came into the room, uninvited, with the glass of whisky and the revolver. But as suspicious as I was, I couldn't have even guessed at how Machiavellian he was being. Even so, I told the Prime Minister, he should tweet it out, that Michael had pledged his support. We raised our doubts, but Simone Finn, who was in the outer office, the Gove ex-girlfriend, she was the one absolutely insisting that Michael wanted to support Boris;

we were like, what, really? We asked Simone whether she was sure that was what Michael was coming to do and she reassured Boris, who always runs straight to thinking the best of someone, and he trusted her. I mean, it's an absolute fucking disadvantage this thinking good of people malarkey, especially in your world where it's like working in a nest of vipers, and she said, "No, it's all absolutely fine; he's coming over. He just wants to show you his support, I promise."

'Gove then came into No. 10 and he says to the Prime Minister, "I think this is a conversation you and I can have alone, together, Prime Minister." Simone just disappeared at that point; she slipped out of the room and shut the door behind her and I caught her expression, and I thought, *Hang on, does she know something?* I think I knew right then, but it was too late, the die was cast. So, we all followed her and walked out of the room, and then, when it was over, when Michael left, Boris came out to us and said, "Michael has just told me I should go, I should resign now." We had quite literally been told by Simone, who Boris and Carrie regarded as a personal friend, that he was going to do the exact and total opposite. I said, "Oh my God, I'm so sorry, I had no idea." Then it was time for PMQ prep, which we had to go straight into, and the guy in the room who was rehearsing Boris to give his best performance, on what would likely be his most difficult day in the chamber ever – and he's had a few – was Gove; the main guy rehearsing him was Michael Gove. I was, like, *I don't know what planet I'm on at this point. This is completely irrational. Right?* It was, like, so surreal. He insisted on coming in before the hardest part of Boris's day, before the cut-throat theatre of Prime Minister's Questions over in the chamber, where Boris would face not only Starmer and the opposition, but the mutinous MPs on the green benches behind him. It was obvious, Michael knew exactly what he was doing. He wanted to destabilise Boris, to unnerve him before one of the biggest moments of his life. We had been psyching him up, getting him ready for the bear pit in the chamber, and Gove, via Simone and foul means, got into the room and blew Boris up. They fucked with his mind and they knew exactly what they were doing.

'What followed Michael's little performance in Downing Street was bizarre and the penny dropped very quickly as to what he had come over to do. The limp drizzle of resignations that had come before, they were probably about to fizzle out, right? Rishi's just hadn't had that immediate impact they had hoped for. Not everyone was rushing out to the cameras to hail Rishi. The people who had resigned so far, they didn't really get the juices flowing: they were insignificant; the situation was salvageable. We were talking about a reshuffle. Getting some of the key agitators onside. And then, suddenly, reports started flashing up on Sky that Cabinet ministers were turning up at Downing Street to tell Boris to go. They weren't doing any such thing. It had only been Gove. I regret that terribly because I think had the No. 10 comms people been slightly more on their game and rebutted it and said, "Actually, that's not true," it would have helped, but then I find out that the people working in the comms office are Govites and on some Gove-adoring WhatsApp group. Later, when Boris famously fired Gove, two of them ran out of the building crying and screeching like banshees. In case you didn't know this, that is not normal behaviour in the workplace.'

His agitation, and dislike of everyone around Boris, was palpable.

'There were no ministers in No. 10, no MPs, and yet Sky was reporting that there were. There really weren't at that point, just the bad aura that Michael had left behind, but they were being fed lies. When Michael left, someone called a journo at Sky and said, "Ministers are here, telling him to go," and Sky, they were just broadcasting it as though it were fact because obviously they had the information from a reliable source, and I don't think it takes a huge amount of time to guess who that reliable source was. But then, because Sky was broadcasting it, that it was happening, it was like a self-fulfilling prophecy. Ministers were then falling over themselves to run across from Westminster and into No. 10, as they didn't want to be the last ones left on a sinking ship, already calculating that if that was what was happening and Boris was falling, they didn't want to be seen to be loyal to him in case that precluded them from being offered another ministerial job by the next person to be Prime Minister. Their moment to jump ship and save their political skins had come. Once they then get the news out on the media, that was it: the ball was rolling. You see, Gove had told Boris that tons of MPs had spoken to him and that Boris had to go, and we laughed out loud when Boris told us he said this. We thought, *Hang on, that's a lie, surely?* I was thinking to myself when this surreal prep for PMQs was going on, *What's he up to? Why is he sat here and acting like this?*

'Then, of course, the ministers did start arriving, once it was being broadcast on Sky news and the BBC, they were just turning up unannounced and milling around in that white dining room upstairs, and we were, like, *How did they get in?* Upstairs there was a guy working the room, talking to them all, working them and telling them that they have to go downstairs and tell Boris to go, and I thought, *Hang on, Boris brought you in; what the fuck are you doing? You work for Boris. Don't you dance with the guy who brought you here?*

'They're so duplicitous. I honestly thought to myself at that moment, *I totally get why people hate politicians. Ninety per cent are just a bunch of self-serving little shits, the worst kind of people.*

'Anyway, that was all surreal. The point I'm trying to make is that the Prime Minister was unable to control his own space, who was in it, who came into the building, and to be able to have trusted people in there, in No. 10, surrounding him. The people around him, they weren't working for him, they were working for Gove, or someone else; it wasn't Boris. We only got there very, very late in the day. We tried to get the office to function around how he wanted it to function, in a way that's best for him. It's better to have a six-and-a-half-out-of-ten decision now than a nine-out-of-ten decision when it's too late. Right? So the change of Chief of Staff from Dan Rosenfield to Steve Barclay bought us important time to settle, regroup and just say, *Okay, if we avoid mistakes, right?*, because there were a lot of bad apples in that No. 10 basket and we needed to work out who was doing what. Where was it all being coordinated from, both in No. 10 and over at Westminster?

'They got Dan Rosenfield out after Cummings left, and of course, they were always going to, he didn't stand a chance. And that's when there's the ... you know, the bottom-pinching guy ... what was his name? Chris Pincher. They were so primed, so organised; one more fuck-up and they would come for Boris.

'And that's also a moment of real regret, because actually, you know, it didn't need to be that which finished him off. I mean, for fuck's sake, the Carlton Club is full of shit-faced Tory MPs every night of the week. Pincher, a gay man, had too much to drink in the bar and wrongly grabbed another man's arse; that was what precipitated the beginning of the end. Does that make sense to you? The reason why it doesn't is because they were waiting for anything to get him, and once that anything, no matter how small, came along, they would blow it up, using Twitter and social media and every Remain journalist, the BBC, Sky, every leftie, but mostly, Conservative MPs. Once they used that network to drip poison in the ears of the journos and set the hares running and spread the rumours, they thought it would be enough to tip Boris out.

'Maybe it does make sense to you, because you're from that world, but Jesus, it's seriously badass in my book. You all behave like gangsters. But, you know, the Pincher thing, that in itself was very badly handled. Look, we can call it a conspiracy; it sounds like a conspiracy when we talk about it here, but it doesn't smell like a conspiracy or look like one, and that's the point isn't it? And the reason it doesn't look or smell like one is that they kind of dropped their own guard as a result of their own arrogance and were pretty public about it. And that's because they've been causing mayhem in the Conservative Party since they started out as Portillo supporters with Maude years ago and they are still doing it today, and people in your world, they have factored in their bad behaviour. Look, it's an accepted thing, right, that there is a person in No. 10 who practises what everyone calls "the dark arts" who everyone is shit scared of. [He was talking about Dr No.] That's the bar, that's why no one pays any attention to all this badass behaviour. You guys, you think it's fucking acceptable, that your little world is more important than any world anyone else works in, and you wonder why the public hate MPs. That's how they all got away with it; the way people get their information is through journalists, and half of them, they are in on it. They have Hague onside now, but it seems odd to me that a man who suffered at their hands back in his day has been playing their tune now as the biggest Rishi cheerleader. Why is that?

'Okay, so take Dougie Smith. I don't think he could have been any more direct, you know; he's employed by Central Office. And he phoned Boris about six months before it all fell down after Cummings was thrown out, and he told him, go now or we will get rid of you. He said to him, if you go now, we will let you back one day. Can you believe it?

'This man, the faceless employee in Central Office who has been paid a grand salary for what? Twenty, thirty years maybe for doing what, exactly? I'll tell you what: controlling the Conservative Party and who becomes MPs, putting into play the dark arts that are so dark people are too scared or intimidated or whatever to say what they actually are, arts which have destroyed the careers of numerous ministers, the vast majority of these arts are used against your own party and people and whoever is leader or prime minister, and by doing that, in my book, they control the country, everyone and everything.'

I knew about the phone call Dougie Smith had made to Boris, he had told me about it at the time. He had been perturbed, I could tell. He was oblivious to the network, to the means they would use to destroy him. It is not how Boris works, not something he would ever think or say. As he explained the conversation to me over the phone, I could tell he was having trouble comprehending what had just been said to him.

When Boris had wanted to sack Dougie Smith, he had been warned, 'If you do, you won't be able to deal with the disruption. Just leave him.' I remembered the words I had been told: *Michael is the glue that binds them all together. All roads lead to Gove.*

I remembered what Iain had said, the words he had used were the same as this man was using now. That the minute he sacked Mark MacGregor, who had been one of the earliest members, *it all came tumbling down like a pack of cards.*

'The advice Boris was given that Dougie Smith was more dangerous outside the tent than inside was clearly the right advice. The same applies to Dr No.

'I mean, there were a number of key people inside our tent and it was very clear that they were trying to do Boris in, and every time the Prime Minister would talk about his interactions with the Chancellor, Rishi, any rational assessment of that conversation was, *Hang on, none of that makes sense; what's he up to?* So, you know, he's the Chancellor, he's on Team Tory, isn't he? Boris could never get through to Rishi to talk to him, did you know that?'

I didn't.

'Boris used to make excuses for him, and so did others who knew what was actually going on. "Maybe Rishi is just having a bad day or is especially busy; that's why he can't take your call, Prime Minister." "No, apparently Rishi can't do any press today, he's too busy, Prime Minister." Boris would say, "I'll have to do it because Rishi is really busy with meetings." I said to him, "Boris, you are the Prime Minister; no one's meetings are more important than yours. What are these supposedly very important meetings?" Boris goes, "No, I really shouldn't ask him; he's obviously too busy." All of it was so fucking obvious. This guy was basically not wanting to play as part of the team, really not on our side, definitely working against Boris and had been doing so for a very long time, and he also was useless at his job and definitely wasn't providing the economic environment and policy environment that a Conservative government needed in order to survive, and this was really concerning to Boris. The man he had appointed as Chancellor was letting the economy and the country down, that was why Boris needed to speak to him. Rishi was doing a bad job.

'I'm very sure Rishi would have made a great middle manager, no doubt about it, but as a chancellor he wasn't cutting it. Clinton's campaign line still applies, you know: "It's the economy, stupid." Mess that up and you're toast, and Rishi had messed up. He was about to raise corporation tax and everyone hated that. He refused to put policies in place to tackle the impending financial difficulties that Boris feels we can only survive if we are focused on investment, and growth. Rishi knew, the disaster train was coming straight at him, and he wanted to get out of his job and into Boris's chair, fast, and to rewrite the story. I mean, even basic stuff, like, "Will you share the media duties on an obviously busy day for the government?", he would refuse. He just wouldn't play ball on anything. So it's bloody obvious, his plotting, led by Rishi and his Chief of Staff, Liam Booth-Smith, it was hiding in plain sight. And then we find out that Rishi had asked his ministers in the Treasury to back him in a leadership election, back in February, five months earlier. Rishi's duplicity was the unspoken elephant in the room. It was there, but it was too incredible when we were facing war in Europe and post-pandemic; it was too unbelievable that Rishi would be putting his own ambitions first, above those of the country and the people. Right? So what I'm trying to say is no one can argue that everything was right. But when I look back and replay the tape and look back, you can go, "Well, okay, that was pretty bleeding obvious what you were up to, Rishi, wasn't it?"

'So just before it all happened, on the Sunday night, Boris went back into London early to have dinner with Rishi. Boris was really concerned that so much of our fiscal policy was just plain wrong, especially our position on corporation tax. He was very concerned that Rishi was just making the wrong calls on things like NICs. He wanted the dinner with Rishi to tell him, "You have to get taxes down." So, they had dinner together that night, and of course the next day Rishi blindsided Boris and resigned. Yeah, genuinely, even for a cut-throat world that was very shitty behaviour. You have dinner with the boss the night before and you don't have the bottle to even give him a clue? Perhaps say something like, "I'm really unsettled, I'm creaking here; don't be surprised if I need to resign." Like, man up. But he didn't. Rishi wasn't a man about it at all. He didn't have the guts to say to Boris face to face: this is what I'm thinking of doing, Prime

Minister. I'm afraid I may have to resign. He was all chummy and hail-fellow-well-met and "see you tomorrow" as they parted. But they didn't and he knew they wouldn't.'

'And what about the lockdown parties?' I asked.

'Yes, we should talk about them. Because it's really odd, really odd, right? First, I must say, had the initial response been, we were helping to save the country, and a few of the No. 10 staff had a few beers in the offices on a Friday night, those who were working all day together, when the PM left for Chequers. That's it, right? That was what was happening. Boris wasn't at parties, the staff were. Simon Case was the man all over No. 10 and responsible for running Downing Street as an office. Then I think all this would have been much easier. As it is, in the minds of the public the words "Boris" and "parties" are synonymous, yet he was fined by the police for sitting at his desk and people walking into his study, one of whom was Rishi. It is a fact that, thanks to the narrative pushed out by the media, people think Boris was a partygoer.

'Now, initially, I'm not actually judging the staff for having a drink in the press office on a Friday night. I'm not judging Keir Starmer for having a beer and a curry in Durham after a day's campaigning. In my opinion, the Keir event was more of a party by all accounts than anything Boris ever attended, but I don't care, right. But, seriously, the people in the No. 10 press office were literally losing their minds, right? Why? And then the penny dropped with me. So, when the police become involved, normally what happens, if you get pulled over for dangerous driving, and you've been on your phone and the police take your phone and you've been up to something dodgy, what you're really going to be worried about is, what are the police going to find on your phone? If you've been buying drugs, right, or actually, you know, you're having an affair with someone, or all the stuff you don't want someone else to know about, your life all of a sudden opens up to the police, and the police love it. They love that moment.

'These guys around Boris who are supposed to be out there defending him, the people who advised him before he went to the despatch box and was accused of misleading the Commons, they are literally crapping themselves. And all that they've done, as I understand it at the time, in those first days is have a beer after work, in the same rooms they had been working in all day on the Friday. So, Friday: it's a mad busy day in the No. 10 press office, weekend media all of that, you can often not finish until very late at night. Now, those people working in the press office, they may have stayed too long, may have had more than a couple of beers, but I don't think that's all they've done, right, because they are way too shit scared for it to have only been that. So my initial reaction was, *Why are you all losing your minds?* Like, all of them. They're chain-smoking, pacing the room. One of them is having a mental breakdown, I mean quite literally, in the comms team; there's crying and the place just collapses.

'I asked, "What the fuck is going on with that fella; he's in bits?" The response was, "Let him go home, he has to go home, he can't cope with this. He has to go home immediately. We're worried about his mental health." Why? Okay, I'm all for mental health. Making sure we look after people, but this one guy, you'd have thought he was about to be sent out into Whitehall for a public flogging and none of it fitted to me. Something else was going on because the reaction of the comms people who worked in the No. 10 press office was disproportionate to what was happening. So, you walked into the press office and they were having a collective breakdown, and you walked into other offices, the policy teams and the others, and they were all mightily fucked off, right, and worried, but they weren't hysterical. Something very serious was being hidden and covered up, and it wasn't a drink in the office or a party – those people, they were having trouble dealing with it. Every fucking one of them was acting as though they were about to be locked up. They were covering something up. I came away utterly convinced that the reason why they were all so traumatised was that if the police began to open up their investigation, as they almost always do, there would be some really bad stuff coming. I was like, all right, so you're all shagging and you've all got families. And you've all been telling your families that you're working super-hard and long hours and then you're found out? I mean, there were even stories about traces of white powder in No. 10. Were people bringing cocaine and ketamine in?

'So, the things I'm thinking to myself as worst-case scenarios, I find out are actually true. It transpires that parties were held in the press office every Friday night. Boris wasn't there, he didn't know. It was all hush-hush. That's why they were all in fucking meltdown; people were terrified they were going to be exposed and caught out.

'So it's a double betrayal of Boris. But it becomes a triple play. This is what they didn't say to Boris, and to this day the behaviour of those in the press offices in No. 10 has been covered up, and the Prime Minister being implicated in Partygate saved their own skins. Boris is facing an inquiry by a biased privileges committee.

'It's like, first, "We were drinking without you knowing Boris, when you had left for Chequers." Second, "We told you we weren't drinking, we told you it was all nonsense. We lied to you. So now you've made a public mistake at the despatch box by denying that there were any parties, and that has caused you huge issues, but it wasn't your fault: you've been told something, and you obviously believe it to be the truth, because to tell you the truth and to advise you is what we are paid to do, but it will bring you down and cause you a whole world of pain, because we can't go back on our lies since we are protecting ourselves first." Third, "We're also all overdosing on the response of the police investigation because of our own personal circumstances and inappropriate behaviour. Right?" There were rumours of a great deal of sex taking place, it was all a bit out of hand. Everyone covered their backs, they saved their own skins, and the only person impacted by all of these lies and deceit is Boris. Of course, I've just told you this, but every fucking journalist out there suspected it. They know but when they got close, they were thrown a bone to put them off the scent, and on this occasion the bone was Boris. They had to keep the Friday night parties locked down, and the only way they could do that was set a breadcrumb trail leading elsewhere and far away from the press office.

'If instead of losing their minds they had been honest, if Boris had been told the truth, if they hadn't lied in order to protect their own backs and the dark stuff they were up to, it would have been very different. Instead, Boris became boxed in by their lies and deceit.'

'Are we being fair here?' I asked him. 'They were saving them- selves, but they were also saving Boris, because if it had been known that they behaved so badly, the public would have blamed him. They would have thought that there was no way he couldn't know about this stuff, like Sue Gray said in her report: some comment about leadership in No. 10.'

He came straight back at me. 'Sue Gray wasn't talking about Boris. She doesn't regard the politically elected as leaders. She's a lifelong civil servant. She was talking about Simon Case, who she loathed with a heartfelt passion. To her, the leader is the Cabinet Secretary, the man who is the most senior civil servant in No. 10. Politicians come and go in Gray's world. It was Simon Case who was notionally responsible for how staff behaved in the building, not Boris. For one thing, Boris was on the road for half of the week. He made a commitment that he would never neglect the north because the people in the north of England had backed him, and he didn't. He was up and down the motorway like a fiddler's elbow.'

I was not surprised at what I was being told. During my week-long session with journalists, I had heard exactly the same from one newspaper editor and two political editors. One had shook his head at the mention of the press office. 'There was more than drinks going on there. Are you writing about the drugs and the sex in your book?' I was amazed. 'Have you written about them in your newspaper?' I asked knowing full well that he hadn't.

Fresh tea arrived that I wasn't aware had been ordered.

'So when Rishi got fined, he comes in to Boris and in a slightly Victor Meldrew way starts bleating, "Oh, this is so traumatic for me and my family." (We had no idea at this time Rishi would be fined a second time for not wearing a seat-belt. He now has double the fixed-penalty notices that Boris does.) He then decides to blow it all up and writes out his resignation letter. Boris says to him, "What are you talking about? It's a fixed-penalty notice." It then turns out, Rishi's being counselled by a senior hedge fund manager called Mas, and Mas and Rishi are best friends from their days at a hedge fund they worked on together. Everyone who worked there made money, I mean shed-loads, off the scale of even imagining what you would do with it for the likes of you or I, proper loads of money. I think it was started by Christopher Hohn, who is friends with Dougie Smith, and Hohn employed Mas and Rishi. And they remained best friends. Now Mas is a board director at NewsCorp – Mas Siddiqui is his name – and Rishi is Prime Minister and probably a billionaire without ever having won a single vote.

'So, Mas is coaching and counselling Rishi, and I'm not being funny, but Mas knows less about the UK political scene than the

Polish waiter who just brought our drinks here – and I'm not being disparaging to the waiter – and then it becomes necessary once we learn this to ask Rupert [Murdoch] to speak to Mas and tell him to cease and desist from counselling Rishi to resign over an eighty-quid fine, because it was insane and dangerous advice. I mean, what the fuck? Rupert, who does understand British politics and is an incredibly intelligent man, got it straightaway; he was on the side of the angels here. I mean, seriously, what the fuck? I don't believe that Rupert knew Rishi was being counselled by Mas, until he was alerted to the fact. If Rishi had resigned over the fine, Boris would have had to resign too. The whole show would have come down. I mean, while Putin is invading Ukraine, Mas advises the Chancellor to resign as Chancellor over a fixed-penalty notice, which would have meant that Boris would have had to stand down as Prime Minister. No choice but to resign and the government would have been totally rudderless. This is the point about Rishi hiding his intentions to get Boris out in plain sight. His conversations with Mas were about how to get Boris out.

'And we still kind of trusted Rishi and his crew, that's the frustrating thing. So the party stuff, for me, is more egregious than the sort of Cummings bullshit to drive up north to Barnard Castle. It's people doing the opposite of their public service. Everyone involved, they thought only about themselves. They literally thought only about themselves. And when it all came tumbling down, the entire response of the machine was to protect the individuals involved, not to protect the Prime Minister. And the definition in my mind of public service when you are inside No. 10 is that you protect the Prime Minister and help him to perform better for the country and create an incredibly efficient decision-making environment where he's at his best. And these people did the exact opposite. So I think it's a genuine betrayal. That's why I'm so cross.'

He sat back in his seat. For the last couple of minutes his own emotional response had been apparent. I felt it too. I mean, he hates MPs, that is quite obvious, and I suppose I should be grateful he's agreed to speak to me, but his points about public service and betrayal are bang on the nail. Boris has been gone for months and, at a crucial time, the government has been frozen. Rishi has, without a single vote from the public or even party members, been installed as Prime Minister. Jeremy Hunt, the man who had been plotting to bring Boris down for years, was Chancellor. The plotters had won.

'Did Boris have any chance?' I asked him.

He shook his head, 'Never. They were way too organised. All this bullshit about Gove being a Brexiteer. Whichever way you look, it was incredibly difficult for Boris. And so they sat there after Brexit and, of course, there was never a chance of anything happening unless it suited Rishi because no one believes Brexit is in his DNA, right? It's a political tool to keep him in with the right of the party. It's not like it's what Rishi stands for. In the red wall, it's not like he feels it, you know; it's not. And I'm not being disparaging about rich people, but how much can he feel about what people really suffer when you are what he is, which is probably a billionaire who, when he was Chancellor of the Exchequer, refused to do media because unless there was an amazingly good news photo shot to go with it, it was below him. That is the essence of Rishi.

'The denouement, it was clear: it was Rishi they were all working for.'

'And what about Boris at the end?' I asked him.

'Boris called it himself at the end. He called Lynton Crosby, he trusts Lynton, loves the guy, and it was touching when at the moment when Boris had to make the biggest decision of his life, it was Lynton he turned to for the final advice. They've had ups and downs and, if anything, that has helped to forge the bond between the two of them. Lynton being an Aussie is brutally honest, and he said to Boris, "You're done mate," and I think that's the point at which it actually hit me: it's over. There's no doubting Lynton's judgement, who, by the way, has been around for years and will give you chapter and verse on what he thinks and knows about Gove, Cummings, Dougie Smith, "Dr No", the whole lot of them.'

I had always respected and liked Lynton. He didn't know me. We had only met a couple of times. I had a longer conversation with his wife Dawn once at conference when Lynton was running Cameron's campaign and I thought to myself at the time, *No man with a wife this lovely can be anything but a good person.*

'What would you say was Boris's biggest mistake?' I asked him.

'The main error in his career, all the way through his life, is that he's been too trusting of others. His life has not been straightforward; him, Rachel, the boys – they are survivors of their upbringing. They have known adversity. He's never had any money, and yet any man with his charisma, intelligence, would be richer than Rishi if he had decided to become a banker. Sadly, he chose politics and public service because it's his passion, and despite his wit and charm they never saw him as an equal, those people he went to Eton and Oxford with, especially the likes of Cameron and Osborne. Boris was a scholarship boy. If you read the Cameron diaries, the sense you get throughout is that it was all about keeping Boris out. Cameron, Osborne, always looking over their shoulder.

'Boris, he had made a number of mistakes, big mistakes, and therefore he's far too forgiving of others who mess up. To be a prime minister you either need to be ruthless yourself or have such good people around you they can fire the shots for you, and he didn't have that, the good people, because Gove had ensured before Boris had even noticed that the people around him were all Gove people, and many themselves were being used. Boris was a nice man, surrounded by bad people. He needed a few loyal soldiers around him who were working for him and not others, but they made sure they had taken care of that; they were all on the other side, trying to get him out. And yet, think about it, he had all these people working against him and look how much he achieved, how well he did. You know what happens if Putin wins right? If he wins and then moves into Poland? No one should underestimate what Boris has achieved, but the narrative in his head is, he's made mistakes himself, he knows how that happens and how it feels, that it is unintentional and painful, and therefore he needs to be more understanding of others who make mistakes – and that's not how it works.

'Look at Rupert Murdoch and the mistakes he has made, the marriages, all of it, but look at how he makes business decisions; there is a man who is ruthless, because he has to be. That is what Boris needs to learn, not to get nicer but to get better at decision making, and I think he's there now. He will bounce back, and next time he will be surrounded by people who will do a better job of protecting him; the bastards will work for him not against him next time, because we will be ready, and I hope there is a next time because if there isn't, this will be the biggest travesty, the biggest loss to this country. And why? Because of a few luna- tic fuckers like Cummings, Gove, Dougie Smith and their little gang, and the worst human being of all, Dr No.

'Those men, they lack decency and honour. They saw he was a vote winner, they rode into No. 10 on his coat-tails, Gove didn't get one of the high offices of state; it was revenge. But of course, they didn't have all bases covered, so then they brought in the most important man in No. 10, the Cabinet Secretary, Simon Case and in doing so, they were complete.'

CHAPTER 10

BORIS: FROM THE JAWS OF VICTORY

It was early Sunday morning and he greeted me in the kitchen of his house in the Cotswolds. Both the lids of the Aga were up and I had to take a very deep breath. I'm a woman of a certain age who has had an Aga since I left the poverty of my background. However, you can never escape your upbringing, and the thing about an Aga is, when the lids are up, the heat is escaping.

Boris was pouring hot water into a coffee pot. Carrie, as always, serene, unphased by her two toddlers, has taken both upstairs to bath and dress them and has left us a plate of warm fresh croissants. Dilyn, the dog, has jumped onto a chair and is trying his best to reach the counter and snaffle them. While Boris chatted, I surreptitiously lowered the Aga lids onto the hot plates and my zen returned.

'The blasted boiler broke,' he said, as he caught me with a glance from the corner of his eye. 'It was all the heating we had over Christmas.'

We could hear hysterical squeals of laughter from Wilf as he charged across the landing.

'C'mon!' Boris shouted as he lifted the tray and led the way into the study with Dilyn close on his heels.

I knew he hated this. The unravelling of the past three years, the realisation of who betrayed him and why. It's not what he's about: personalities, game-playing, parties, deceit. He is just not that man, he literally has no time for it. As I placed my bag on the floor and took out my phone to set Otter to record, I looked around me: this room is who he is. A huge volume of Shakespeare's complete works open on a wrought-iron stand, like the type people use to keep a cookery book open on a certain recipe. To his side, a textbook open next to his laptop and a notepad with a well-placed pen keeping his page, and on the other side of the desk stands high a pile of hardbacked books, waiting to be read. I went to sit down in the leather wingback chair at the side of the desk and jumped back up as quickly. Dilyn had got there first and even as I sat on him, refused to budge.

'Get, down, Dilyn,' I said as I lifted him onto the floor and took my place, before he leapt straight back up onto my lap. I noticed that the book on the top of the pile was uniquely a novel, *Act of Oblivion*, by the author Robert Harris. The remainder of the books appeared to be on politics, history and economics; some on the spines were written in Greek, so I couldn't really make out what they were actually about at all.

'Robert Harris, he's not one of us,' I said. Meaning he was far from being a Brexiteer.

I had read a number of Harris novels and loved them. I read *Pompei* when I holidayed on the Amalfi coast, and it was just gripping; the novel brought the place alive for me. I could see the characters in the book walking the streets where, now, only foundations remained.

Boris passed me the plate of warm croissants, which Dilyn eyed jealously. He sat in the chair and picked up his mug, and I began.

'So, you know, I witnessed Rishi's behaviour in Cabinet towards you, his body language, the passive-aggressive rudeness. What did you make of all that? Did you ever notice it yourself?'

He made his deep 'Hmm' sound that I've come to recognise is thinking, but not being happy with the thoughts.

'Yes, I picked up on all of that, of course I did – it was all very odd – but you know … there were more important things to focus on in Cabinet than Rishi twitching in his chair.' He frowned.

Some of us sat around the Cabinet table had found it incredibly childish and petulant, and had commented on it following Cabinet. One Cabinet minister had confided in me, 'Apparently he doesn't like the way Boris chairs the meetings. He says it's inefficient but Boris draws the best out of everyone around the table.' It was true. No one was afraid to speak, and on a number of occasions discussions had become warm. I wouldn't go so far as to say heated, but they were certainly productive.

I have since discovered that Rishi now chairs Cabinet using exactly the same format as Boris, only discussions today are stilted and muted, Cabinet ministers being too afraid to speak openly. A present Cabinet minister recently said to me: 'So Rishi was definitely the product of Cummings. He was Cummings' plan. They could see by the polling that he didn't hack off the Remainers in the way that Boris did, and they were feeding this to Boris. We all began to notice the change in behaviour in Rishi towards Boris.'

Boris confirmed this. 'I remember Lee Cain and Dom Cummings showing me some polling – I can't remember where it came from or who had done it – and they were basically telling me, "Look how unpopular you are and how popular Rishi is."'

There was a Rishi-supporting pollster they had brought on board; I guessed it was his polls that Boris was being shown. They were certainly the polls put in front of MPs when they were being persuaded to do the deed and topple Boris in favour of Rishi, effectively shortening their careers as MPs.

He reflected on his words, and drank his coffee. I desperately wanted my croissant, but thought I'd better not start if he wasn't eating his. It smiled up at me from the plate, with all its buttery richness. I hadn't eaten; I was sure he had, as the detritus of the children's breakfast had been visible in the kitchen. Only the previous week, we had been chatting on the phone as Carrie reprimanded him for eating cheese that was intended for Wilf's lunchbox. He was literally holding the conversation with his head in the fridge.

'The link to the polling, Cummings' plan, Rishi's behaviour, it can't have been lost on him,' said a close Boris ally. 'Obviously, polling would be a factor in any leadership competition, and it moves MPs who panic easily and can't weigh up the bigger political picture, or have no longer-term interest in politics. If you take polling to an MP and say, "Rishi is polling better than Boris, ergo with Rishi you have a better chance of keeping your seat," you are pushing at an open door. MPs don't often question who the pollster is, after all.

'It was probably the plan they would be able to use to remove Boris, to get him to voluntarily stand down, MPs would see the polling and back Rishi as leader, possibly without the vote even being put to the members, and without the lengthy process of a protracted leadership competition. It would have been seamless.'

It would never have worked, even if Boris had acquiesced, which he never would. Rishi massively underestimated his own popularity with party members and the Tory voting public.

'It was clear to me that Cummings and Cain were acting in the manner you would expect from a narcissistic, controlling and abusive partner,' continued the ally. 'They were attempting to emotionally destabilise Boris. They were trying to make him feel shit about himself every day, gaslighting him, to make him feel isolated, subtly hinting at how great they thought Rishi was and how he was failing in the eyes of the voters in comparison.

'The polling they commissioned to show him was compiled by a niche, very pro-Rishi pollster and those niche polls were used to pressure MPs into believing it was over for Boris and Rishi was the future.' Said another, 'Rishi was thinking more about how he could persuade Boris to gently move aside, and avoid a leadership competition.

'I mentioned the tactics to Boris,' he continued. 'He [Rishi] kind of openly asked me to; he actually asked me to do that on more than one occasion, and Boris would say to him, "Look, I mean, I can't think of anybody better than you to take over from me. But I want to go on, you know, I want to level up. I've got a plan. I think you should stick with it for now." And so I think Rishi's problem was that he couldn't see how it worked for him in the longer term. He couldn't see how the partnership really worked.'

My reckoning was that along with many others, Rishi couldn't see how he could fit into the Prime Minister's seat when the man occupying it was so popular with party members and the public. Rishi's body language, his impatience, his disinterest in being Chancellor and the fact that it wasn't enough for him had been apparent. He had been given the impression by someone that he should simply bide his time as Chancellor until the bigger prize became his.

Boris continued: 'The trouble was, by the time we came out of Covid, people wanted a more radical, dynamic plan to kick-start the economy, so I kept saying to him, "Come on, what's the economic plan?" And then I noticed from January '22, he just refused to engage with me. I can see, looking back, that's obviously because there was a plan, it was to remove me, and people were saying to him, "Don't give him anything."'

This idea of Rishi holding out had been explained to me by someone working in the Treasury at the time. 'Rishi was being a genuine dog in the manger. He was sitting on changes he could have made because he didn't want them to be credited to a government led by Boris. That was part of the plot. Rishi didn't think, he knew: they would get Boris out at some stage, so letting him announce policy, to make progress, that was definitely out of the question; and the Treasury, it was the perfect machine to frustrate Boris and to achieve that. There was no financial plan; the country could go to the dogs. Business, families, people, they could all be kept waiting until his priority – to get Boris out and become Prime Minister himself – was successful. That was the focus, where all the energy was spent. Rishi had no interest in the country or the economy. There was just the one plan which was coordinated and extensive and only required patience and time. Playing fast and loose with the economy was a small price to pay for what would be his eventual prize. After all, he was a very wealthy man; there was nothing money could buy that could interest him. From a pair of Prada shoes to a luxury yacht, he could have anything he wanted. There was no material objective left to get out of bed for. Being Prime Minister, that was the prize.

'Certain MPs fluttered around him like moths to a flame, as people often do when in the presence of great wealth. He and his father-in-law were friends with some of the most powerful and wealthiest people in the world. Of course he knew it would only be a matter of time. To men like this, the notion of democracy, of power transferring from the people to the government, to the person they elect as Prime Minister, it's all a joke. Money can and does buy anything, even if occasionally it has to be acquired indirectly and over time.'

'So, Boris,' I said, feeling my way to the question I wanted to ask him, 'in '21, less than a year after you had won an historic general election, Cummings and Cain tried to get you to stand down. It failed. Rishi then openly asked you to stand down, himself. That failed. Then came the call from Dougie Smith, which moved everything up to a new level: not asking you, telling you to stand down. What did Dougie Smith say to you when he called you?'

He hesitated. Again, I could see how reluctant he was to revisit this stuff, but I had to know, so I shifted tack. 'You do know that Dougie Smith lived with Michael Gove and his wife, Sarah Vine, don't you?'

'I mean, not permanently, but before Dougie was married.'

He frowned again.

'What did Dougie say?' I prompted him a second time.

'Well, it was unexpected and fairly unpleasant,' he said. 'I remember where I was when the call came; I was upstairs in the flat in the kitchen.'

That image of Boris nicking cheese out of the fridge came back to mind.

'He was pretty robust and to the point. He said, "I think you should go, you should stand down now and we may let you come back again one day. You are poison, like Nixon. If you don't go, I'm going to take you down. I'll finish you off."'

Having experienced my own telephone call with Dougie and the menace in his thick Scottish accent, I could imagine how disturbing it had been.

'That must have been horrible,' I said.

It was easy to check the dates; it was a concerted effort by those involved and it all happened within a short time frame, when Rishi had a personally high poll rating, which made their efforts to force Boris to go, frenetic.

But personal rating polls are a fickle mistress. Now the much-talked-about Rishi bounce had failed to appear and the Conservative Party was tanking. Of course it was. You can't sustain a shallowness rooted in PR and Instagram shots when you are a prime minister. Self-promotion and confected adoration is not sustainable; eventually, it dies. He may do well personally against Starmer. However, we have been in power now for so long, most have forgotten how that works mid-term for a Conservative government or how difficult it was for Cameron and Osborne.

Dilyn chose that moment to lunge off my knee, seized the croissant and made his escape, diving under a chair beneath a large oil painting at the end of the room.

'How insistent were Cummings and Lee Cain when they were showing you the polls and asking you to stand down?' I asked him.

'Well, I remember Lee and Dom showing me the polls with some degree of uncontained enthusiasm about how popular Rishi was, and I liked Rishi, I thought he was able. There was a long period when I thought, *Look, if I'm going to hand over the leadership to anyone one day, it probably should be Rishi.*'

I had also been told that although this was what Boris thought at the beginning, the truth was, as time moved on, it was apparent that Rishi was turning out to be disappointing as a chancellor and far from able.

He had done nothing about the issues which made Boris impatient for change: Solvency II reforms or lifting the pension cap. The economy was in desperate need of measures that shook things up to deliver for business and to boost the economy. Rishi, though, always seemed to revert to Treasury type. He just wasn't interested in radical tax cuts to deliver growth.

'But he just talked about putting up corporation tax and it was an anathema to me,' said Boris. 'That wasn't what we were supposed to be doing; that wasn't in the spirit of putting a rocket up the economy. I just couldn't understand why he was doing it, but he kind of kept saying, "Well, it's basically because the

Treasury wants to keep the money coming in," and I was very frustrated with this response.'

Boris was right. Rishi had a different, very non-Conservative view of the world. It was hard to know to any degree what his view of anything was.

'Do you remember at Party Conference, Rishi's speech?' I asked him. 'It was all about California and how great California was.'

It had happened again in his leadership hustings against Liz. It was all about tech and California. I found this interesting. Tech had been my sector in the department, and I had found tech leaders to be very unimpressed with Rishi. 'He just isn't listening,' one had told me. 'If you want to get tech companies who start up in the UK to stay and list in the UK, you need to reform your pension regulations and make it easier for them, and make the UK a desirable destination for them to invest in.' I asked the tech founder if he had spoken to Rishi and he replied, 'Repeatedly. He just isn't listening. His response is robotic.'

I relayed this story to Boris.

'I mean, say what you like about George Osborne, he at least had a vision about what he wanted to do. You know, the Northern Powerhouse or whatever; he had a plan. I kept saying to Rishi, "Come on, what are we going to do here? Are we going to deregulate, cut taxes, corporation tax? Let's get it down. We need an economic narrative, where is it?" And there was just nothing coming back, and he kept saying to me, "Look, we're doing so much, let's just keep focusing on what we're doing."'

It was quite astonishing. Our Chancellor sat on economic reforms in order to ensure that one day, when they were eventually introduced, he would take the credit. His intransigence, his sitting on policies for the best part of a year, holding them back until the plot had worked and he became Prime Minister in order to make the Boris-led government appear moribund, was unforgivable.

'Look, I'm not saying interest rates aren't a global problem,' I said. 'But isn't it interesting, it's those high interest rates which exposed the fact that we had £500 billion pension investments which were precarious as a result of poor regulation and yet, Rishi had been Chancellor during this time for three years, and Sajid and Osborne before him, and to divert attention away from that and themselves, they all pointed the finger at Liz? Interest rates and gilt prices are higher under Rishi than they were under Liz, and yet, they forced Liz to stand down. There was no £60 billion black hole that dominated the headlines, it was only £30 billion as it transpired because interest rates came down and we fared no worse or less than countries in the EU. Did they somehow create that narrative around the markets? Did they create the turmoil that affected so many to get Liz out and Rishi in?'

Boris sighed. 'God, I liked Rishi. I'm just shattered by what he did. I'm very upset about it. People forget Rishi was there with me in 2016 when we were fighting for MPs' votes and people were coming in to see me; Rishi was with me during that time, before Gove stabbed me in the back. So Gove had decided very early on during that campaign that Rishi was to be my wing-man and to stick by me, and he did. He was with me, at my side always, with me throughout when I was meeting with MPs and canvassing their votes.'

I stopped and looked up as he spoke. Rishi had been an MP for less than a year at this point. How did Gove even know him and why would he think Rishi, the brand-new, wet-behind-the-ears MP (because he truly was) was the person to shadow Boris all the way back then and why? Had they decided as long ago as 2016 that Rishi would be Prime Minister? It felt so familiar to me. Always the same people, the same Tory fault-line of the past almost forty years. The power rested in their hands, and when it didn't, like petulant teenagers, they created such disruption, they destabilised the country and our economy.

'Was he of any use to you during the 2016 leadership campaign, before Gove stabbed you in the back? He was only a new MP then.'

Boris thought for a moment.

'Well, Rishi would say to me, "You know, I realise you really think that that MP you've just met with was with you and you have his vote, but I'm just not sure about him."

'I remember thinking at the time that he was very, very kind; he was nice, in this very charming manner that he has. This is before Gove blew it all up.'

I spoke to someone who was there in 2016. 'Oh, Rishi behaved towards Boris then like people think Rishi is today; you know, before we cottoned on to what he was really up to. Look, I think Rishi was turned into the snake in the garden by the temptations of the system. I think he was turned by others who played with his mind, and by the sort of temptations they put in his path. I think very early on – I mean, very early on, possibly long before he became Chancellor – I think there must have been some sort of conversation in which Dr No, Cummings, Gove, Dougie Smith and the rest would have sort of said to him, "Look, here's what … here's what needs to happen; you know you need to get rid of this guy. We know what needs to be done, we can't control him. And you're a perfect fit. He has to go." And so I think he decides at some point: that was his path. They would have said to him, "You need to clear the stage" and made him think it was all there for the taking. And I think there was also a little sub-part of him that is kind of ruthless, the part that is the Goldman Sachs banker guy, and his basic calculation became "Johnson goes before '24 and I take over, or he fights '24, wins it with a small majority after Covid, and maybe it's a miserable time in those next four or five years, and then I'm the tail-gun Charlie, who gets, you know, swept out with the end of the Tory epoch. Much better if Johnson goes now; he's had a good innings. Three major election wins. Twice Mayor of London and once as Prime Minister." I mean, he would sometimes say things to Boris, like, you know, "You've done so much in your career and you've … you've delivered Brexit, you've done this, you've done that. You know, isn't it time for you to go? Your legacy is already there." And then he'd say to him, "Look, I really feel sorry for you because the inflation and the economy is going to be so bad over the next few years," and it was like he was saying, "Why don't you evaporate?" And yet, it was incomprehensible to us, because Boris had just won an eighty-seat majority, the biggest Conservative win in over forty years and would probably keep the Conservative Party in power for another ten years. If Labour win it's because Conservative MPs removed our winner, Boris Johnson. But, you know, here's a problem: some of those MPs are so young they don't even know what a socialist government looks like, they don't even know what life is like under a Labour government.'

'You know all roads lead to Gove, don't you?' I said to Boris, not for the first time. 'Cummings is Gove, Gove is Cummings. Smith is Gove and Gove is Smith. Dr No, he is everywhere and everyone. Whenever any of them are exposed, it's Gove who dives straight in to protect them. He fights for them all.'

Boris turned to the window and clasped his fingers together on the desk. He thought for what felt like an age.

'I think you're right,' he said. 'I think you're right. There were people telling me, I should have sacked Gove long ago. He wasn't delivering; he was insubordinate.'

That would not have worked. If he had sacked Gove, they would have got him out a lot sooner than they did. The plan to install Rishi had been well entrenched for years. They would never have let Boris get away with that. I knew MPs despaired with him for bringing Gove into Cabinet but they just weren't thinking it through.

'Did anyone advise you to sack Rishi?' I asked him.

'No, not really, it was hard to see what they were up to, what their plan was or how they were going to achieve it. It was all compounded by the confusion and the help they had from the Remain media [he meant the BBC, Sky, ITV], whipping everything up into a frenzy, and they knew just what they had to leak out there to whip it all up. That was why they did it. That frenzy then exploding on social media, then hitting MPs, played with their psychology, particularly the 2019 intake who had only been around for a couple of years and for much of that they had been at home due to lockdown and Covid. They couldn't cope with it; they were unused to the cut and thrust and then being radicalised into thinking that the only way they could purify themselves and the party was to kill Johnson. These MPs, they kept saying to me, "My personal integrity is being attacked."'

At this point, I wanted to laugh out loud. Your personal integrity being attacked comes with the turf of being an MP. It happens all day every day.

What those MPs were saying to Boris was also indicative of the naivety of our new MPs and the negative impact of social media. They were experiencing the opposite of the dopamine hit they got every time they checked their Twitter feeds or Facebook accounts for likes. Social media is designed to be addictive, that's how it works, and it increases feelings of anxiety, doubt and insecurity. It is triggering and exacerbating, and maybe what Boris had been dealing with was the first generation of algorithm-distorted MPs to enter Parliament.

'When someone begins to talk about themselves and their own reputation in the context of what's happening to you, the government and the country, it's quite an unusual consideration, isn't it?' I said.

Maybe I'm old-fashioned, but in the context of Rishi's behaviour and what MPs had been telling Boris, perhaps this was a new era, each man and woman for themselves. Maybe that old political chestnut, party or country first, was now old hat. It was quite patently the case that each man or woman was for themselves. Had it always been this way? I guessed it had; after all, regicide runs through the veins of the Conservative Party. We are the party that brought down and removed Margaret Thatcher. Nevertheless, in the days of social media, I predict that the political landscape will become far more turbulent regardless of who is in power.

We discussed the polls.

'Blimey, the polls are dire,' he said.

'Even Gordon Brown got a 4.3 per cent bounce when Tony Blair was persuaded to step aside for him,' I said. 'When they got rid of you, they shot the golden goose.'

Half of those who got rid of him – the Westminster contingent of Mark Harper, Andrew Mitchell, Steve Baker – they weren't worried about Boris losing the next election; they were worried that he would win it and they would spend longer on the backbenches. The way some of these MPs viewed the chance to get themselves into Cabinet was to do the work of the plotters, to attack him vigorously and frequently, and that way, Rishi would be indebted to them. It was either a plan of action decided early on, or they were taking their chance and hoping Rishi would one day be Prime Minister so that they could go to him and say, "Look, I helped you to become Prime Minister, I helped to bring Boris down", and it would be a legitimate case. The former seems the most likely option to me. That's why they were attacking him from so early on: because they thought that out of the 365 MPs we had, their place was to be in the top few that sat around the Cabinet table or to be given rewards and gongs and plum seats with a bird's eye view at the forthcoming coronation.

We were moving away from Rishi onto the MPs, and while I reflected on the irony of the fact that the downside of winning a big majority is that, for some, it just means there is more competition for the top jobs, I felt I had enough information about that not to need his input. I heard Wilf running down the stairs shouting for his daddy.

'Let's finish,' I said, packing up my bag.

Boris walked me out to my car and, as I drove away and passed the gate, I could see Boris and Wilf in my rear-view mirror, waving. Dilyn had run alongside and accompanied me all the way down the drive. He stopped when we reached the gate and ran back to retrieve a ball he had spotted on the grass, after which, I have no doubt, he ran back to drop it at Wilf's feet.

When I got home, I looked up the book that was on the study desk, *Act of Oblivion*, the Robert Harris novel waiting to be read, and I checked out the reviews. The *Guardian* reviewer had described it as apt for the political time we were living through now. This was written at the time Boris was removed:

From what is it they flee?

He took a while to reply. By the time he spoke, the men had gone inside. He said quietly, 'They killed the king.'

CHAPTER 11
DANCE INTO THE FIRE

When writing a book, it is always an immense relief to write the words, 'The end'. I start out on all of my fiction-writing journeys, consumed by my characters and the world and situations I create for them. I rapidly slip under the surface and it's a tricky time for my family as I become slightly lost to them. My characters wake me in the night as I groggily turn on the bedside light and scribble down whatever words or lines they have woken me with, or on a drive, I stop the car to get Notes up on my phone to do the same. My rule is, if they wake me at five or beyond, I get up, make a pot of coffee and head for my desk, where I know it's easier to just give up on sleep, switch on the computer and give my demanding characters a free run. Throughout the writing process, I'm distracted until I'm done, and by the time that final day arrives, I cannot say goodbye to the manuscript or my characters quickly enough. I have spoken to other authors who have reassured me this is an entirely normal process. That the journey takes so much of you that your mind and body are craving freedom and re-entry into the real world. That your imagination reaches a point whereby it needs to rest, recuperate and fill up the well.

This book is different. I have no use for my imagination. I am being given more information than I could possibly cram into one book.

* * *

My next interview was with someone whom I am at a loss to describe. If I begin to try, even in cryptic terms, everyone in the Westminster bubble will know who it is.

'Look,' he began, 'I wondered about whether or not I should speak to you. I mean, you may bleed the poison out of the party, but I think there is a strong chance you may destroy the party with this book and so I had my reservations. But then I thought to myself, you know, the party, it's bigger than this, it will survive. It will come back stronger and better without these people plotting at its heart and creating the havoc they have over so many years. Their networks, they are only strong because they as individuals are, but their strength does not come from place of duty, or responsibility for the country; it is driven by their desire to serve self.'

Needless to say, a good lunch was consumed, and instead of waiting for the sommelier to top up his glass, I did it myself.

'I hate it when I hear people say he had the wrong people working for him and surrounded himself by bad 'uns,' he continued. 'It's simply not true. Boris has good loyal friends and there were lots of really good and loyal people around him, but they had been pushed out to the periphery by those determined to do so in order to control the centre. It wasn't until it was all over and you're left thinking *What the hell just happened?* that you realise, they weren't enough to save him, and that's because of the bad people – they were everywhere, and God, they were organised and skilled. There were people pushed out of No. 10 who Boris wanted to be there and they were ruthless at it. Those guys were focused and the only time they lost their pace was when Covid hit and we were all thrown into a period of the unknown and unpredictability for a time.

'You remember that scene they kept showing on the news of Dominic Cummings running from Downing Street? When Boris was hospitalised? Well, I'm very sure the reason he was running was because he thought the world was going to end; I'm not kidding. His reaction was sheer panic. That's why he headed to the wilds of Durham; he probably thought that was the place to go to survive. He read a book on the Spanish flu that he kept spouting from as though history was about to repeat itself. For a man who claims to have a scientific mind – not that I ever saw it, I think that's all fake too – he acted like a catastrophist, as though modern drug therapies had yet to be invented. When Covid hit, he became lockdown obsessed. He was all doom and gloom and the world was going to end. He and Michael Gove, they acted as a force against everyone who was advising the Prime Minister to be cautious about lockdown.

'The truth was, Boris railed against lockdown like a wild animal. He hated it and when it came to the second lockdown, he wasn't sold. As it was, the first lockdown was totally necessary. When it came to the second one, there was a meeting at Chequers. Gove, Cummings and Hancock, all three were lockdown hawks. When they left, they knew Boris wasn't convinced, but he knew he had lost the battle; in the face of advice from his Chief Medical Officer, the NHS (which wasn't coping very well at all with bed pressure, staff burnout and sickness), he was outnumbered. SPI-M-O data* and graphs added to it all, and the three lock-down hawks: they were on form. Boris didn't have a leg to stand on; he knew what he had to do. Now, all three of those men were known to be leakers to the press, but only one of them was suffi-ciently well practised in leaking in order to bounce someone into a policy position and that was Cummings. When they left

* SPI-M-O: Scientific Pandemic Influenza Group on Modelling, Operational Subgroup – a subgroup of SAGE providing expert advice to the government during Covid.

Chequers, Boris had taken the decision, but in my opinion, he was bounced into it. He liked to think through difficult decisions and chew them over and throw them around. He was on his way back to London to the press conference and apoplectic when the press began to report there would be a second lockdown, because the moment that happened, he had lost control of the narrative. He knew that the markets, the media and the opposition, they would seize on it. Once the media had run with it, it was impossible to phrase it so as not to cause alarm, impossible to be temperate with the language or even reverse the decision if he had wanted to. He is rarely angry, but he was that day.'

We were on to coffee and the spoon clinked repeatedly against the side of the cup as he looked up and his eyes met mine. He placed the spoon on the side of his saucer with great care. I had sat myself too close to the fire and it was burning the side of my leg, but I didn't want to move and disturb him.

'You know on the night it was announced that Rishi had been put into No. 10, without a single vote from a member or the public, the staff working at their desks in CCHQ stood up and cheered. Did you know that?'

I shook my head.

'They were staff who, since the day Liz had been elected, had almost refused to work. Over a period of time, CCHQ had become infiltrated and were mostly Rishi supporters. There was a key woman, one of Rishi's Spads, who had been placed in CCHQ and had overseen this process. On the day Rishi won, she left CCHQ and went to work for Rishi in No. 10. It was then I realised how far the net had spread, they had their hands on every lever of control, and then you realise Oliver Dowden had been party chairman; of course it was easy for them. Oliver was Team Rishi. Ask yourself the question: why? Look at the number of emails that are now being sent out from Kemi Badenoch to party members via email from Central Office? Do you think that's a coincidence? The positive press briefings? No, it isn't. It's the poison, setting up the next person they want to put in place, because they are addicted to control and power, they get off on it, in the perverse way some people are addicted to sex, but power is also sexual for some I suppose.

'Rishi will be useful for now but he's just another Michael Howard to them; he's a stopgap and his time will be short. First though, they will use Rishi, they will benefit from Rishi. Then, when they have done so, they will remove him and replace him with Kemi, the person they have been preparing for many years. And it is because Kemi is an abrasive, often-difficult, sometimes very rude person who is so closely linked to those who have spent decades causing havoc in our party, that I can't actually stand by and watch that happen. If Conservatism is ever to survive, these people have to be driven out. Kemi as leader would mean more of the same. The MPs who are allies of Dougie Smith are already out whispering in the corridors of power, telling MPs what an excellent leader Kemi would make. She is very, very close to Dougie Smith. I more than most know what are the essential qualities required in a prime minister and Kemi doesn't come anywhere near the bar. I do believe that once these people are gone, the Conservative Party can become a great party again, and I think your book is necessary in order to achieve that after the swamp is drained. I suppose I had hoped over the years that they would become weary, tired of anarchy or maybe fall off their perches, but they show no signs of disappearing into the shadows; on the contrary, they are more powerful now than ever before.'

Kemi Badenoch was elected as an MP in 2017 and, during the latest leadership election, had been backed and supported by Michael Gove. Kemi is perceived as being on the right of the party and it was assumed this had been done in order to split the party vote with Liz and allow Rishi to come in down the middle. Like so many connected to the small but powerful gang, she had previously worked at *The Spectator* magazine who pump out regular copy which is so bizarrely obsequious it could be announcing the coming of the new messiah.

'The campaign to get Boris elected in 2019 was phenomenal,' he continued. 'He was surrounded by people who wanted him to succeed. The election was well underway, and I noticed, Dougie Smith along with Oliver Dowden, they were always around, but they never read right to me, do you know what I mean? Occasionally, they would be with Dr No. They were all saying the right words and, on the face of it, they were gung-ho Team Boris, but I was never quite sure, it was like they didn't really believe it. Dowden, Rob Jenrick and Rishi put an article in the papers saying how they backed Boris and the narrative quickly spread that it had been an article which was influential and instrumental in bringing other MPs on board to back Boris, and that was the biggest exercise in smoke and mirrors I've ever seen. All three of those MPs, they have no influence or following. It achieved little or nothing. No one really knew or rated any of them. I knew then, it was an act of the dark arts and Dr No was probably behind it, but he is so good at it, Dr No, the narrative just flew and no one questioned it at the time. Anyhow, I kept my reservations to myself because everyone else was perfectly fine with the two of them and we were very, very busy, you know, and no one ever said anything to me, but I have to say, I wasn't in the least surprised at the people they turned out to be.'

I believed every word of this. On my first day as Secretary of State in 2021, I arrived at my new department at around seven o'clock in the evening. Around three hundred messages had arrived on my phone on the short journey from Downing Street to the department. I had been allocated a car and a kindly temporary driver.

I had been sat in the House of Commons' hairdressers deep down in the basement when I got the call telling me to make my way over to No. 10. The two lovely hairdressers, Kelly and Lynn, and I stared at each other in the mirror. They could hear the voice on the phone; all three of us had our mouths open. Lynn dashed to the door and locked it from the inside as they both frantically set about drying my very wet hair. I had not expected this. I had just parcelled up all of my old ministerial clothes and donated them to charities supporting Afghan refugees. I had done two years in the Department of Health during Covid and, frankly, I was knackered. I had already made the decision: no more ministers' jobs for me, I was done. I hadn't asked for or even considered Cabinet.

When I reached the department, I was greeted by my new Permanent Secretary and Principal Private Secretary, and the look of fear and trepidation on their faces was the first thing that struck me.

As they escorted me up the stairs, I was met at the top by the junior ministers who had endured a year under Dowden before me. 'Thank God,' they said as they greeted me and escorted me to my office. Within half an hour, I had a sense of my predecessor.

Back to my current interviewee. 'So, I was wary of Dougie Smith and Dowden,' he said, 'and then, almost at the last minute, Boris said, "I'm going to bring in Dominic Cummings." He'd been under a considerable amount of pressure. Lord Frost was a big Cummings fan and Frosty was someone Boris respected and liked, so he took his requests to bring Cummings into the tent seriously, but honestly, I think Frosty, just like everyone else, was taken in.

'During the election campaign itself, Cummings did nothing, but used to say to people things like he was working on the data with statisticians, and when he had left the room, it was like we were living in an episode of *Black Mirror*, and we knew he was talking nonsense. It is a truth that Dominic frightened people. He ran No. 10 based on a culture of fear. Sacking people without notice, telling Spads at the Friday meeting, "Not all of you will have a job on Monday" – all of that macho bullshit crap. He went home feeling like the big man, Spads went home feeling sick, wondering if they would still have a job and could pay the rent at the end of the month.'

Once again the phrase, *you are only ever two pay-packets away from homelessness* made by another No. 10 passholder came to mind.

'It became clear very early on that Dom was leaking to the media. Long before Covid, and it was incredibly destructive. It was like a fifth column was operating inside No. 10 from day one.

'Now, I was never taken in,' continued my source, 'by all the Rishi-will-do-better-in-the-polls nonsense; I could see what they were up to. They wanted the man of connections and big money to be indebted to them. They were moths flapping around the flame of wealth and influence. I felt sorry for his wife, Akshata. She's very polished; like Rishi she's done an MBA at charm school; but you cannot take away from her that she is a wonderful mother and has created a secure, calm and stable environment directed towards Rishi in order for Rishi to thrive in, like that was also part of the plan and I'll be honest, a Prime Minister needs that. It's a sad fact, but it's true. My personal belief is that he became someone ridiculously vain and ambitious. He exposed his rather wonderful wife and children to these plotters in a way he never should have. I mean, he lost to Liz Truss. He was in the lead. He lost, she didn't win. Some of that is definitely down to your own involvement.

'I know you persuaded Jacob [Rees-Mogg]. Once yourself and Jacob publicly endorsed her that was a huge boost to Liz. I'm not going to say much more, but I just wanted to make sure that if you are looking at the group of men who live in the shadows of our party, who truly decide who the Prime Minister is, then you should look a little closer at Kemi. They are always one step ahead, and if you want to see how that works, who her friends are, who she takes her holidays with, who the people are who are whispering in corridors, then I think you may find that a fruitful path to explore.'

CHAPTER 12

THE WRITING'S ON THE WALL

I needed to know more about the press office parties. About what actually happened on a Friday night in No. 10 during Partygate. I've already been told this: 'The case of wine that was carted in, in a suitcase, that's been happening for as long as anyone can remember, back to Blair days, certainly. The press office Fridays can be fifteen hours long; everything needs putting to bed for the weekend papers by the end of a Friday, so it wasn't a new thing by any means. It was just they took it to a new and frankly, debauched level, and that was nothing to do with Boris; he was totally blindsided when he found out. The problem was that the people he turned to for advice, to inform him as to what the hell was going on when he was in Chequers, they were the very people who were up to their necks in potential rule-breaking, and apart from anything else, they had a huge amount to hide. They had families and marriages as well as careers to save.'

Getting to the bottom of what happened in Downing Street on a Friday night has been the most difficult part of writing this book so far. I needed to speak to people who were close to or attended the press office parties, someone who was fined or gave evidence to the Sue Gray inquiry. Someone who even had had sex on the sofa maybe? I knew it was a long shot, finding a person who would tell all, but as it turned out, it was not as unrealistic as I had at first thought. I was about to discover that my digging around would take quite a dark turn. Out of the blue, I received a message from an unknown number on my phone: *I'll talk to you.* This was the first of such messages as the news of what I was doing began to spread.

We spoke over Zoom; she didn't want to meet in person in case we were seen.

'I just want to tell you what I saw,' she said to me. 'There were times when I knew more than others because of my job, but I kind of knew what was going on all along since many of us are on group WhatsApps and, you know, some of those WhatsApps are totally locked down – no one would ever leak from them – but something happened to me which I think needs to be known. I don't want to be the one to put my name to it, but I could give you the names of the women who were compromised. They would never talk openly because, I mean, imagine, you work in a world of journalists and comms, and you blow the whistle: how is that going to work out for your career? It would be terminal.

'With regard to Lee, he has always been an arrogant twat. Always bragging about his pay. He would get very excited about the fact that he spoke to editors of newspapers; and now I hear, Lee is back inside working for Rishi via his own new comms organisation. Lee only ever referred to Cummings as the Dark Lord. Dom is very much Lee's boss, not just professionally, but kind of emotionally too. Lee was terrified of upsetting Dom. When I look back, that first year, in 2019, it was obvious, whatever Cain had been to Boris before the election, he wasn't the same person after. It was Dom who placed Lee with Boris for his leadership election campaign, and he worked as a team with Dom and Cleo Watson, who was very close to Dom, and they were all working against the Prime Minister. I think things just got worse and worse, week by week. The thing about Lee is that he also had poor judgement. I'll give you an example that was all over one of our WhatsApps.

'There was a visit up north somewhere to a police station for a Boris speech. Lee wrote it and anyone who knows Boris will know that he writes his own speeches. Lee told the visits team, I want Boris with the police lined up behind him as though he's Kim Jong Un, and I want him to make a Brexit speech. He said all this the night before the visit. What he never did was talk to Boris. When Boris was handed the speech he was really uncomfortable, and he said, "We're at a police station; I can't make a speech that's overtly political." Boris was seriously unhappy; he looked at it and said, "No sorry, I'm not giving that," and they were herded into this room at the police station and Boris sat down and began to craft his own words, which, of course, he would have done the night before if he had been warned. He had been told something entirely different from what he was being presented with. One of the police officers who was stood out there fainted because it was a really hot day. It was awful. They tried to pull a fast one on Boris and it backfired.

'They often briefed things out to the media without having cleared them with Boris first. I think it was to stuff him up and it was so confusing, but there was always this plausible deniability factor when they were challenged, which confused you even more. They were actors and they presented excuses to Boris to confuse and distract. His link to the public, his popularity, no matter how hard they tried to destroy him, they couldn't get around that one and it drove them nuts. They tried everything. They bullied him, lied to him and sidelined him, and none of it worked, he remained popular because people loved him. But the thing was, Boris is only interested in what gets done, the task in hand; whether it's getting vaccines or levelling up; his mind becomes all consumed by it, contrary to the stories which were constantly briefed out to the media to discredit him.'

'Was it just Lee and Cummings?' I asked.

'No, but the others, Dr No and the dark arts lot, they were never actually around. Dr No, he was this man in the shadows. People would whisper that he was there and say to be careful, so no one really ever mentioned his name. I never saw him once.

'I absolutely hate all of this stuff; it makes me feel sick to talk about it.'

I could see she was becoming distressed and so I brought my dog into the conversation; he was barking at a squirrel in the garden. I knew she also had a dog and so I put my Westie, Teddy, on my knee to calm him, and her, down.

Teddy did his work well by putting on his most endearing, inquisitive face. She picked up her springer spaniel with some difficulty and we chatted about our beloved animals before we resumed, and then without prompting she said, 'There was some-one who came into No. 10, sick. He came into No. 10 with Covid. He had symptoms, took a test on his way into work, and then came in to organise a Friday-night party in the press office while he waited for the results. My guess is that much of what has been leaked out to journalists was a distorted version of events to keep all the attention away from what the press office were up to on a Friday night, because some of the journos were becoming suspicious. It's an absolute joke that this culture was inspired by Boris. He was working his arse off and went straight to Chequers from his constituency or a visit on a Friday.'

I pushed her on this. 'Wouldn't one of those people have squealed?' I asked.

'No, because one way or another, he had them in the palm of his hand. Lee's press office staff were all really loyal to him, of course they were. He cut down on the numbers of all of the comms staff who worked in departmental comms teams and then gave loads of members of staff working in the No. 10 comms team a massive pay rise by bumping them up a whole grade. So, funnily enough, guess what, they were all very loyal to him. He bought their loyalty, or silence, whichever way you want to look at it. It was an absolute abuse of power and process and I've no idea why Simon Case allowed it. It was like, everyone who works in a government press team is shit, but you guys here in my team in No. 10, you are the best and they have to know that, which is why I'm going to bump up all of your salaries. It was appalling: he bought them. He had this kid called Damon Poole; if Lee didn't like what the journalists had written, he sent this kid out who was, what, twenty-two, to shout at them. I honestly think the journalists just laughed.'

'Damon Poole?' I said. 'He was sent to Health when I was there, to work as a comms guy to Matt Hancock.'

'That's right, he did. The people who work in the departmental comms team have usually been doing the job for years and doing it really well. Many of them spend time in No. 10 and then move from there into the departments; it was bizarre that they would send anyone with as little experience as Damon Poole into Health, where you were handling a major pandemic; just so odd.

'Cleo Watson – now, she's another story. She was brought into the Prime Minister's private office, right at the heart of Boris's operation.'

'Everyone came across Cleo,' she continued. 'She used to complain all the time about having to clean up Lee Cain's mess. I'm not sure if she meant emotionally or the cushions on his sofa, and Boris didn't have a clue. He was just in back-to-back meetings or out on the road. He would be prepping for PMQs or an appearance in front of a select committee or hosting tech leaders at a dinner in the dining room, whatever it was. When you are

Prime Minister, it's full on and Covid just made that a million times worse. Cleo had a really charming manner about her, which was a front. She and Dominic were so horrible and disrespectful to Eddie Lister; they pushed him out of every meeting. He had worked with Boris for years at City Hall and he was the one person who had Boris's back, and they knew that, so they wanted him out. Anyone who would have been on the lookout for Boris was soon identified and got rid of.'

'Were they like that with Rishi?' I asked her.

'Oh no, not at all. It took me a while to cotton on because Rishi and his wife are so utterly charming, but then you realise, it's a learnt skill with Rishi, even though the smiling mask occasionally slips and he can be very petulant. I'm not sure about Akshata – she is lovely, despite her financial privileges – but Rishi, he can become irritable and snappy very quickly, like in a flash. At first, Boris really rated Rishi, I mean *really* rated him, but then you realise, Boris had just fallen for the Rishi patter and the charm offensive Rishi uses when he wants something to go his way. And the Rishi circle, who were supposed to be working for and promoting Boris, they were constantly praising Rishi to Boris and gaslighting Boris, but over time you saw the quizzical look in Boris's eye and his brows furrow, and when they had finished prattling on about how much everyone loved Rishi and how popular he was, Boris would say, "Really, why is he raising corporation tax to 25 per cent then? Why isn't he doing something about Solvency II or pensions or creating an economic environment for the tech companies to list here rather than in New York? Where are his big ideas for the economy? What about him tells you he's a Conservative? I'm still waiting, eh. C'mon, don't tell me how great he is; show me."

'When Boris began to do this, they would um and ah and scuttle away. It took me forever to click, to be honest, that Rishi was the project. By the time I realised it was too late. Even if it wasn't, I'm not sure I would ever have had the confidence to walk up to Boris and say, "Prime Minister, I think this is what is happening," because why would he listen to someone like me at my pay grade? I don't know if you remember, when Boris was on his way to Kent to announce funding for cancer care? Well, that morning, when he was actually on his way in the car, the Treasury pulled the funding and the announcement from under the wheels of the car he was travelling to Kent in. Rishi was in the convoy and he was behind Boris, and they had to find a police station with a secure room to sit in and thrash it out. Boris was flabbergasted. Someone dropped the ball on that day, because Rishi would never have been in that convoy if he had known that was what they were about to do and would never have wanted the face-to-face confrontation with Boris. That isn't Rishi's style; he's a coward. I think Rishi persuaded Boris that it was the Treasury machine, that it had all been lost in the process because they always had a really good and very convincing reason why things happened as they did, all totally plausible. It was really obvious at all the meetings I was at that Boris came into power thinking that everyone in No. 10 was committed to public service and they were all on board Team "Get Things Done". But the only team that existed was made up from a certain group of individuals who were on the team "Get Boris Out", and that was very obvious from Friday morning 13 December 2019.'

'If Rishi is a Cummings project, why is Kemi being raised with me?' I asked her.

'Well, if there comes a point when suddenly Rishi parts ways with Cummings you will know about it because Cummings will begin to publicly attack Rishi via his blogs and Twitter feed because that's how he operates. If at any point Michael Gove went on leadership manoeuvres, and everyone knows he will never give up because surely, all the plotting and leaking has to have been for something, Cummings would be out there doing his bit to tear Rishi down first before Gove could be built up. You will absolutely know the day Rishi and Cummings part ways.'

Cummings, a barometer of Gove's intentions as I write this, is totally silent. I had already made a note to find out why Kemi Badenoch was Gove's preferred candidate, it's hard to find anyone who thinks he genuinely endorsed her and that in doing so, he wasn't just moving another piece on the board.

I asked her if she could tell me a bit more about the parties, about the Sue Gray investigation and what was on the locked-down WhatsApps.

'What I can tell you is this: we were all utterly gobsmacked. In her published report, Sue Gray says about the garden event organised for all staff, that Lee Cain said he had just popped out to see how many people had attended. She reported what he had told her, as an actual fact in her report, as in, I've been told this and it is a true fact. She did not do that with a single other person, only Lee Cain. Why was that? That was weird. And it's literally in there now, in the report. Why would she believe him and no one else? Repeat word for word what he told her without challenge and do that for not one single other person?'

When I looked this up in the Gray report, I found that what she had actually written was, *Lee Cain informed the investigation that he attended the event for a brief period to ascertain who was present in the garden.* So while not quite the categorical acceptance of what he had said, it was nevertheless odd that he was quoted defending himself in this way, and no one else had been.

On the previous page the report says:

211

Lee Cain, the then No. 10 Director of Communications (a special adviser), also received the invitation. In response, he emailed Martin Reynolds, No. 10 official (1), and Dominic Cummings at 14.35 on 20 May 2020 stating: 'I'm sure it will be fine – and I applaud the gesture – but a 200 odd person invitation for drinks in the garden of No. 10 is somewhat of a comms risk in the current environment.' Lee Cain says he subsequently spoke to Martin Reynolds and advised him that the event should be cancelled. Martin Reynolds does not recall any such conversation. In addition, Dominic Cummings has also said that he too raised concerns, in writing. We have not found any documentary evidence of this.

What is undoubtedly true is that nowhere else in the report is anyone quoted in a way that might be deemed to exonerate them. And if in neither case was the evidence verifiable, why quote it in the first place, if only verifiable evidence would be included in the report for anyone else?

So, on the one hand you've got Gove, whose links with Gray go back years, and on the other are the weekly parties run by the press office – not just a few people sitting at desks with a glass of wine, but proper messy affairs where things got broken and wine got spilt up walls, and although Lee Cain's name is never linked to these parties, he was the head of comms, head of the press office.

'Also, the thing about wine-time Fridays is that this was just the press office,' she said. 'It's not any of the other offices that seven out of eight of the people in No. 10 were working in. It wasn't most of the civil servants or the policy teams or those working in the Prime Minister's private office or anyone else working damned hard in No. 10. It was the press team. People don't get that 10 Downing Street is a big house, a listed building with a huge number of rooms on lots of different levels. It's not open plan or even proper functioning offices. That's how they managed to keep secrets; it's the logistics too. You know what it's like inside, but people reading your book won't know that. You could sometimes see a journalist slipping in the back door on a Friday night to speak with Lee Cain and Dom Cummings. We were like, "What the fuck is this famous person from the telly news doing coming in through the back door?"'

'Can you tell me who they were?' I asked her.

She hesitated.

'I'd rather not, but I think you can guess those who had engaged in the most negative reporting against the government and the Prime Minister.'

She moved back onto Rishi. 'During the General Election campaign in 2019, Boris was on a tour of the country and went to stay at Rishi's house. Some were at the house, some in bed-and-breakfast accommodation but they all went to Rishi's palatial house to be fed by his housekeeper and his staff, all very Downton Abbey, and that's when they were all together. It wasn't as obvious to some who were there at the time, as it is now, that Lee Cain was up to something. He weaved his way around the gathering from person to person asking people to put pressure on Boris to sack Eddie Lister, who was a great man and a good friend and so loyal to Boris. It was clear, he was the first person they had to remove to start destabilising Boris, and he hadn't even won at this point. He was saying to people, "Boris will listen to you. Can you persuade him to get rid of Eddie and put Dominic Cummings in as Chief of Staff?" Throughout the referendum, it was clear that Cummings was gearing up for a big role in No. 10 at the centre of government.'

We moved on to the removal of Boris from office.

'Look, the people who have had the most negative impact on Boris are Gove, Cain, Cummings and Gavin Williamson. I add

Gavin because he had a few old spies among MPs from the 2015 intake in the Westminster camp, he was useful. There were a number of those MPs who would listen to Gavin when he raised the flag, when it was time for them to remove Boris. Gavin may be back in Cabinet now [October–November 2022], but he won't last, his level of unpleasantness is far higher than his IQ. He will mess up again and be out.'

Just then my mind went back to someone whom I had spoken to earlier who put my source's comments into context. 'Boris Johnson had too many toxic people clamouring around him, like no other leader ever has before or will again, and if they can be exposed that must be the point of your book. To make sure that men like Iain [Duncan Smith] and Boris aren't attacked and removed in this way and that professionalism and democracy can return.

'He's surrounded by people who compete for his friendship, his influence, his patronage, his protection. Everyone he is in contact with wants something from him and asks him for something or begins speaking to him with the words, "what you need Boris is …" like they are telling him something he didn't already know.

'Simon Milton, who had been at his side in City Hall, passed away, which is why they made removing Eddie their number one priority, and then it was Carrie they went for next. They knew exactly what they were doing.'

When my source and I came to the end of our Zoom call, our dogs woofed goodbye to each other. It was clear that her whole experience of working in No. 10 had been traumatic. I asked her, if she knew of anyone who could confirm any of what she had said, could she put them in touch with me. Shortly after we ended our call, a civil servant sent me a copy of a text he had sent to his boyfriend on 18 December 2020, when he was leaving Downing Street for home.

Walked to the top of the stairs and there's literally sixty people all gathered and drinking and laughing and cuddling in the No. 10 press office.

He posted an angry emoji at this juncture and continued:

Like, to the point I had to walk back downstairs and go another way to avoid it because I couldn't have physically got through it if I had wanted to. Unbelievable.

That date, 18 December, was a Friday.

CHAPTER 13

BORIS: WE WILL STAND TALL

I'm back in the bright and sunny office overlooking the river. Boris has been writing in a notebook and I think it was Carrie who told me that he makes a note at the end of each day, before he goes to bed, which is an impressive New Year resolution many writers set and fail to achieve. He is bouncing around the office like Tigger, driving everyone mad. It never fails to be uplifting when you are in the presence of his infective, effusive energy. He finishes writing something and I thought it would take someone with the skill-set of a hieroglyphologist to decipher his handwriting. If a thief took his notebook, he would throw it away.

I wanted to talk about the Owen Paterson affair, which played a huge role in his downfall. One of his long-suffering staff popped her head around the door. 'Tea?' she asked, smiling. It is mid-afternoon and I accepted gratefully as I opened my laptop.

'No, I'm fine,' said Boris.

'Let's get a photo,' she said as she reached into her skirt pocket for her phone. Boris and I turned to the camera, both smiling. I do have the sense that I am in a very privileged place to be given the chance by so many people who are trusting me to tell the truth, including Boris. In the eyes of many, once the Paterson affair blew up, the troubles Boris was facing turned a corner. I've heard many conflicting versions, and so I wanted to hear his.

Owen Paterson, a former member of the Cabinet under Cameron during the coalition years, had been facing suspension from the House of Commons following a report by the Standards Commissioner. He had been found guilty of lobbying and paid advocacy. The inquiry had dragged on for a very long time and I simply couldn't understand why Paterson, so obviously caught bang to rights, had not resigned his seat and given himself a far easier life.

'That was an awful thing, the whole Paterson case,' Boris said as he reached into his box of notebooks to the side of his desk and lifted one out. 'Aha, here we are; it was, let me see, the 18th or 19th of November.' I was utterly amazed, not only that he remembered the date, but that he put his hand straight into the right box and extracted the right notebook and turned with minimum effort to the correct pages. I had given him no warning about what I was going to ask him. That's where it ended though, as he slipped his new and very smart bright-green reading glasses up his nose and, squinting, asked me, 'God almighty, what does this say?'

I immediately thought, *Oh no, the deciphering is going to fall on me*, until he threw the diary down, folded his hands in his lap and, swivelling the chair around to the river view, said, 'Right, so I'm at COP, flat out …'

He squinted his eyes. 'Yes, I was in back-to-back meetings from 6.30 in the morning at COP26* in Glasgow until 9 p.m. at night, and during the day I made what looks like five speeches. Hang on [he consulted the notebook], I met and greeted 135 heads of overseas governments and delegations, and then I find, flicking over, the next day on the Tuesday, I was doing exactly

---

* COP26: the 2021 United Nations Climate Change Conference held in Glasgow.

the same thing. Some of the speeches were from the central platform. We negotiated with heads from overseas governments
about moving beyond coal, and had numerous bilateral meetings
with key heads of state. I can see listed, Monday: President
Jokowi of Indonesia. I see Prime Minister Modi of India. I see
Tamim bin Hamad Al Thani, the Emir of Qatar. I met about a
billion people from around the world those two days,' he said.

I glanced over and smiled at the humour in his overestimation.
He grinned at me, knowingly; he was very much on form.

'I met with Prime Minister Kishida of Japan, President Nguesso
of Congo, Prime Minister Bennett of Israel. They were all for
bilaterals.'

He was clearly still thinking as he clasped his hands behind his
head.

'I make speeches about trees and about global warming. About
UK leadership – all these things. So we're getting, we're moving
towards an agreement. And it's been, it truly is turning out to be
an incredible success. We are moving towards getting the whole
world to compromise on using coal-fired power stations. Massive
commitments are made to stop the use of internal combustion
engine cars around the world. We are raising the money that we
didn't think we'd raise to support the Third World, the develop-
ing world, to move away from carbon from fossil fuels, and we
have countries who are coming with big commitments on reduc-
ing their carbon budgets, which is the basic thing you have to do
at the conference. That's the big question for everyone: "Where
will you be in 2050? What will you have done?" And we're
getting more and more commitments to move to net zero by
2050. So in Britain we are the first country in the world on course
to do this, to achieve it. There were people who said it was
wrong, but it was them, they were wrong, because this is this
thing, this goal that makes money for the UK. It delivers hundreds

of thousands, millions of jobs. And actually, it saves the planet too, and it's totally the right thing to do.'

I agreed with him. The people in our party who whinge on about environmental pledges and objectives to make the planet a safer place, with cleaner air; who say we should run on oil and gas forever; are totally wrong, and those of us who manage to live another twenty-five years will know this. We can do much, much better, and why wouldn't we? Why wouldn't we create those jobs in nuclear, in green energy, green technologies of the future, and lead the modern world? I had attended COP26 myself; it was a massive success.

'I flew out of Glasgow as planned on the Tuesday evening and flew into Stansted, but instead of going straight back to Downing Street, I went to a dinner.'

'You went to a journalists' dinner at the Garrick Club?' I said to him. 'Weren't you knackered by the time you got back to London?'

He picked up the tea, began to drink it and frowned.

'I'd agreed, rather sort of vaingloriously, to go in and to be supportive of a group of former colleagues. You know, I'm always very proud to be a journalist. I love journalism and love journalists. I think it's a great profession and a very important profession. And one of the things I liked doing for a long time was writing editorials in the *Daily Telegraph*. I did it on and off for decades. And so there was a college of leader writers that we were all members of in there and they invited me to this dinner at the Garrick Club. Charles Moore was there; he was one of the instigators and persuaded me to come. I did, and at that dinner I think Charles mentioned this whole business about imbalances and Paterson and what an injustice it all was.'

I reached out for my tea; it wasn't there. He was drinking my tea. 'Boris!' I exclaimed, and jumped up, opened the door, and said, 'Any chance you can get this tea leaf his own mug? He's nicked mine.'

I've asked a number of people about the Paterson debacle and they all say the same thing: Boris was getting on with the job of being a prime minister. He expected those who were running Westminster and No. 10 to get on with the day-to-day issues, and that included in the parliamentary party. His job wasn't to be a nursemaid to MPs. His job was on the world stage, banging the drum for Britain. One person I had spoken to said to me, 'The problem with the PM's diary was that it was almost incompatible with being a human being and there was very little room to accommodate side-swipes and unexpected events. The diary didn't allow for issues which blew up without any notice. Those who were working against him, they knew this, so if you look back, every time an adverse situation did blow up, whatever story it was which was all over the BBC and the media, with media tart MPs out on the green hunting down cameras to complain to, he was either out of the country or his diary was jam-packed full, limiting his ability to respond.'

'How long had you known Owen Paterson?' I asked him.

'Oh, I had known him for a long time. I first met him I think in 1989, when I was on a plane to Prague or some such place. Anyway, it's been a long time. His brother-in-law is Matt Ridley of the *Telegraph*. Look, he had a long, distinguished parliamentary career, he had served in Cabinet. And so I was willing to listen to people who said that he'd had a very rough deal, but I didn't have any of the details about what it was he had been investigated for – none of them.'

This wasn't surprising and was in fact part of the problem. The whole investigation had taken place in the utmost secrecy.

An aide has told me that it was almost impossible to verify what anyone was saying in Paterson's defence and once the details were public, they had virtually no time to do so. Charles Moore had apparently been very clear at the dinner as he sat next to Boris and as Boris had huge respect for Charles, a man of God and a man of integrity, he would have listened to him. He told Boris that Owen's wife had taken her own life in the most dreadful, awful circumstances.

During my time as Minister for Mental Health, I had spoken to Owen not long after and it was his testimony along with that of so many others that reinforced my commitment to making the online safety bill robust and workable. The impact of suicide on a family is bewildering, painful, and utterly devastating. And for the most part, they have to deal with that alone.

The following morning after the Garrick dinner, Boris attended the morning meeting in No. 10, a further meeting, and then went into PMQ prep. Most prime ministers have prep twice, once on a Tuesday afternoon and then again on Wednesday.

'Did you miss prep on the Tuesday because you were at COP?' I asked him.

He shook his head. 'I never had it on a Tuesday. It took up too much of the diary, too much to do. I only had the one on a Wednesday morning before PMQs.'

It was that Wednesday morning at PMQs when Boris was first asked about the Paterson inquiry.

'Starmer went straight in on it,' he said, 'because we had decided we were going to vote down the motion from the Standards Commissioner. That's what the whips were asking MPs to do.'

Starmer was uncannily prepared. I've heard from others, it was like Starmer had been in the PMQs prep himself.

I vaguely remember almost calling Boris at the time, only to realise he had been at COP26 and so deciding I didn't want to disturb him. I was full of sympathy for the situation Owen found himself in and for the loss his family had suffered, but it seemed to me that although there were huge concerns with the Standards Commissioner and how she had conducted her investigation, acting as judge and jury, which by any measure is totally wrong, the substance of her findings was unavoidable. However, Owen should have had the right to appeal, that is a fact. There had been a Standards Commissioner, Kathryn Stone, who had received a great deal of criticism about the conduct of the inquiry. The plan was: rather than vote to agree with the findings or not, to introduce an appeals system, which so many MPs had asked for so often. In Owen's case, it was particularly relevant because he was obviously not a man capable of defending himself. He was destroyed by grief. I mentioned to Boris that the perception had been that the process had become conflated with the findings.

'I think that's right. I think it was that very day that I had to explain things at PMQs. Back in No. 10, while we were trying to differentiate between Paterson's culpability and the process, he had asked a number of questions. I had been assured by those advisers in No. 10, those in authority in the parliamentary party and by a whole bunch of MPs, that we had to defend Paterson, and as Boris was trying to do so, at the despatch box, it fell apart in his hands, and it just didn't make sense. It didn't feel right. Paterson had either done it or he hadn't. It seemed like an open-and-shut case. He had been paid lobbying on behalf of a company, Randox. It was of no relevance at that point that the process may have been flawed; the findings were conclusive.'

Boris had been told that we should vote on the process in view of Rose's death and the House would understand that.

An aide told me that all the Gove people said to him, when Boris expressed his concerns, '"You have to power through this, you cannot back down. Just keep going," and I'm afraid we had been so busy, back to back with COP, he just hadn't had time to think about it. I had no idea what was coming, we were in Glasgow while all this was kicking off back in London. I wish there had been more time in his diary; we worked him hard and he was pretty euphoric, actually, because we'd done brilliantly, and the UK looked good. The UK had demonstrated real global leadership hosting one of the best COPs ever. Global Britain was really back and we were delivering. By the time he started to read the thing and to say, "Hang on, we're being asked to defend the indefensible here, we cannot do this, this is wrong," it was too late: the troops were already being marched up the hill and it had been leaked out to the media what we were going to do. This was always the perennial problem: the leaking to bounce the PM into decisions was utterly extraordinary.

'I knew he had gone up to Owen in the afternoon during the vote and I said to Owen, "Look, you've got to apologise for what you've done. And you know, you've got to make it clear that you feel you know that you are at fault, but that you think the process was flawed. And you know, people are going to want to hear some contrition from you," and he absolutely refused to listen to Boris. He then went out on the radio and said, "This is a great indication Boris Johnson has backed me," which totally infuriated everyone.'

That day was one of the most bad-tempered I have ever known in Westminster and it occurred to me that the party looked and sounded nothing like the party I had been elected to in 2005. I had been sat at my usual place in the library and had witnessed an altercation between two colleagues that had frankly disturbed me. The MPs in question were openly bad-tempered and pretty foul-mouthed towards each other in a place where, as a matter of courtesy to those who are reading and working, no talking is allowed, and I remember thinking to myself, *Is this the kind of*

professional environment I would like my daughters to work in?
And I answered myself without hesitation: *No.* Many MPs of late
appeared to have a problem containing their emotional response
to the mildest of irritating situations. The levels of animosity and
unpleasantness had reached a new level during the Brexit debates.
We had a responsibility to set the tone of the debate, and we did:
we set the bar low.

Despite Brexit, the level of aggressive hostility shown towards
Owen was not something I think I had ever witnessed directed
towards an MP in the chamber before, and many had been guilty
of far worse. I had never in the past seen so many MPs enter the
lobby at night very much refreshed, lacking good manners. I had
mentioned this to one of the MPs even older than me, who had
said: 'It's like back in the day and Maastricht. But, back in the
day there were no cameras in the chamber, there was no Twitter,
and there were not many ladies to mind the language for.'

The rise in social media usage and the mainstream media
meant it was all lapped up. Every MP today was an actor and the
chamber his or her stage for new and frequent outbursts of
emotional incontinence to be posted, make the news and to go
viral if they were lucky.

Christian Wakeford, one of the 2019 intake of MPs, walked
up to Owen Paterson in the lobby and aggressively called him a
'fucking selfish cunt'. Whatever you thought of what Owen had
done, and it wasn't killing firstborns or mugging a granny, he
was a man deep in painful grief. New MPs hadn't lived through
the expenses crisis of 2009 and then put themselves up for
re-election in 2010 when, for the first time, we broke the strong-
hold of a sustained Labour era. If Twitter poked them, they
squealed and they squealed. Some MPs from the 2010 intake had
told me during interviews that they had found the behaviour of
some of the 2017 and 2019 intake of MPs so toxic and bewilder-

ing, so alien and bad-mannered, that they no longer spent time on the parliamentary estate. They came in to vote and left straight afterwards. I soon discovered that some of the good people in the 2017 and 2019 intake did the same thing. This is not what they had signed up for.

I closed the laptop. 'Let's leave it there,' I said.

You would have to search for a long time to find anyone who disagrees with the assertion that Boris got every big call right. It was the little calls where others had the most input and leverage and created the most mischief that were difficult. Successful prime ministers had a full political machine working behind them, on the same team, moving forward as an army, loyal and united. It was becoming clear that Boris's huge achievements came about in the masked face of adversity, and that in the corners of Whitehall, where he assumed his loyal support was based, there lurked his worst enemies, whispering in the corridors of power.

It had been well over an hour that we had been chatting and, as I left, Boris picked up a cricket bat, which was leant against the wall in the corner of the room, and rocked it gently, then swung it through. He grinned. 'Look at that!' he exclaimed as he caressed the bat and turned it over in his hands. Normality was truly restored.

CHAPTER 14

THE WORLD IS NOT ENOUGH

Rishi became Prime Minister without a single vote being cast by either the general public or a party member. It was as good as a coronation. It didn't pass me by that if this had been France, there would have been calls for a revolution and carnage out on the streets. On the Monday morning when Rishi began to announce his first reshuffle, Boris Johnson sent him a personal text message asking him to be kind to those ministers who had worked hard, arguing that they were all good men and women. Within seconds that message landed onto the phone of an aide to Boris; it was sent to him by Dougie Smith. Rishi had simply forwarded the text from Boris on to Dougie. The message being sent straight back to the aide from Dougie Smith was loud and clear. He was making the appointments; he was in charge, not Rishi.

We slipped into the back of the smoking room in the Commons, which is for the use of MPs only. It's called the smoking room but no one has actually smoked there since the days of the smoking ban. The last MP I saw lighting up in here was David Cameron. He was perched on the sofa beneath the window facing out onto the Thames, opposite the heavy creaking oak door that announced your arrival as you walked in. On that particular night, as I opened the door, the air was thick and blue with cigarette smoke. I waved the smoke away with my hand as it hit me in the face and involuntarily I screwed up my eyes. I spotted David opposite through the haze, who shouted across, 'Get out if you don't like it.' I had been raised on a council estate and yet it was the bad manners in men who were supposed to be well bred that had constantly surprised me since I had become an MP. I tried to imagine my bus driver father, or my late husband, speaking to anyone in such a way. I couldn't.

Today, the air was clear and the room was empty, but the memory and vision of a grumpy David Cameron prevailed. My colleague and I plonked ourselves down on the red leather seats below the same window. We had both bought tea in takeaway cups from the members' tearoom, and as I peeled back the lid from mine the steam that rose reassured me it was still hot. The carved wooden bar was set in the corner for the early-evening rush. It was 4 p.m. Votes were at seven; in a couple of hours, MPs would start filing in. I scanned the carpet for mice before I settled back in the seat nursing my tea. It hasn't been so bad in recent years, but I am still scarred from the number of times I have been sat in the Commons and a mouse had run over my foot.

'I'm really interested in this book you're writing,' said my colleague. 'Are you mentioning Dr No? Did they really used to smoke in here?' He looked up at the ceiling as though checking for hidden packets of fags on the light fittings.

I sipped my tea and nodded my head at the same time.

'Wow, no wonder the average lifespan of an MP has risen. They all popped their clogs in their fifties back then, didn't they?'

His initial question had surprised me. How did this new MP know about people like Dr No? I moved straight on and asked him.

'Do you know about Dr No?'

'Oh, God yeah, he's been in the background for the twenty years I've been an activist and he was around long before that. There's him and the other one in the shadows, Dougie, he's in charge of candidate selection now since Theresa May's days which is why most MPs today are totally shit. That's how I got to know Dougie, but it's Dr No who is in charge, he's the big man. I'd been told years ago, Dougie will help to get you a seat if you want to become an MP. You have to sell your soul to Dougie, but he will get you a seat. There are MPs in the party who wouldn't be here today if it weren't for Dougie. He has this way of preparing MPs for selection meetings in front of associations and he's good at it; he's really good at manipulating associations too.

'So, back in the day, Dougie Smith, Robbie Gibb, Mark MacGregor, Gove, all that lot, Dr No in the shadows, a bit later Cummings, they were called "the movement" and they were incredibly militant plotters. They were mad Michael Portillo supporters, close to Francis Maude all of that lot. It's the reason William Hague stood down the morning after the 2001 election; if he hadn't they would have made his life hell. They never stop, it is all an addictive game for them. You know there was this disgusting dirty dossier circulated about Liz Truss during the leadership?'

I nodded as I wiped my glasses and placed them back on my nose.

'Well, no one used it. The knowledge of a dirty dossier in existence leaked out. When that happened, MPs who would have voted for Liz became nervous about doing so because they had heard about the dossier and they thought, *I don't want to nail my colours to that mast in case it all comes out and it turns out to be true and then I am going to look like a really poor judge of character.* It's the rumours of a dossier, even if it's all lies, which creates as much trouble as the dossier itself.'

I sat back against the hard leather seat. It made sense.

'When the whole Portillo leadership bid fell down,' he continued, 'they learnt from that experience and they just became more organised, more strategic. Portillo was the man. I suppose it could be said that's where they learnt the beginnings of their craft. Do you remember the television programme *This Week* that Andrew Neil used to present? It was on after the news on one of the week nights. The permanent resident guest was Michael Portillo. Who do you think the editor was when the programme launched in 2003?'

I shrugged my shoulders.

'Robbie Gibb.'

'No, really?' I said.

He leant forward and retrieved his tea.

'When Munira did her big resignation thing over Boris throwing the Jimmy Savile criticism at Starmer for never having prosecuted him when he was the Director of Public Prosecutions, it was so obviously the "time to kill Boris" trigger. When you know how they operate, you can sniff out what was behind it and how it was staged. When Munira wrote that she was upset about the Jimmy Savile comments and resigned from her policy job in No. 10, it was so utterly ludicrous. She had worked for Boris for fourteen years, and yet she chose to make a huge public announcement about that? And Boris was right. Munira was a policy adviser not a minister, and yet her letter was leaked to journos. The timing? In order to cause as much harm as possible, the letter went straight to the press. Just ludicrous. It was all obviously part of a plot, but the thing is, most of the MPs who have arrived with my intake, some of them have only been political for five minutes. They don't know anything or anyone. They haven't got a clue. Half of them had never heard of Munira until the day she resigned and have no idea who the players in the background pulling the strings in No. 10 are.

'And do you remember also, in 2016, when Michael Gove stabbed Boris, he said it was a last-minute decision and then gave a five-thousand-word speech almost straight after. It takes a week to craft a five-thousand-word speech, right, not an hour. It was all bollocks, and what was even more bizarre was the speech Michael gave in the Thatcher Room the day before. Remember?'

I did remember Michael's words from the time. He said something like, 'I never thought I would be stood here saying this, but I endorse Boris for leader.' It was a very odd, bitter-sweet, passive-aggressive, not what anyone fully endorsing someone would say. The room fell quiet for a second; it was just odd. He said afterwards: 'Oh, I was in torment.' It just didn't ring true. None of it did. If you're the running mate to someone and you're backing them, that's not the way to do it, and there was something about his manner – Gove is so theatrical that sometimes his melodramatic acting style lets him down.

'Because I know these guys, I could see straightaway what was going on, but I couldn't do anything about it,' he continued. 'What can you say? Who would believe you because no one would ever put all the pieces together. That five-thousand-word speech, it was a speech which needed to be meticulous and precise; it had been written long before.

'So you remember on the day when Gove stabbed Boris in the back, the nominations had to be in by noon?'

I did, only too well. Gove withdrew at ten past nine.

'Yeah? So I spoke to someone who was close to what was happening. I don't want to give a name because these guys can be … well, anyway. I said to him, "What the fuck was that all about?" And he's a mate, and he said, "Michael thought all of the people who had declared for Boris would come over to him." It's the collapsible slate theory. Gove gets everyone to sign up for him and Boris, and then, at the last minute, Gove pulled out, expecting the slate to fall behind him. Boris withdrew because they had probably been gaslighting, they do that so well and told him MPs are only signing up because of Gove, not Boris, so we ended up with May by default. The accounts written up following this act are very Govian and Cummings-inspired and incorrect, and were probably handed over to journalists by Cummings.

'No one ever said "Gove the backstabber" before. Everyone, even taxi drivers, know him as Gove the backstabber now. He was so caught up in these games he had lost all sight of what was reality. If Osborne did back Gove, you can work out why. Interestingly, Gove spent a weekend at Dorneywood with Osborne just before it all happened; you can see he is in the visitors' book. Think about it, Cameron and Osborne: their careers ended in failure at forty-nine and forty-five years of age. I'm not sure that was ever meant to be how it ended for either of them. Did you hear, Cameron shot two stags on the Isle of Jura, his father-in-law's Scottish island? He named one Gove and the other Boris.'

At this point my source, without warning and out of the blue, dropped a bombshell.

'And don't forget Kemi. Gove backed her during the leadership, not Rishi, but that was for a number of reasons. He couldn't be seen to be putting the knife in, not again, and it was useful to keep Kemi right in the race, and keep her up there and relevant in the mind of MPs. When Kemi spoke at the hustings, you could hear the voice of others coming out of her mouth. You know Kemi and Dougie Smith are very close, don't you? He's been coaching her for years.'

'I've been told by others,' I said.

'I'm not sure if Rishi has any idea how close they all are to Kemi; he thinks they are all about Rishi. They always have someone in reserve. There has been no boost in the polls for Rishi, and if there isn't they will start to dish the dirt on Rishi and manoeuvre Kemi into place. But do you know what? I just can't see Gove wearing that and I think they may have another mini war between themselves. With Kemi, you just need to join up the dots. *The Spectator* has written numerous articles about her; I mean, articles with titles like, "In Praise of Kemi Badenoch", and yet I can't listen to her without hearing Munira's voice who apparently wrote all her speeches for her when she ran for leadership. Dougie prepping Rishi, Munira prepping Kemi. So, just so you get it …'

I think I had it. He must have heard my brain whirring.

I suddenly remembered Kemi's words at *The Spectator* awards dinner and googled her exact phrasing, where she had joked about her own resignation during the toppling of Boris Johnson: 'It really was like the *Avengers Assemble*, with Sajid Javid as Captain America to take down Thanos.'

I quickly looked up Thanos: 'And there came a day unlike any other when the earth's mightiest heroes found themselves powerless against a threat too formidable to comprehend. On that day, Thanos declared himself supreme ruler of the universe.'

It was all so Govite. For all I knew, Kemi was probably on the Order of the Phoenix WhatsApp group too. They were like children playing games with British democracy and they thought no one had noticed. It was so student politics it was breathtaking.

While I looked up Kemi's acceptance speech I came across Jeremy Hunt's at the same event, where he had stated that Liz Truss had painted over the gold wallpaper in the flat above No. 10 by the time he had got there, only he knew that wasn't true. She had lied. He joked that the gold wallpaper had begun to peel off, and he had told his children to scratch over there, that there was gold in those walls. His comments ripped across the media. I honestly felt despair. Did the British voters not deserve better than this? The joke backfired, as Team Truss acknowledged they had painted nothing. They didn't have time and of course, as journalists who ran the story well knew, the gold wallpaper didn't exist and never had. It was always a red painted wall.

'The resignations, they weren't just coordinated, many of the ministers were bullied into doing it,' said my colleague. 'Kemi was threatening to remove people from WhatsApp groups and was hectoring, aggressive, it was all in the press, as we know. It was desperate, like we will punish you if you don't do it now. Once Sajid handed in his resignation, they had begun the process of toppling Boris and they could not fail; they had to keep going because they had exposed their hand, and if they failed, they in turn would be exposed. Kemi's messages to MPs were both revealing and unedifying, she is not fit to be Prime Minister, I'm afraid, more suited to a schoolground bully.

'Rishi was the central part of the plot, he was the axis it rotated on and has been for years, but he is also totally unaware that they won, and now, the same people, they are plotting against him. I remember when everything came out about his wife's non-dom status and her financial affairs; he thinks he's survived it. What he doesn't realise is that they don't give everything away at once. They will have more and when it is time to remove him, it will all blow up again, and when it does they will milk it. They keep the best for last.'

My teatime companion had been around No. 10 during the Truss administration, although fairly low down the ranks.

'What was it like?' I asked him.

'Awful. There was a lot of panic. When the Asian markets opened on the Monday morning after Kwasi's budget and offloaded sterling, which drove the price of the pound down to its lowest rate ever against the dollar, we knew something weird was going on and it wasn't going to end well.'

'Where's it all going to end?' I asked him.

Suddenly the door swung open, and an MP entered and glanced at the still-closed bar. 'Isn't he here yet?' he asked us of the barman.

I shook my head, my companion looked at his phone. The door closed again. Our bubble had been burst.

Our meeting was over. I checked over my notes, as he stood to leave. As he got to the door, he turned back. 'I do wish you luck but, you know ...' He hesitated and looked down at the handle, twiddled it around in his hand noisily. 'Just be careful. I mean, this has been their life, their addiction, for nearly forty years and you are about to ... well, you know what you are doing. Just be careful.'

I hadn't even checked my phone before the MP who had come to see if the bar was open popped back in and walked over to me.

'Hiya. Look, I just saw him leave. I hope you don't mind, I've heard, well it was in the press ...' He inclined his head towards my notebook. 'Do you mind if I tell you what I think?' He was a known Rishi supporter, so I was slightly wary.

I patted the bench next to me and told him to sit. I knew from the unique role he held that he may have had something interesting to share. He didn't need any encouragement. He perched on the end of the bench, his hands clasped together. He didn't look at me as he spoke but turned to look out of the window.

'Look, everything has its day, doesn't it? And with what has happened, we have had ours now, and I reassure myself with the thought that one day the party will come back, but we just have to get rid of the malign force; well, it's dangerous, isn't it? Is that what you are writing about? This is anonymous, isn't it?'

I reassured him that it was. 'But you are a Rishi supporter, aren't you?' I said.

There were many MPs who were unhappy at the installation of Rishi Sunak into No. 10. MPs aren't wholly stupid and even those who were anti-Boris Johnson had begun to wonder: had they actually been played? Was he one of them?

'You know Dougie Smith was about to be sacked by CCHQ the day before Liz fell? They had to go through an HR process, he had been on the payroll of the party for so long. I supported Rishi, you know that, but at the beginning, I didn't know what was going on. I still don't know, but I've heard enough to know it doesn't sit right with me.'

I asked him what his thoughts were on the fact that for Rishi it had been a coronation. The transfer of power from Liz to Rishi had lasted over a weekend, with Boris withdrawing on that Sunday when it was made clear to him that if he ran and won and regained his place in No. 10 a rump of MPs would make life so miserable for him, they would destroy the party in the process in order to remove him again.

'Brady and Hunt did not want the members to have a vote. CCHQ were ready to launch a two-day online members vote. It was sorted in three hours with online security in place. They set the number of MPs who would have to support Boris at a hundred, knowing that Rishi had been at this for a very long time and already had his list sorted. When it was announced that Rishi was to be Prime Minister, someone who works in CCHQ told me that three-quarters of the staff in CCHQ jumped to their feet and began cheering. It was like watching a super sleeper cell in cold war East Germany come alive.'

We chatted on for a further twenty minutes, during which he confirmed some of what I had been told already.

The brass screens on the window of the door rattled as the

door swung closed behind him as he left, and as I crossed the room to drop the empty tea cups into the bin behind the bar, a startled rat that had chewed its way through a black bin bag, and that was cleaning its whiskers after having dined out, stared up at me.

'You don't scare me anymore,' I said. 'I've met bigger rats than you in this place.'

CHAPTER 15

CASINO ROYALE

From the day Liz Truss resigned, Thursday 20 October 2022, days of chaos ensued. Boris, Carrie and the children were on holiday on a Caribbean island and were urged to fly back, and a weekend of campaigning began in earnest. He was the only man in the country who had a genuine mandate to serve as Prime Minister. He had been voted for by MPs, party members and the country. Rishi was also in the game but not a single vote had been cast by anyone for Rishi. Boris secured 102 nominations but withdrew on the Sunday evening, and then Rishi entered No. 10 on the Tuesday.

My next contact and I met in a casino that I noted was dangerously close to Westminster.

'Why here?' I asked him. 'I didn't even know this place existed. Are you a regular here?'

'Why here? Well, let's just say a dickie bird told me you met with a certain someone in the Two Chairmen pub a few months ago, and when I heard what you were doing I thought to myself: *Interesting*. I know you will forgive me for this, but I really don't want to be seen talking to you, I still have hopes for promotion.'

'Fair enough,' I replied. 'No offence taken.'

He ordered two espresso martinis and I settled into a booth. I looked around; the place was empty.

'How do you know it's safe here?'

He didn't answer me at once.

'Did you know that MPs get into so much trouble in here that in the office back there they have a number which is a direct contact to the whips' office, all parties, and when they think someone needs help they call that number and then, Bob's your uncle, suddenly a friendly but firm soul is at your elbow and says, "Come on Michael, it's time to go home now; follow me."'

He laughed.

'So, let's say I know the management is friendly,' he said as I took my first ever sip of an espresso martini.

'You aren't going to say who I am, are you?'

I shook my head as I wiped the crème from my upper lip. 'Definitely not.'

'Good, right then. They never stopped, you know. When Liz won the members' vote and she was elected as Prime Minister, they simply did not accept the result. They think the party members are barking mad. The thing is, these guys, they are an ace hit squad at destroying things, but putting it right and making it better, that's harder; they were absolutely determined this time that they had to win and they were prepared to do whatever it took. The economic shock, that wasn't what it seemed. You have some of the richest men in the world behind Rishi. Liz didn't do anything she hadn't said she was going to do during her campaign to be elected.'

I sipped the martini again and wondered how I would sleep that evening.

'You can't prove that, though,' I said. 'It's all speculation.'

'Oh, I agree. It will be interesting to see what happens to Rishi when interest rates rise higher than they were with Liz, will the Treasury mandarins be screaming for him to go like they did with Liz? So, when Boris fell they went after Nadhim Zahawi first and really hard. As far as they were concerned, he was a risk and had to go. Ruthless. No one matters to them. Take everyone else out by fair means or foul so that you don't need a members' vote and one MP is left standing and has so much support; so many MPs' votes, they go straight to being leader and bypass the members. Win so big, there would be no leadership contest. It happened by default with Theresa May when Michael Gove fucked it all up, as he so often does.

'Nadhim is a wealthy man and if you are a wealthy man, whether your name is Gary Lineker or Nadhim Zahawi, your tax affairs will be complicated. Just like Rishi's as it happens. Our tax system isn't set up in a way that makes it easy for anyone who does well. He has done nothing wrong, he's a man who has always been successful and ambitious, so of course he was always going to have his tax affairs in order. He knew, being in the public eye, they would be scrutinised and he has always been fiercely ambitious.'

As he said this, I remembered my first meeting with the Queen when I was appointed as a privy councillor. Nadhim was with me, he had just been appointed too, and we witnessed each other's private conversations with the Queen. I'm not sure I have ever met an MP apart from myself who looked as proud as he did in that moment. As a nine-year-old boy, he had arrived in the UK as a refugee from Iraq, not speaking a word of English, and there he was, in conversation with Her Majesty. His gratefulness for the position he had reached was apparent every time you met him and the people who worked with him, loved him. From day one, his enemies were not only out to destroy Nadhim, but in their campaigning they were totally aggressive with other MPs. They knew they could buy off any other contenders with the promise of jobs. Rishi wasn't really worried about them. But Nadhim was a good man and he had a track record of delivery that none of the others could hold a candle to.

'Rishi was never really concerned about Penny [Mordaunt], however, Nadhim, he really worried about him. He was clever, an excellent media performer and communicator and he had totally gripped every ministerial role he had taken. Like most of them, he's got a huge ego, but he's one of the nicest men in that place. He was a real threat.

'By the time we got to conference in the October, Grant Shapps – who was steaming that Liz hadn't given him a job in Cabinet – and Michael Gove were telling journalists that they would bring Liz down by Christmas. Once the leadership competition got underway, Gavin Williamson and Julian Smith (Theresa May's former Chief Whip) worked the tearooms hard. Julian Smith is a good man at heart and was so scarred by the May years, he just wanted the party to survive, but he wasn't remotely subtle; he was pulling MPs out of the chamber to pressure them into supporting Rishi. Because Boris had resigned and there was no big dog to coalesce around, the votes of MPs were far more splintered than they had anticipated. They had expected MPs to flock to Rishi, and they didn't. Those MPs who backed Penny Mordaunt and Tom Tugendhat, did so because they were either diehard Remainers in Tom's case or trans community advocates, or anyone but Rishi-ites in the case of Penny. They hadn't expected that.

'When it came to the wider party and MPs, they had expected everyone to just fall in and it was a bit of a blow that it was proving to be harder work than they had at first thought it would be. With Williamson and Julian Smith, it was like the old team were back in town. They brought in some of the big hitters to drum up the support for Rishi, but it was so unpleasant, more reminiscent of a press-gang. Just look at what they are up to now that Rishi is languishing at the bottom of the polls. If you go into the tearoom on any Tuesday or Wednesday afternoon, you will see MPs waiting at the tables to talk to Julian Smith, who is really a sort of chief whip. He's offering out gongs, chicken-run safe seats, anything he can to keep MPs on board and to stop them agitating. I can give you a list if you like. He has no official position, this is all done behind a screen, but you can see him walking up Downing Street every morning to attend the 8 a.m. Prime Minister's meeting.

'It's around twenty-five MPs who have been offered safe seats, because that's the going price if you have a vulnerable seat and they want you to be loyal to Rishi. It's how they are holding the government together and that, to a degree, has always been the way. It's just in overdrive right now. Some MPs were smart, they did deals and bartered long ago when Rishi was canvassing support. All those northern wall MPs who are always banging on about how much they love their constituency are about to be put on shortlists for safe seats in the south; I wonder how they will explain the chicken-run away. They disposed of any pretence of principles when they removed Boris.'

The martinis were neither shaken nor stirred, and I sipped wide-eyed and steadily as he spoke.

'Their tactics, the bribery, it was so brutal. I know of half a dozen MPs who over the past year had been asking each other, "Why doesn't Boris sack Rishi? He's not a Conservative Chancellor, he lets the officials run the Treasury, he's planning to hike up corporation tax. Why would anyone invest here? It's madness. Why hasn't Boris just sacked him? Rishi is all PR, and Instagram. There's nothing to the guy; he's not even that smart." The MPs who had been saying that for eighteen months were quite literally press-ganged by some dirty tactics into backing him. And now, around that Cabinet table you have some fairly toxic people. I know someone who has been to a number of small-group meetings in No. 10 just recently and he told me that

Dougie Smith is in all of them and Dr No is on the speaker phone. How is it that a man who was arrested for threatening to kill someone and who ran sex parties, for God's sake, who no member of the general public has ever heard of, how come that man is controlling Rishi? How come Dr No who allegedly tried to burn someone's house down, was alleged to have swindled party donors out of money, taking one poor donor's American Express card for such a ride, who has spent nights in prison, how come these people are there with Rishi?'

He thought about his own question for a moment.

The rest of the espresso martini slipped down like a coffee as I thought about some of the other stories I'd heard. Many I'm unable to include here because of possible 'legals', but they are very real.

'Right now, these people operate in a very small group around Rishi. Dougie Smith, Oliver Dowden, Robert Jenrick, he's been in on the Dougie gang for a long time now. MPs were asking themselves, "How come he got into Cabinet five minutes after he became an MP with no discernible talent?" Now they have the answer. If you want to know why Dougie Smith currently has the hold over the party that he does and why we have the MPs we do, it is because he oversaw the selection of MPs and had control of the candidates' list in the last two intakes. He's always done that – look at Rishi and others – but it was very much so for the 2019 intake: if you weren't approved by Dougie, your name wasn't on the list. That buys you plenty of loyalty, plus of course the suspicion that as far as possible he selected people who he was able to control, because they are not very bright.'

'How does he keep getting away with it?' I asked.

'He has friends, and his biggest ally is Michael Gove.'

I laid down my pen. 'What is it with Gove?' I asked him. 'Why is he like this? What does he get from all this disruption?'

'Ah, well, you are making a big mistake there in thinking there is a purpose to what he does. Someone else once asked me that question. It was a minister. She said to me, "Michael Gove is so tricky to work with; I think you have to work out the end game in order to survive working with him." And I said to her, "You're wrong. There is no end game. It. Is. Just. A. Game."'

CHAPTER 16

BORIS: FOR YOUR EYES ONLY

He answered the door with his phone in his hand. 'Nads, have you heard from Matt Hancock?' he asked me by way of a greeting.

I shut the door on a beautiful day as Dilyn escaped just in time and charged down the lawn.

'Coffee?' He marched through to the kitchen, which was flooded in early-morning sunlight.

'Why would I have heard from Matt?' I asked him.

'I dunno, he's sending me messages saying he needs to speak to me urgently. Let's take some coffee into the study and give him a call, shall we?'

Recently, Matt had been at the front of the queue outside No. 10 when Rishi had arrived at 10 Downing Street about to step foot over the threshold as the new Prime Minister. Matt was standing in line as Rishi walked down shaking everyone by the hand and, rudely, Rishi blanked him and purposefully walked straight past him. That had been painful to watch. Someone had set Matt up. Steered him in front of the camera when Rishi drew up in the limo in order for him to be humiliated live to a global audience of millions. Matt has been described as many things during his time as Health Secretary and since. A Duracell bunny. An over-enthusiastic puppy dog. Industrious, vain, absurdly ambitious, a narcissist. After having worked with him for two years, I have to say there was an element of truth in all of those descriptions, but whatever anyone thought of him, he worked the longest hours and he did so in his ruthlessly upbeat and optimistic way, with never a word of complaint. He didn't get everything right, but he didn't deserve such childish rudeness from Rishi. Boris hadn't seen Rishi blank Matt, and as he poured the coffee, I told him what had happened.

I'm here because I want to talk to him about the interim period between Liz standing down and Rishi being installed in No. 10. There had been no end of stories flying around social media over the previous weekend, but the main one was that Boris didn't have the numbers to run when Liz stood down (which was untrue and obviously being spread about to influence the opinion of MPs who were wavering).

'That's a shame,' he said as he poured. 'But maybe it's not such a surprise. They hated Matt, you know. Always briefing against him.'

'Who?'

'Lee Cain, Cummings – I could never understand why.' He handed me my mug. 'You know what my impression of Matt was: he had this incredible pachyderm quality. He took so many bullets, and they just flattened on his hide. He just kept going, nothing stopped him. He was like a rhino, and look, I always liked him. He was obviously very ambitious, but he always wanted to be Chancellor, and maybe that was the origin of the briefings. I think they were quite wary of that.'

I had put this point to a Cabinet minister, whom I had served with, earlier in the week and he was slightly more forthcoming.

'It was Rishi too,' he had said. 'You know they hunted as a pack. Rishi, always looking over his shoulder to see who might be after his job. Rishi is quite insecure and wary of MPs who have potential. Remember how Kit Malthouse and others used to quite rightly challenge Rishi on the performance of the economy at Cabinet? Do you remember what Rishi's face would look like? How the smiling mask would disappear, that sudden slip from charm to a flash of anger?'

It was easy to see how Matt and his naked ambition would have hacked them off. The amount of attention he received, and created for himself, during Covid – it was unprecedented. So many when commenting on Matt have made the point that he became infected by hubris, always desperately seeking publicity and a camera – but not the one in his office to catch him kissing an aide and there are huge questions around how that happened. The publicity ran away with Matt and one very senior civil servant had made the comment, 'It felt like every decision Matt made during Covid was based on would it get him on the news, or behind the daily press briefing lectern, and would it make him look like a hero, and yet, this was people's lives and that never seemed to cross his mind. To Matt, every decision was about how did it benefit Matt?' Ouch.

Matt's ambition was so naked, so overt, so wrapped up in publicity stunts that it was always going to come back and bite him. When there was no major announcement, he would leap over the very low fence in St James's Park and get someone to photograph him to place in the press. To fill the gap. Matt was in the job of Health Secretary when Covid hit and the poisoned chalice landed in his lap. Despite his desperate thirst for publicity, I shudder to think what would have happened if Jeremy Hunt had still been in the job, a man who advocated a zero-tolerance Covid policy and told me when I was a Health Minister that people who tested positive for Covid should be removed from their homes and placed into quarantine for two weeks.

Boris continued. 'Yes, it was always very clear, Matt's ambition was to be Chancellor; he couldn't hide it and they didn't like that.'

I was reminded of the secret dirty dossiers sent to journalists which had been circulated about various ministers who became rising stars. Matt's career had ended painfully, when cringeworthy security footage of him kissing Gina Coladangelo in his office was handed to the *Sun* newspaper and became a public scandal. Whatever Matt thought of himself, he was never going to be Chancellor after that.

Boris was checking messages from Matt on his phone. The security camera in Matt's office had been tampered with, we knew this for sure. Even though it had been reported in the national press, no one had paid any attention to this fact. Matt was a scalp to the opposition and no one in the Conservative Party was inclined to defend him. The news that the cameras had been set to spy on Matt in his office fell on stony ground and died a death due to a lack of interest. It was a piece of information no journalist picked up and ran with. My office in the Department of Health was directly across the hallway and opposite Matt's; I had a camera on my ceiling too. Both of our cameras faced away from the inner office outwards, looking towards the windows and the large glass doors out to the exterior balconies, which were considered to be a security weak spot; that's why the cameras were there. The day after the story broke, I checked the camera in my office; it was still directly facing the balcony. Both of our balconies spanned the same side of the building. Someone had tampered with Matt's and turned it in to face the interior of his office, towards the door, stating that his office had refurbishment works taking place.

Did people in No. 10 know about Gina? She had attended enough meetings in No. 10 with Matt. The photograph of him striding out of No. 10 with Gina behind him, Matt adopting his favourite pose, staring down the barrel of the cameras opposite No. 10 as though he were modelling for *GQ* magazine and Gina, in full frame behind him, was front pages in the media and that in itself was unusual. An aide would have normally been removed from the frame, and that should have been a red flag. I thought this was odd and asked Matt why they had kept Gina in frame. The media love a pretty face, he told me, to brighten up the front pages.

Gina had also attended a G7 health meeting in Oxford with Matt, and they were undoubtedly sharing the same room. I know this because at the time I asked someone who was there, 'Are they sleeping together? Because, if so, that doesn't look good at a G7.' The friend was embarrassed and instead of answering no, he said, 'I asked; I was worried too. Matt has promised me they aren't,' but he sounded far from convincing. If I knew, Matt's enemies definitely knew too.

To recap, when Matt was caught kissing Gina, the security camera was facing Matt's inner office and inner door when other cameras were turned away from the offices and out to the roof balconies. The inquiry found that the camera had been facing the door because of access to the roof, only the door it was facing didn't have access to the roof: that door was on the opposite wall, the opposite way to that which the camera was facing. The camera had been tampered with.

Boris had telephoned Matt and his phone was ringing out.

'Hi, Matt, how are you? I've got Nads with me. What's up?'

A very non-urgent and incidental conversation began. It was obvious that whatever Matt wanted to tell Boris, he didn't want to do it knowing I was there.

Eventually the call ended and Boris put the phone down and smiled. 'Look, I liked Matt,' he said, defensively. 'I think he tried, he worked really hard. And we had to make some pretty bloody appalling decisions. Cummings, he called him a bull-shitter. He used to say that when Matt reported to me that things had been done, they hadn't. Care homes: that was a massive nightmare. Sometimes Matt would say things that it transpired we couldn't rely on, but, you remember, we were in the middle of it all and he got a lot right and overall he did his best.'

This was also true. I was there and saw it all at first hand. Covid landed in the middle of the Department for Health and Social Care like an unexploded bomb and was met with the same degree of urgency and fear. MPs, the opposition, the people, they wanted answers to everything on the morning of day one. Neither Matt nor any one of us ministers was a qualified epidemiologist, but apparently there were more of them than we thought, as overnight, everyone from journalists, MPs, broadcasters and Twitter trolls became an expert in contact tracing and infection control at the click of a mouse. We didn't have data, information or knowledge on day one, and had to depend entirely upon our Chief Medical Officer, Chris Whitty, and what the Chinese were telling us. Chris Whitty was a man who had spent his working life tackling the worst viral outbreaks, such as Ebola, in the poorest parts of the world in the most difficult of circumstances. He had some of the answers. The reality was, we were dealing with a virus as yet unknown, and it could just as easily have been a relatively harmless outbreak, or the black swan – the name we gave to what could have potentially been a dangerous mutation of the Covid virus that we feared might come sailing into the picture. That was an eventuality we planned for should Covid or any of its mutations transpire to be something far worse than we were already dealing with.

Matt worked seventeen hours a day for weeks on end, as did many people working in the Department for Health and Social Care, including the civil servants and the Prime Minister. The critics, they slept each night and woke to fire their barbed words through a keyboard at all of those who were trying desperately to find a way through what was a catastrophic event and to keep everyone safe. As our intensive care units filled, the fear of running out of hospital beds was a very real one as we began to receive the data that told us how many available hospital beds we had across the UK on a daily basis and how many doctors and nurses were turning up for work and not going down with Covid. It was a practical problem rarely acknowledged.

I could sense Boris felt for Matt being humiliated by Rishi with the spurned handshake. If you know Boris, you know it is not something he would ever do. He has fair words of polite greeting and a smile for everyone, even those who do him harm.

'I suppose, to be fair to Rishi, Dougie may have decided that now that Rishi was in, they needed a bit of distance from the past,' he said.

I thought this was an interesting comment. Boris, without question, was aware it was Dougie Smith who was running the Rishi show and No. 10.

'I found Matt very obliging, very determined to do well. My God, it was pretty overwhelming. No Secretary of State has ever had to deal with what Matt did ever before and that should be remembered.'

We move on to what happened in the hours that Liz resigned and Rishi was appointed.

'Well, we were all set to go to Santo Domingo, the oldest European city in the Americas. We are in this tropical paradise, the kids in the car seats, and Carrie says, "Have you seen what's happening? Liz is about to resign." We watched her do this very brief resignation statement and I thought, *For heaven's sake!* And then, my phone just explodes and, you know, I'm getting inundated with messages from everyone saying, "You've got to get back and save the party. It's all falling apart," and it looks like almost everyone is messaging me, dozens of backbench MPs. I'm desperately trying to field them all.'

This is something else about Boris that is unique. When MPs message Rishi, he opens them but never replies. Boris replies to almost every single message, even if it's last thing at night and it's just a thumbs-up emoji. He tries to be courteous and let MPs know that he's read their message, even if he hasn't time to respond fully.

'We weren't due back for another thirty-six hours or more. There was a painting I had to finish, things I'd promised to do with the children, so I have to work out what I'm going to do, and it's pretty clear my duty lies in trying to do what I can to rescue the situation. We were thirty-six points behind in the polls. I clearly had to help. So I spent quite a lot of that day on the phone to people, asking: "Is this really right? How I'm reading it because I was out of the country. Am I right in thinking I should come back?" People said yes. We flew back, World Traveller class, eleven-hour flight with two kids under three on our knees. So on zero sleep I went straight to the office, got there at one o'clock on the Saturday, and you know the situation just develops from there.

'We finally learn that the nomination threshold has been set quite high by Graham Brady [Chairman of the 1992 Committee], probably for good reason, to get it all over and done with quickly, to get people over the line.'

Many MPs believe that the number was set high in an attempt to fell Boris at the first hurdle.

'It becomes clear as the day moves on that there is a very effective operation taking place. People are being telephoned and told to ring me and tell me not to run, not to do it. I was very happy to [run] once we got to the number of MPs required to support me; it was one hundred. I wanted to go and make my case to the members.'

I thought this was an extraordinary thing for him to say. He had a mandate from MPs, members and the British public, with an eighty-seat majority to serve as Prime Minister until January 2024 and yet he still felt he needed to go back to the party members in order to speak to them directly.

'I wanted to make my case. All talk of an early election had to stop. We needed to get back to the 2019 mandate. We had to continue with levelling up and we must not return to the measures of austerity. I make my pitch to the colleagues I speak to and everyone is, "Yeah, do it." There were a lot of loyalists but it was becoming quite clear to me that MPs were being told that the privileges committee was going to be absolutely fatal. MPs were repeating to me all of the unsavoury stuff that they had been told by Team Rishi.'

The thought crossed my mind, how did Team Rishi know the privileges committee findings were going to be fatal? It was early days. At that point in time, no one made that assumption. Did they know more than the team of lawyers and KCs who were advising Boris, when no evidence had yet been heard or made public? Unless they thought they had an infallible way to make it fatal. How did they know enough at that point to tell MPs considering backing Boris that they would end up with a Prime Minister who would fare so badly with the privileges committee, that he would have to stand down as an MP and leave his post? Did they have a crystal ball?

We decided to top up the coffee and chatted on as Boris told me that on the Saturday night, he thought what would be best was if he could do some sort of deal with Rishi, but Rishi pushed back. He didn't want to meet him or to talk with him, and this went on for hours. He refused to meet. Boris felt sad because he felt obliged to do it to help, a thirty-six-point deficit in the polls is wipe-out in an election, but he could also see that it would expurgate all the Partygate stuff. It was pretty unpleasant being made to feel that he had been drummed out of office because of something that was fundamentally untrue, and he thought it would give him the chance to put all of that straight. But we agreed, that wasn't a strong enough reason. As I watched him talking, facing the garden through the window, his hand on the kettle as is came to the boil, it felt surreal that we were even having this conversation. This man making the coffee was the man the people had voted for to lead the country.

He didn't mention to me that the MPs on Team Rishi had made it very clear to him and the people running his operation that they would make his life impossible if he returned. They had no interest in the party or the country, or in democracy, only in the jobs and positions they had been offered to back Rishi and to keep Boris out. Others told me that as MPs spoke to Boris, they as good as threatened him because his return would mean the jobs they had been promised by Team Rishi would not transpire if Rishi didn't get in and Boris did. Boris didn't do deals.

Boris could see that the message was getting through to the team, who weren't particularly bullish about the future. He knew the threats weren't idle and he knew the party was bigger than him. He couldn't put everyone through that. And so by the Saturday evening they were considering pulling anchor and he had said, *Well, let's just see.* By the Sunday morning they had about eighty MPs; the personal target was two hundred. But as the day wore on he thought, if so many MPs are against me, like two to one, and determinedly so, it was just going to be unfair to everyone who would be trying to make it work.

Finally Rishi agrees to meet Boris at about seven o'clock in the evening. It's the first time he had talked to him since he toppled Boris, and Boris had apparently said to him, 'Look, there is no point in us going back over that painful era, but we need to try and unite for the good of the party – here it is, here's what we could do' – and Rishi says, no. He believes he's got the numbers, that it's his because he knows all about the economy. He's been talking about it all summer, he's been proved right.

Given the price of gilts I wondered what it was he thought he had been right about. Boris had made his point to Rishi about the need for a winning team, getting everybody back together again to campaign in the red wall seats to keep those seats; that we needed a big campaign that gets everybody motivated again, be determined. He offers Rishi the big role but it's clear he's not interested. Rishi was full of that fake personal warmth and all of that stuff which he does very well. As Boris left the meeting he joked with Liam Booth-Smith, who had been sat outside, that Rishi had agreed to be Deputy Prime Minister and Chancellor.

There was just the two of them in the meeting. It was about eight o'clock when it was all over and he made his decision as they reached one hundred and three MPs.

I mentioned to one of my sources that I had been told Penny Mordaunt had said that she fully expected him to stand aside for her. He didn't confirm.

Boris told Rishi that Suella had confessed to him that Rishi had promised her Home Secretary if she backed Rishi, and he denied it completely. Suella was appointed Home Secretary.

I had also been told that Boris had a number of conversations about Suella over the weekend, because John Hayes negotiated for her and was insisting that Boris offer her the job, and in those conversations she then told Boris herself that Rishi had offered her Home Secretary, so she was wanting him to make the same offer. But he just wouldn't make any offers.

'Once you start doing that ...' Boris said. Suella backed the man who guaranteed her the job.

Boris was right. People had to back him for the right reasons, not because they had been offered a job. Loyalty and party first over self-interest still surely has some place in our democracy. I asked him if maybe he should have offered jobs and he said, 'I just wouldn't do it. I wasn't going to offer people jobs in return for backing me.'

Rishi obviously had a different approach.

'Anyway, I'm pleased Suella got the job she wanted,' said Boris graciously.

Suella getting the job was a less questionable appointment than Andrew Mitchell. Mitchell, who along with Mark Harper and others who had been appointed to the Cabinet were among the most vicious when it had come to attacking Boris in the media. Mitchell was a man hoping to be raised from Plebgate to the equestrian order and receive a knighthood. It looked like his plan was working.

I mentioned Mitchell to Boris.

'Good luck to him. You know, even when people have absolutely no basis and no reason for thinking that they are going to be offered a place in Cabinet they kind of project onto you this idea that they absolutely are prime material for such a position, and then when they don't get it, because there is no reason on earth they should, they become incredibly disappointed and bitter.'

We talked about Rishi's Cabinet. 'What Rishi has done now is actually quite clever,' I said, 'bringing the toxic material out of the Conservative Party and putting it into a sort of Chernobyl-like container in the Cabinet. And that was a thing which really struck me: there are promises which could have been made for a very long time. I mean, if you look at Harper, Williamson and Mitchell, these guys have been on your case for ages.'

All three had made some of the most obnoxious comments about Boris on both broadcast media and in the press for the best part of two years. They sat and shook their heads as Boris spoke in the chamber. Had they been offered jobs in the Cabinet if they helped to remove Boris some time ago? That's certainly how it looked.

I could add a few others to this list. These were the voices who set the anti-Boris tone in the party and out in the country. Lone voices at first who whipped the herd into moving. MPs who spent half of their lives on College Green in front of cameras calling Boris Johnson a liar and then heading out for the evening with a woman that the wife back in the constituency had no idea about. Experienced MPs who played the newer MPs like finely tuned fiddles. Was it corrupt? Who measured that; who called it out? Do the public accept that is how it works, how the country is run?

'I mean Harper, he was absolutely harsh and unrelenting,' I said.

Boris nodded his head in recognition of what I had said.

He was in my intake in 2005 – if possible, slightly more ambitious than Matt Hancock – and he arrived thinking he was destined to be a future prime minister. He will have known Dr No from his time when he was Chief Whip for Cameron.

Harper had been particularly disloyal. Hypocrisy gone mad, given he had to stand down for employing a cleaner who was an illegal immigrant while he was Immigration Minister. Another, who had successfully been raised from his own previous failings?

'I mean, Williamson ...'

'Seriously, don't waste your breath,' he told me.

'Let's get back to your conversation with Rishi,' I said.

He tells me it was a wholly amicable conversation. Rishi made it clear that he hadn't particularly enjoyed the means to his ascent to power. Boris had asked him why he had done it and he had told him that when it came time for Boris to go, he would be ready to take over. Why did he jump the gun? And Rishi wouldn't engage. He just kept saying, 'Look, I don't want to go over all of that with you.'

Boris said, 'It was after the meeting when I got the message from you, Nads, saying, *Boris, you don't have to do this.* That was actually quite important to me because I thought, *If Nads is saying this to me, maybe I should just jack it in.*

'Your advice is always very specific, and if you were saying to me that we don't need to do this now, and they were your words, maybe I had to be brutal with myself. Maybe Rishi will get us through the next election. I felt that, fundamentally, it looked narcissistic and selfish to keep going in the face of the disquiet and comments being made by MPs in my own party and I had to respect that. I could have bludgeoned my way to victory, but it would have been a Pyrrhic victory. Those who didn't want me there, they wouldn't have stopped, I think that much was obvious; the chaos would have continued. We could have turned it around, got a new team in No. 10. We'd have had a very different approach, would have been much tougher; we'd have focused on the economy. But, you know, that did require Rishi coming on board.

'Rishi wasn't going to do that. I could have pushed through, but the party, it had been through enough.'

'It has. Some MPs are actually looking forward to opposition in the vain hope that some sanity will prevail among those who are left. When I was in Cabinet, it always seemed to me like Rishi was very hands off as a Chancellor. Like he just wasn't engaged,' I said.

'Ah, well, he was very unlike Osborne. The thing about Osborne is he was very creative. He was always coming up with weird little ways to do things. He at least had a vision. Whatever you think of him personally, the Northern Powerhouse was a big idea. I mean, austerity was just wrong, it was terrible, but at least he had ideas, and whatever they say about Truss, most of her pro-growth ideas were sound.

'Look, Nads, I've done it, and I'm very proud of what we did. We achieved a huge amount. I have a happy life, I'm incredibly fortunate, and you know, throughout all of this, the Queen was massively supportive of me in my time as Prime Minister. I was inordinately fond of her and I was lucky to have served her. Some of the MPs who backed me were very disappointed when I pulled out, but I had to, for the sake of the party, I had to.'

'You will be back, one day,' I told him, but as he cleared the coffee cups onto the tray, I could tell he really didn't believe me and for the first time, I'm not even sure it's what he now wants.

Boris and I met again shortly after and arranged to talk over a Sunday lunch in the pub with families and friends, but with children and chatter, it just didn't work. Instead, we reconvened on the phone when I reached home and they were in the car on the way back to London. The children provided a backdrop to our discourse and it made me smile. A conversation about the most serious of events accompanied by the innocence of toddlers singing. The lunch, in the kind of country pub you have to search hard for these days, had seen Boris on top form. He is earning serious money, they have bought a beautiful home that he is obviously excited about, and I did wonder, *Has the political boat sailed?* Life is stress free and good again. Why would he ever want to come back?

'C'mon, fire away,' he said as the car transporting them all motored up the M40. I dived straight in.

'Did anyone ever warn you about the seriousness of the intent of those who were working against you in No. 10?' I asked. The line was clear; I was hopeful.

'I was once warned early on by someone about a group who were working together, and he said, "Be careful of these guys, they are working as a gang."'

I asked him who that person was, and he told me. Separately, he had been warned about Michael Gove by many people, including senior members of his Cabinet with their own observations, but this appeared to be the first time anyone had indicated to him that there was a collusion at play at the heart of No. 10. If Boris has been guilty of anything, it has been of turning a blind eye to the number of warnings he was given about Gove, the most stark coming from Lynton Crosby, his trusted election guru, who had no skin in the game of governing. Winning elections is his business; it's up to prime ministers what they do and who they appoint once he has helped them to succeed.

'What was your reaction when you were warned for the first time that they were working in an organised way?' I asked him.

'I suppose I thought, *Well, we'll see about that.* I mean, we had an eighty-seat majority, a democratic mandate from the people.'

The idea that individuals inside No. 10 would be working to take down a prime minister with such a strong mandate from the people must surely have sounded preposterous to him at the time. Who of sane mind would think that there were people in the party so willing to dismiss the vote of the nation? But, an event equally unimaginable had taken place in Theresa May's government when her own Remain ministers negotiated with Labour to remove her and impose a temporary David Lidington/Jeremy Corbyn-led government while we re-ran a second EU referendum. The party had been imploding for some time. It was only when Corbyn insisted on being the named Prime Minister that the plan fell down. If they had reached an agreement, the very ministers May thought were her allies would have had her removed too.

Boris had said to me in the early days, 'I rather naively thought that in this country, power flowed from the people into electing a prime minister.' We all thought that.

'How did he know this, this person who warned you? What made him suspicious?' I asked him.

'In retrospect, I think he must have been at some meeting or event where they were working together, not in the interests of me or the government, and I remember thinking about it and concluding at the time that surely there wasn't a problem. It's good to have tightly knit groups of motivated people working together, and he was the only person to raise this; if there had been more who had raised it with me ...'

I was told Dougie and his wife Munira had been spotted with Rishi and Akshata many times by staff in No. 10. I asked Boris did he know this.

'I saw them in the garden together ...' We lost connection.

I dialled him back. He joked, 'If only we'd had a Cabinet minister who could have sorted out rural wi-fi.' That had been me. The scars were yet to heal.

I asked again about his rapprochement with Michael Gove. 'I'm not really sure there was one,' he replied. 'He was profoundly sorry and said he bitterly regretted what he did in 2016. We had a job to do, you know ... we had to put that sort of nonsense behind us and get on with the job of governing; the people had put their faith in us, in levelling up ...'

There had been lots of rumours swirling around Westminster about George Osborne – how he was set for a return – and the number of times he was appearing on television to denounce Boris and praise Rishi gave those rumours legs. I asked him if he thought Osborne had been involved in the plot to remove him.

'Well, I have no evidence to support that theory, but he did go into No. 10 to advise Rishi just recently, didn't he?'

He did. The idea that George Osborne would go into No. 10 for a meeting to simply impart his thoughts of wisdom and not leave with something to benefit himself almost made me laugh. My theory, so far unshared, was that he probably went to talk to Rishi face to face about his own return and to discuss which safe seat a retiring MP was leaving vacant, which he would prefer for himself. It was possible, but not something Rishi would have welcomed, I'm sure. He could also have been making a plea for his former Chief of Staff and friend, Matt Hancock, to be returned to Cabinet.

'Look, I've no idea. I suspect that he's been advising a number of people.' Boris laughed. 'He's an addict, George, he's incorrigible. He loves it all, all the intrigue.'

'I'm sure he's been talking to people,' I said. 'I'm very sure it would be gratifying for George to have had a hand in pulling all that off and getting rid of you, but as always there is no evidence.'

We were cut off again. Via a series of text messages, we arranged to reconvene a few days later. The question remained, why?

Was it all about payback for Brexit?

'They all just wanted to pay him back,' said the close ally who had warned him about the forces against him. 'Every single one of the Remainers in our party was involved in the effort to remove him. By '22 it was like a perfect storm – the media, MPs, who just don't understand politics or what was going on, those who felt unloved, and I don't blame them, it was very hard for them all. They had barely been MPs for months when Covid struck. Those who were just desperate for ministers' jobs. It was the Cummings machine, Dr No and all involved within the fifth column who since the day he had been elected were trying to remove him, and yet, to his mind, we had a massive task to do and we had done so much. When I warned him that I suspected something was going on he just said, "C'mon, we have to shake the country up after Covid. You are seriously saying the government is going to be destroyed by these people, for what? What's the alternative plan?"

'What he couldn't understand was, what was their purpose? Why? What was the agenda? There was no rival agenda, no kind of radical thinking going on, no point of principle. It was all personal ... personal ambition and hostility towards Boris for Brexit. I mean, am I not right? What was the purpose other than self-interest? They simply wanted to gratify their lust for revenge; that was all it was about. I mean, in getting rid of Thatcher, you could argue that there was a plan to bring in a gentler, kinder Toryism, rub off some of the hard edges which existed in the minds of voters, turn a new page. What was their big plan? Now, we're losing levelling up, losing all radicalism on Brexit, we're tanking in the polls. What was the point? And anybody who thinks that he was having unauthorised parties in No. 10 with his mates is out of their tiny mind. The idea that he was partying with people or that he knew about unauthorised social events, we didn't have social events in No. 10, we didn't have them, we were basically fighting a pandemic, the whole thing is nauseating. If I look back on it now, I feel angry with myself for not being aggressive enough in how I communicated with him and failing to persuade him to be more assertive, but I wasn't Lee Cain, the person preparing him to go out to the despatch box at the time. Others did that and they got it all very badly wrong.'

'Why did he keep apologising for something he had no knowledge of and hadn't done?' I asked the ally.

'He was being urged to, mostly by Oliver Dowden, who kept saying to him, "You can't apologise enough, keep on apologising." Bullshit, it was a disaster; the apologies just made him look culpable but Dowden was part of it. I should have been much more assertive; I should have made it much clearer. The repeated apologies meant that in the mind of the public, he had been partying the whole time. I mean, what was he apologising for? He knew nothing. As for the police he called in to investigate any work gathering he had attended, he assumed the Met were the highest authority, that he was going higher than a mickey mouse, witch-hunt-motivated, biased privileges committee led by a left wing Labour chairwoman. It was a total sham.'

I repeated to Boris what I had been told.

Before me was a man the public still flock to support. Who shout out his name on the streets and who desperately want to have a selfie with. The man who inspired those who are tired of empty promises and identikit politicians. Those who go out and vote for him. In good part because he does makes mistakes, he gets stuck on zip wires, he gets divorced, he falls in love, and he has been belittled and vilified by an entitled and vindictive Westminster elite who are determined to destroy him.

'Frankly, the event I was fined for, the bloody cake that wasn't even taken out of its box, I was sat at my desk,' said Boris. 'It's not like I organised a social event. It was utterly mad. It was kind of like Salem. The idea of an illicit party. I mean, people think No. 10 was like 1920s Chicago with illegal raves taking place. Absolute nonsense. There were people working around the clock to save others from a virus. My efforts were totally fixed on getting us a vaccine; that was the way out of this mess. Nothing I attended in the way of thanking people, to keep morale up in the office with those I was sitting down with and working with all day long, went on for longer than was strictly necessary. It's just nauseating, the whole thing. It, of course – the notion of Partygate – was a fantastic piece of media. BBC and Sky, they ran with it.'

e

'You made the mistake of trusting Sue Gray to do the right thing. You called for the inquiry; it was you who wanted to get to the bottom of it all,' I said.

'I literally asked for a report because I didn't know what had happened.'

'Did you expect that Fisk-like report, which cherry-picked information, which bundled together a list of allegations that painted a picture of debauchery, of people vomiting in toilets, and karaoke, and all of this sort of nonsense?' I asked.

'We tried after Sue Gray's report appeared to track down the sources of her allegations. It all just crumbled away. It was a very shoddy piece of work. As a result, most people think, as a result of her narrative, that I was either at illegal parties or knew about illegal parties, and I did not.'

If it looks like a stitch-up and it smells ... it was a stitch-up.* We moved on to talk about the fact that it was reported that Cleo Watson is to be working for Rishi's wife Akshata (though those rumours didn't appear to come to anything in the end, as far as I know when writing this).

He shook his head in disbelief.

I had been told about a meeting that took place the day after Dom and Lee Cain were ousted from the building – and Boris was ruminating about Dom, because Dom's father is a sort of oil-rig project manager or something (he's not exactly Red Adair, but he manages big projects), and at the meeting Boris had said, 'I think Dom, in his own self-image, he's this guy who drives big projects, he loves that conception of himself. I think it's all about

---

* Certainly, in the course of researching this book, it would have been a great deal easier if the report had given some indication of who Sue Gray had spoken to. Trying to verify anything – other than the most obvious facts – is almost impossible.

his father really, something going on there.' Suddenly Cleo burst into tears and ran out of the room.

I asked Boris about this.

'Oh, yes, I thought, *Blimey!* I mean, I was very struck, shall we say, about the obvious intensity of her feelings. I'd obviously touched some nerve in her. I felt absolutely terrible. I thought, *Oh crikey, what on earth have I said?*' Others who were in the room, elaborated further ... 'He obviously felt very bad, mortified. She obviously feels very emotionally connected to Dom and [Boris] had no idea, he just doesn't know about that sort of stuff and seemed to have put his foot massively straight in it.'

'People tell me she was a mean girl,' I said to him. He wouldn't engage.

Getting Boris to say anything mean about anyone is almost impossible. I had been told by others who worked in No. 10 that Cleo was mean and a satirist and had a sort of slight public-school malice in the way she often made fun of people, imitated the way Eddie Lister and Priti Patel spoke and frequently made fun of Priti in meetings when Priti wasn't around; 'across the globe and around the world', she would say before she collapsed laughing – it was a favourite quip when imitating Priti. She would sometimes phone Eddie, pretending to be Priti and make outlandish requests and she was so good, he would be taken in. A lovely man. All very funny to them, but this was No. 10, the building which was the engine room for the country, and she projected this air of entitlement she had adopted from Cummings. One staffer said to me, 'In an Enid Blyton book, she would be the sharp-tongued Alicia in *Malory Towers* who brought everyone down to size.'

I changed the subject back to snippets of information others had given me: that Rishi had been a dog in the manger. How he sat on and obstructed policy.

'Can you give me an example of how Rishi did that?' I asked Boris.

It's difficult enough to get a policy signed off and through Cabinet, you need all ministers to agree. If any Cabinet minister chooses to try and block policy via a process called write round, where each minister's opinion on a proposed new policy has to be sought in writing, it makes life difficult. If it's the Chancellor and the Treasury objecting and there are financial costs attached to a policy, it is almost impossible to get the policy through, even if you are the Prime Minister. Rishi was a serial blocker ...

With regards to Rwanda and illegal immigration, Rishi constantly objected and pushed back. As soon as he was Prime Minister, it became the only shot in the locker. He opposed and obstructed policy which had huge implications until the time came for him to be Prime Minister and to take the credit.

'Look,' said Boris, 'I just wanted Rishi to work as a team, together. It was all I asked of anyone in Cabinet.'

This was ironic: Rishi had never done that whereas Boris had lived and breathed it. If any ministers were in trouble Boris would support them in whatever way he could for as long as he could. I probed further even though it was sad to see how let down he obviously felt at how Rishi had betrayed him.

'I don't think Rishi ... I mean, did you ever, ever, hear Rishi stand up and say anything positive about the government, the Cabinet, No. 10, or you even?' I said. 'How many times did you and others praise him and say what a brilliant Chancellor he was? When actually, he wasn't really; objectively, all he tried to do was hang tax rises around your neck. National Insurance contributions, corporation tax. And by the way, we had the money, we didn't need to do it that way. He wanted to blame you for the tax rise. It just wasn't team work.'

Boris smiled. 'We were meant to be Batman and Robin, Wallace and Gromit, Achilles and Patroclus, and it wasn't.'

'No, it wasn't,' I said. 'It was Caesar and Brutus the whole time. He was basically endlessly measuring the drop for you.'

I wanted to tell him that someone he respects had told me he thought the plan was to get Rishi in and manage the decline of the party and for it to lose. To give Starmer a term to reverse some of Brexit and the idea that Boris remained, for what could be another two or three elections was an obstacle to achieving that because Boris had championed Brexit. Gove's words to Iain Duncan Smith, that the party needed burning down, had come back to me. Had Gove finally got his way?

'Gove came in to see me right before PMQs on the worst day, the Wednesday,' said Boris.

'At the worst time,' I said.

'I thought, *Oh God, here we go, Gove part two,* and it was exactly that; he sat there all pompous and said to me, "You've got to go, resign; you have three minutes. I've been talking to MPs. Kemi Badenoch, Alex Burghart, Lee Rowley, Julia Lopez – those MPs are going to resign if you don't."'

We drank the coffee and chatted about why they did what they did, what good has come from it, and how well the party is doing in the polls. Today, the Labour Party is nineteen points ahead.

'I mean, what are they doing? The people are hearing nothing from the government. What was it all for?' I asked him.

He shrugged. 'There's no particular sense of a mission from this new government,' he said. 'Maybe it's all kind of rope-a-doping. Maybe the strategy is: soak up all the pain, all the media abuse, all the punishment, and then when things start to turn around, come off the ropes. That must be what this is all about. These polls have got to mean something. I accept they don't mean what's going to happen at the next election, but what they're showing is that the public aren't hearing anything from the government about what the government is going to do for them. They've scrapped social care you know.'

Social care reform was one of Boris's huge achievements. He went where no other Prime Minister had dared to tread and it was a precarious path which had been the undoing of Theresa May.

He was enthused by the subject.

'When I was visiting hospitals on the General Election campaign in 2019, so many hospital beds were full of people who didn't need to be there. That's why A&E is full; they can't get patients through. And now they've dropped it, so what's the plan?'

My source in the Treasury had told me: 'Rishi was so against it, Hunt was for it, until he became Chancellor. He banged on about it the entire time he was chair of the Health Select Committee. Where are his speeches on social care now they have done away with it?'

Boris spoke again. 'They should be doing some really big things now, measures to shake up the economy and make us world leaders. They should be cutting corporation tax to lower than in Ireland even, and campaigning around the world: come to Britain to start your company. In the Midlands, the Northeast, Scotland, come here. And instead he's putting it up; totally nuts.

'Do you know what I really think? I think this country is going through the crunchy–soggy cycle of UK history. We're going through one of those now. There are over fourteen million people registered disabled in this country; fourteen point seven, right. We haven't changed the laws on anything that made the labour market more productive, the Treasury was very against that, and, you know, we're becoming a nation of bludgers [scroungers] again. The idea of having a Labour government now, while we are going through all this: Starmer would come in, put taxes up; he's quite left wing. He'll hit the City with a financial transaction tax, may well do symbolic stuff like whacking independent schools, and his devolution programme would break up the UK.'

It was time to wrap up and I fleetingly mentioned what a Boris return would look like. There are Conservative MPs who would rather eat their own eyeballs than have him back, and that's the truth of it. They have the tribal guilt of the regicide upon them. The only way to expiate that guilt is to show that it was the right thing to do.

'One thing Rishi was good at was talking to MPs,' I told him. 'He was always having parties in his rooms in No. 10, always had parties in there. You never did.'

Boris pulled a face at me. 'Well, I never had the time and, I don't know, maybe I should have been more like Rishi, maybe I should have. Maybe he was right.'

His phone rings and we have a three-way conversation with a former Cabinet minister who wants to talk about the 'appalling behaviour of Cummings and Gove in the removal of Boris'. About how Gove is falling out with everyone in Cabinet, how Cummings has been at it for years, how they all have and it is exasperating. 'They have wreaked havoc and it's still happening; they just get bolder and more audacious. When are they going to be stopped?'

Boris muttered something half to himself before we said our goodbyes and ended the call, 'the twitch upon the thread'.

I wasn't going to pretend I knew what that meant, so I looked it up once I was alone.

A twitch upon the thread. A metaphor from G K Chesterton. The metaphor speaks to a line long enough to let us wander to the edge before God gently brings us back.

Did he think these people would be pulled back by God from the edge of their own peculiar madness? Dr No was said to have tried to set fire to a house when people were sleeping in their bed. There was a whole family in the house at the time, including a child. They say when a young woman spurned his advances, he chopped up her little brother's pet rabbit into four and pinned it to the front door to greet the child when he arrived home from school. Cummings had been described to me as having a dark triad personality. Smith had run sex parties and intimidated people. Whoever put these people into No. 10, it surely wasn't God.

CHAPTER 17

GOLDFINGER

Simon Case, the Cabinet Secretary and most senior civil servant in Whitehall, could be described as the power behind the throne in No. 10. However, given that he was appointed by Dominic Cummings, he has operated under a cloud of association for almost the entire time he has been in post. His performance has often been under the journalists' spotlight and found wanting.

He is the final person the Prime Minister would turn to for advice, and when it came to Partygate it was glaringly obvious that he dramatically failed in his role to advise the Prime Minister and to care for the civil servants who became embroiled in the Partygate row.

Case is inexperienced, humourless, lacking the emotional intelligence such a seismic event at the heart of government required from the country's most senior civil servant. He recused himself from the Partygate inquiry, a move that baffled and stunned the Prime Minister. Regardless of who I spoke to, it was hard to find a civil servant with a civil word when it came to him. It is a known fact and the worst-kept secret in Westminster that Sue Gray and Simon Case cannot stand each other. Whenever Gray is criticised, this is mounted in her defence, as in, 'Yeah, but she has got the measure of Case, so she can't be all bad.'

I have been told by a source that Case was 'let go' from No. 10 during the time of Theresa May and went to work for the

271

Royal Household as Private Secretary to Prince William. During the time he was there, he lunched with Michael Gove on a regular basis. He does not come out of Prince Harry's book, *Spare*, well, as previously noted. Gove's early relationship with Case was established when the latter worked in Brussels. There were many issues around key meetings in Brussels being leaked to British journalists during Brexit within hours of those meetings taking place. I just have no idea why no one asked, where is Gove? But, then I remembered, Robbie Gibb was Theresa May's head of comms. There were issues also with unauthorised negative briefings around the two Princes William and Harry when Case was at Buckingham Palace. The first interview disclosing a rift between the two was broken by political editor, Tim Shipman in the *Sunday Times*. It was quite something that a political journalist like Shipman would break such a seismic story relating to the Royals and not the experienced *Sunday Times* Royal Editor, Roya Nikkhah. In the article, Shipman described having lunch with his source. Speculation is that the source was either Simon Case or Michael Gove, although no one will ever know.

The word 'salad' I was given to describe Case by civil servants covered everything from liar to snake. It appeared the sentiment came from the fact that he was wholly untrained, unqualified and unable to do the job of Cabinet Secretary. The response from permanent secretaries across Whitehall was one of universal utter amazement when the announcement was made that Cummings had demanded he was given the job.

When Case was brought into No. 10, my suspicion is that this is the point at which Gray, who had been loyal to Gove for so long, had maybe had enough and moved over to Labour, possibly with Gove's knowledge and blessing. I'm sure given that Gove has put his neck out so often to back Sue Gray that it would be useful for him to have someone on the inside of Labour HQ. Now that a Labour landslide is looking likely, maybe he needs a foot in that camp, too.

I was in 5 Hertford Street again and met with a group of people who worked closely with Case. Glasses of cold white-wine spritzers arrived with a generous dish of nibbles for us to share in the middle of a silver tray. It was evening, after votes in the Commons had finished, and the departments of government were done for the day and almost empty. It was a clear night, chilly, the stars bright in the sky, and the fire in the small sitting room once again blazed. The outer sitting room was completely empty as most guests had left for the dining rooms, so we had the upper floor to ourselves.

'Does anyone have any views on Simon Case? Because I don't really.'

We are a few sips and nibbles in and I switch on Otter and take out my pencil. They are talking rapidly between themselves and I have to get down what they are saying fast, as every point is important.

'Simon Case was appointed by Dominic Cummings, but Simon said he had only met Dominic once before he appointed him, but obviously Case was more familiar with Michael Gove, his Brussels mate and later lunch buddy. Dominic was desperate to get Mark Sedwill, the former Cabinet Secretary, out. Cummings, in his role as de facto Chief of Staff, just couldn't control him; Mark was a pro. For one thing, Mark would have walked into the PM's study and said to him, "Prime Minister, can I have a word?" Mark would have exposed them. Case was not only out of his depth when he took the role, those people were his point of reference for how to behave, they told him how the place was run and who he answered to.

'And anyone who thinks Cummings doesn't still have his hands fully on the levers of government is out of their tiny mind. We will know the moment they fall out and Rishi decides Cummings is a liability. Cummings will erupt. He will take to his blogs and start his ranting and tell everyone how Rishi needs to be removed. Hard to imagine that Rishi was the project, the person he worked so hard to get into place, though I could be wrong.'

I asked them, 'If Cummings wanted Sedwill out and to get Simon Case in, was that his decision or was it Gove's too?'

One of my guests leant forward and picked at the nibbles. 'Ah, well, it wasn't as easy as they thought it was going to be. Boris was neither convinced, nor impressed by Case. He rejected the idea out of hand and it was yet another one of those occasions when Cummings didn't get his way with Boris, so Cummings, as he did every week, went nuclear. I lost count of the number of times Cummings burst into Boris's office and told him he was going to resign, and the appointment of Case was one of those occasions: he was in and out, interrupting meetings, banging on about how he was going to walk if Sedwill didn't go. He had to fight really hard before Boris would agree, because Boris stood up to him and just wouldn't cave. Boris wasn't impressed with Case, thought he was a lightweight. Eddie Lister had given him sage advice. He had arranged a dinner with Sedwill and Helen McNamara [Deputy Cabinet Secretary] just before Boris got in and they were in a good place. Then suddenly, you find lots of extra urgent meetings being popped into the Prime Minister's diary, even his time for phone calls being eaten up. This is the difference between Boris and Blair. Blair's people were solid Blairites; they protected and supported him. Boris's were Govites; they worked for Gove, not Boris. If Gove wanted his friend Case, then they would make that happen.'

I was intrigued as to why Cummings survived and why Boris hadn't told him to walk.

'Good question. He nearly did sack him. Remember Barnard Castle, there were three people allowed into the room with Boris when all of that kicked off. They were Dougie Smith, Dominic Cummings and Lee Cain, with Dr No on speaker phone, and all of them reinforced the narrative that Cummings had to stay, that Boris could not allow the mob and MPs (God, how they hated MPs) to dictate via social media and pressure via the whips the decisions to be taken by the Prime Minister. I mean, it was intense. I'd say Boris was bullied into keeping him. I'm guessing there would have been hints of: "If Cummings goes, we all go and we will bring the whole pack of cards down with us." These guys, they were masters of manipulation and control, and they were all in Team Gove, and they had been at it for years. Boris wouldn't have stood a chance. No Prime Minister would. And two weeks after Case was in, Boris knew it had been the biggest mistake and wished Sedwill was still there.'

My questions were all over the place in this interview, as I have just realised (a) how difficult it is when you have a number of people to control and ensure that only one speaks at a time, for the benefit of the recording; and (b) how much they spark off each other, which is a huge benefit. They are leading the conversation, reminiscing with each other, and I decide to give up with questions and to just listen, observe and write. I am so aware, given the company I am sat in, how privileged I am to be here and that their voices are far more valuable than mine.

Let's refer to them as V1 (for voice 1), V2 and V3.

V1: 'Did you know that Dougie and Rishi have been friends for years?'

V2: 'Oh yes, he and Munira have been to Rishi's place in California a number of times; they holiday together regularly.

Dougie was up and down to Yorkshire to Rishi's grand palace up there. Maybe it was Dougie who demanded the swimming pool. He likes the high life.' They all laugh. 'They are best of friends and it has always been that way; Rishi was always on the cards to be Prime Minister. Rishi and all the wealth and opportunity he brought with him, he excited them. Boris didn't have a bean, he was suddenly small fry. They just had to manage and handle it into being.'

V3: 'How?' (V3 doesn't go back as far as the others.)

V2: (laughs) 'Dougie is a genius at how to manipulate Conservative associations. He's really good at it; he gets MPs into seats and then they become so grateful to him that he controls them.'

V1: 'He does, he's been doing it for years; that's how we end up with MPs like Oliver Dowden and Robert Jenrick. With Rishi it was all far more strategic. In Rishi, they had brains, good looks, money, pliability; he was their dream puppet. Here was their robot. They had to get him into a safe seat, then let due process be seen to be observed to keep his progress free from suspicion. Into a ministerial job, into Cabinet, into being Chancellor – and by the way, he's done fuck-all along the way other than screw up the economy with tax rises – and then they put the plans they had already made in place to get Boris out. These guys – Gove, Cummings, Smith, Cain, Dr No – they have an entire network singing to their tune. They are the power and the throne; the voters, they are just players in their game.

I had to speak. 'It didn't work so well with the leadership election and Liz,' I said.

V3: 'Well, you and Jacob kind of blew that apart, didn't you, as you both have traction with association members, and you quite rightly framed Rishi as a backstabber and as someone who wears Prada shoes to visit deprived communities. You guys burst their bubble and Liz surged ahead.'

V2: 'But even when she won, they never stopped. You really think those men were going to let her stay in post? Look at the economy now. Does anyone ask, hang on, it wasn't this bad when Liz was removed? Does anyone think, were we played there? Liz's problem is she is socially inept, awkward, scared, never a leader. It is a problem. She should never have been Prime Minister; geeky Chancellor was the perfect role for Liz if what you want is an economy which grows and puts money into people's pockets. Her ego and ambition got the better of her. The big question is, not how did they get Liz out – we know how, big money and money institutions joined forces, aligned against her and rocked the economy – but why did they do that? Who and what for?'

I'm lost. I don't have the knowledge of the politics of money and finance and how it works to ask further questions on this. I've never had any interest in how money works. I can barely manage my own savings. My interest lies in the democracy we are supposed to be living in. If the people who live on the road I was born on, Breck Road in Liverpool – one of the most socially deprived areas in the country – have a vote that, in reality, is a farce, a fake, then what power do ordinary people actually have? Are we totally disenfranchised by a group of men who are linked into the richest financial network and the biggest money players in the world? Is money at the root of this? Are people like Dr No, who is apparently on and off yachts, and Dominic Cummings, are they benefiting financially in some way? I know what they are doing, but I have yet to understand why. Are they getting rich on distorting democracy?

'Where did it start with Rishi? How did he even get into the political scene?' I asked.

V1: 'So, Rishi comes back from California. He's married Akshata and, suddenly, he doesn't need to work as hard as he's married into this billionaire fortune. James Forsyth, husband to Allegra Stratton and political editor at *The Spectator*, is a close friend from university and was his best man when they married, and what happens is, he gets interested in politics and no one can quite understand why; it's not like he has any overpowering political principles, not like he ran for president of the Oxford Union or anything. Anyone will tell you, he just isn't remotely political. But he suddenly wants to do it and I've always wondered, was the father-in-law an influence? Or James? Does he need to do something to prove himself in the eyes of his daughters? That he is a bigger and more important man than grandpapa? That he can secure a job and a position that money can't buy? But actually, oddly enough, of course his money mattered and had influence and inadvertently did buy him his job. If that was his motivation, he's proven nothing to grandpa. Anyway, James Forsyth says to him, "I'll introduce you to Dougie Smith" and Dougie then began to exert his influence, which he does with everyone. He meets Dr No and then he's passed for approval and he's on his way.

'A whole other story is how they establish think tanks and use them and how people from think tanks end up in the Lords and who facilitates that. Anyway, Dougie got Rishi a job at Policy Exchange and did all the preparation for him to become the MP for North Yorkshire. Dougie would have introduced him to the key players in the area, who would have arranged all the drinks parties and dinners – I would think that was William Hague – and he, Dougie, would have rehearsed the life out of Rishi. I was told that there were planted questions in the audience which Rishi was given prior notice of, and he was given advance warning of which other candidates were there and the questions that he would be asked. Some of the members weren't totally discreet about that fact after the event. It was a stitch-up. Dougie also imbued in Rishi the Conservative philosophy, because Rishi just wasn't even particularly political. He had to be taught to think like a Conservative.'

V2: 'They knew that if Hunt got in, they were going nowhere. Hunt was never in their network and would never be a winner, so they needed Boris in. That was all they wanted him for: to get in, win a big majority that would cushion the party, give them the headroom they needed to play their own power games, and then get Boris out and Rishi in. It was surely the plan all along.'

V1: 'Remember, there was a transition team in place. I know someone who was at those meetings. At every meeting there was Dougie, Oliver Dowden – who is Dougie's lap-dog; and that, honestly, is a generous description – and Rishi. Robbie Gibb apparently attended a few of the meetings and he was desperate to stay in the game, at the heart of No. 10, but it was decided that with him having been in May's government his reputation was toxic and he would have to stay on the sidelines for a while. He was desperate to get back into the centre and to exert influence; one of the addicts of the game. May's people didn't know he was doing that. Apparently, every time the Cabinet discussions came up, as in general conversation around who was going to be in it, Dougie would say, "But of course, regardless of who Boris puts in as Chancellor, that role has to be Rishi's soon." And Rishi was sat there, and the person I know who was there told me only last week, he could not remember one thing Rishi said at those meetings. He was as quiet as a mouse, never spoke, let Dougie do all the speaking for him. Dowden apparently talked endlessly, as he does – you will never meet a man who is more scared of Dougie Smith or loves the sound of his own voice more than he does. Rishi, not a word.

'The interesting thing about Robbie Gibb, as he's a good case, is to look at what motivated him. He was supposedly an ardent Brexiteer, but he spent his time trying to persuade MPs to vote for May's deal, which did not deliver Brexit. Some would say, well, he was loyal to May, wasn't he? That's not the point. He was in the bunker, and actually some of the advice given to May was utterly disastrous, but being in the bunker with May, with whoever was in office, that was all that mattered to all of them: being there until they could engineer the placement of the person who actually was their choice.'

V2: 'That is why it's wrong to think that any of them have any love for Rishi. If they began to lose control, if others in Rishi's life had more influence, or rose to positions they didn't want them to reach, well, they would do for them. They don't like anyone they haven't chosen to progress on the board. Matt Hancock, I mean wow, for a blatant narcissist, he had done far too well in the first stages of Covid; he had to be blown up. Richard Sharp, chairman of the BBC, Rishi's old boss, he had to be got rid of: pow, gone. Nice one Simon Case. Did you read the Heppinstall Report* into the furore over Sharp and the loan to Boris from his cousin? It cleared Sharp. Cast a huge cloud over Case, but they spun it to protect Case, he survived. They will definitely go for the wife, Akshata, again. You will see stories about her crop up when they are ready. They've had the first run on her non-dom status; you can bet your life they will be holding more back. Rishi, he may not be as easy to control as they thought, and my guess is that he won't last too long, because the next person will be Kemi.'

* The Heppinstall Report was an official inquiry into the public appointment process of the Chair of the BBC Board, led by Adam Heppinstall KC.

V3: 'Oh, she's a great friend of Dougie's going years back, very abrasive, upsets a lot of people, just like Dougie.'

They all laughed. This conversation was roaming all over the place. I decided to let it keep rolling.

V2: 'It's no laughing matter is it though, right now, that we have a Dougie Smith in Cabinet and Dougie has total control over government, and hardly anyone has ever heard of him or knows who he is? These guys all go back to the Eighties; they've always been around. It wasn't until Cameron demoted Gove that it all started to go horribly wrong. And they will get rid of Rishi soon, too. But first they will have to take Ben Wallace [Defence Secretary] out. He's very popular with members after the Putin invasion and Ukraine. At some stage, when they make the decision to start moving the pieces on the board again, whether it's to move Ben to the backbenches or to get him out altogether because he's a leadership threat, you will begin to see unpleasant articles drop and it will always be in *The Times* first. Ben will see it coming, he's been in Cabinet a long time. My guess is, the first time a negative headline attacking him appears in *The Times*, he will announce he's standing down because he knows how they roll and he won't let them trash his reputation. Right now, because he's good at his job and popular, he stands in Kemi's way, or rather, their way. They will remove everyone until the only viable option left to save the party is Kemi. They will be worried about Penny. They did for her last time and she has risen again, they will be steaming. They put her in as Leader of the House not knowing what her ceremonial role during the Coronation would be. I would have loved to be a fly on the wall when they discovered that one and frankly, she didn't put a foot wrong. She aced it.'

Everyone fell silent and raised their glasses to their lips, which was a relief as I scribbled down some notes.

V2: 'Dougie is a complicated person. He is a bully and a genius, a man most describe as intimidating, and he has total meltdowns. The only authority he answers to is Dr No. He will call people when he is unhappy at all hours of the night and scream at them. He has done it with Dowden. Dowden had sent a nice tweet to an MP who is trans, Jamie Wallis, but he did that without Dougie's approval and the fall-out was explosive. What had happened was that Dowden had done something that Dougie hadn't given him permission to do; it was a tweet sent not under his control. I think even Munira was really concerned that night when he lost the plot and rang around friends. His behaviour was so odd.'

V3: 'They are all odd. Have you heard the whips office story about Cummings? What he did in the early hours of the morning in 2016, when Gove stabbed Boris in the back?'

We all sat up and paid attention. I checked that Otter was working.

V3: 'Well, you know how the official story is that Cummings didn't know, he wasn't around, was no part of it according to the reports, yada yada. Well, back in 2010, when Gove was Education Secretary and creating havoc, after he'd promised Cameron he would keep Cummings under control, it was decided in No. 10 to send one of the whips to see Gove and to tell him it wouldn't be long before Cameron flipped and demanded Cummings was sacked. Gove needed to rein in Cummings and was told he would be doing himself a big favour if he sacked him first. So the whip, who was doing Gove a favour, he was kind of signalling, if you don't get rid of Cummings it's not going to go well for you and that was Gove's warning that the demotion may come. Anyway, the whip went to see Gove in his office in the department and Gove was pathetic, he went into meltdown and pleaded, on the verge of tears, "I can't do anything, I can't be without him. I can't do my job without him. He has to be here." It was a very bloody-weird conversation and the whip, shocked at how pathetic Gove had been, duly backed off – men just can't deal with other men crying – and carried the details back to the Chief Whip.

'Anyway, fast-forward to 2016 and the night before Gove so publicly stabbed Boris in the back and Boris declared he was pulling out of the race because of it. Gove did that, what, at around 9 a.m.? Well, earlier, at 2 a.m., that whip – he was a known Boris supporter and had been helping to organise the troops – had been sound asleep in his bed when his phone went off and woke him. It was Dominic Cummings and he asked the whip, "I just want to check: you are going to the Gove–Boris running ticket for leadership announcement tomorrow, aren't you, when Boris announces he's running, with Gove as his No. 2?" The whip, half asleep, is confused; thinks that Boris has got Cummings, as Gove's right-hand man, ringing around to make sure everyone who is supposed to turns up, and, muddled, he answers, "Yes, of course, I'm a Boris supporter, I'm working on the team; of course I'll be there." Cummings replies, "Good to hear it; just confirming," and puts the phone down. In Cummings' petty mind, he wanted that whip to be there, to witness Gove pulling out, to see Boris withdraw, and to pay back the whip for being sent to Gove to tell him to fire Cummings all those years ago. That's a measure of how vindictive they are.'

So, those journalists who were told by Cummings that he wasn't even in London and wasn't a part of it, that he hadn't agreed the plan with Gove, all reported in media and books, it was all totally untrue.

V3: 'Dougie and Cummings, they go back forever, way back, best friends way back. They fall in and out like lovers, but they all do that with each other all the time. Dougie tried to insist he had nothing to do with Gove stabbing Boris in the back, so did

Cummings; they were both obviously up to their necks in it, because the one thing you learn about Gove when you've been around him for years is that he does nothing unless these guys tell him to. Osborne, with the help of [now] former MP Nick Boles, made sure the backstabbing took place but there is no way they all weren't on board. He's such a coward, Gove would never have done that alone or without the Dark Lord's approval. It then later fell on Dougie to tell Gove that he didn't have the support of MPs he thought he had; that actually, everyone on the slate had wanted Boris, not Gove. If he hadn't done that, he was about to be No. 2 in the UK, partner to Boris, probably Deputy Prime Minister and Chancellor, and he totally blew it. MPs in Westminster are mostly onto him, and so this destruction of the party, the managed decline which looks more like crash and burn – he thinks he will be one of the survivors, as that is the only way he will ever get to be party leader in opposition, and one day prime minister. Because his Machiavellian network is so tight, once he is in, no one will get him out.'

I swallowed the nibbles I was munching as, wide-eyed, I listened. One of these men was a friend of Gove's, or at least I thought he was.

'Were these people right to remove Boris? Is Rishi the answer?' I said.

They all came back with a resounding no. If they had said yes, would it be a case that the end justified the means?

V3: 'Dougie thought that Boris was an election-winning machine. He and Boris weren't totally aligned on all policy levels, but Dougie thought that didn't matter. That once he won, they would influence him. But the fact of it was, with the network they had in place, they didn't want to influence, they wanted to control, and the crunch point came when the Dark Lord and Cain were removed. That was the point where they realised, it was falling apart for them, they were losing power and control, and they decided to press the start button and accelerate the plan to get Boris out. Exactly the same thing happened when Iain Duncan Smith sacked Mark MacGregor. The day after IDS sacked him, because he became aware that they were working against him, the sky fell on him and the knives were out. It's a bit like they've written an operating manual: *The A–Z of How to Control a Political Leader and, When that Fails, How to Remove Him*. Bear in mind though, Dougie thinks Rishi is a pussy, and if Rishi ever tries to exert any control himself or push back, he will be out too. The thing about Rishi though is that I believe he knows it, and it would appear that he doesn't care, because there isn't any driving light, no policy he's passionate about. So far, he seems to be very happy for them to be in control, and he will acquiesce. Rishi will never stand up to Dr No, and Dr No will allow Rishi to believe he's in control by not interfering in the macro decisions, but Dougie will one hundred per cent control appointments, candidates, woke agenda, House of Lords appointments, trans stuff, because that is really all he is interested in policy wise, hence his relationship with Kemi, as that's what rings her bell too.'

I wondered out loud, who paid Dr No?

V2: 'The rumours are that many fund him, mainly hedge fund managers, friends of the most powerful people in the land and it is thought he is on the payroll of a number of billionaires. Some say he has connections to Mossad, others that he was in MI5. I personally don't believe any of that. No self-respecting spook finds himself on remand for trying to burn someone's house down or arrested by the police for harassment, or embezzling. I mean, the list goes on.

'He may have spent time in prison, but now he is the Prime Minister's key adviser, but not listed as someone working in No.

10, so he bypasses that process. The billionaires – I would think that they know Dr No has the hugest influence, more influence than anyone else in No. 10, and so they pay him. He has certainly eased the path of key individuals into the House of Lords. Whether he's been paid to do that, I could not know. That's one of the reasons a political bomb always goes off when anyone talks about getting rid of any of them. Maybe this level of mind games and control, the aggressiveness of it all, is because there is so much at stake. Maybe it is actually all about money.'

They talked. I thought. Have I missed something entirely here?

Drinks finished, they were winding up. All had dinners to attend, the London life.

As I sat alone waiting for my Otter file to upload so that I could name and export it, I stared into the dying embers of the fire.

Maybe when it boils down to it, they are just very mercenary individuals seeking wealth.

For the love of money is at the root of all evil.

CHAPTER 18
DIE ANOTHER DAY

An MP is taking me to meet two great men from the party who, due to their longevity, may no longer be around in the near future to ask anything of. Both of sound mind, intelligent and clever. At the end of two and a half hours, their recollections and acuity had provided me with as much material as I would need to write another book, if I so wished.

After many years, events that were whispered about and concealed at the time are spoken of more freely today. I drive up from London and we take my car northwards up the M1 and eventually head out, across country, to the old vicarage in a picturesque English village that is so small, it surely only warrants the status of a hamlet.

The snowdrops, with a gargantuan effort, have forced their heads up through the thick blanket of leaf mulch that lay on the ground and the thin daffodil stalks are yet to be topped by their buttery yellow heads. The first rays of sunshine warm my back as we tug on the bell-pull to the side of the arched oak door, and we wait for what appears to be an interminable time. A robin, at the sound of the bell, lands on a stone pot to the side of the door, as though awaiting entry itself. The sound of shuffling footsteps reaches us and the front door opens on hinges that creak as loudly as the bones of the elderly gentleman who leads us into the drawing room.

The fire is lit, but the log perched on the firedogs must have been damp, as it is smouldering and struggling to ignite. A young woman enters the room from the far side and asks, 'Tea?' – an offer that we gratefully accept. Once introductions are made, I do as I am told and take a seat, feather upholstery threatening to claim me as my five foot two inches almost disappears down the back of a Knole sofa.

I am slightly in awe given the company I am in, and my chaperone, sensing this, explains to the two elderly gentlemen, whom I shall refer to as Bambi and Thumper, what I am doing. He has already done so on the telephone when seeking permission to visit. As he speaks, I expect maybe a warning, a disapproving frown or some degree of kick-back, but there is none.

'Death is waiting just ahead of me,' said Bambi, and I could sense it, almost feel it, lurking in the shadows of the room. The conversation moves from nought to sixty in about three minutes and roams around members of what was known as 'the movement'.

Bambi is wearing many layers and I can sense he's delighted to have visitors.

We make small talk as the young woman reappears through the door; a waft of something still warm and sweet accompanies her. We are served tea in Royal Doulton and homemade short-bread fingers, which look delicious. Oh, to have the time to bake. I'm sneakily dunking while my chaperone and the gentlemen reminisce and discuss their salad days. They begin to casually discuss a wealthy man, a party donor who had some sort of dispute about money with Dr No. It was a story I had heard others refer to.

'He fleeced him, you know. Took his gold American Express card for a ride. Travelled in helicopters, pretended to be setting up a think tank, trashed his house and spent the money. Dr No was nothing more than a petty crook and now he's in No. 10 and advising Rishi. It all ended in tears, solicitors involved, settled out of court. I have the name of the solicitor who acted for the donor if you would like it. Trouble was, the party donor felt like such a nit, he only told a few people about it which allowed Dr No to repeat the whole sorry mess with yet another donor.'

He turned to my other veteran of Conservative Party politics, not to me, and as they discussed the years and the people, I dunked another biscuit.

Thumper picked up the thread, naming an instantly recognisable and well-known former MP. 'When it was all over, this MP, one Dr No was obviously working on, took Dr No to a party in Westminster one night which the donor was at. I mean, he knew nothing about Dr No's behaviour, lots didn't. The donor was so disturbed and visibly shaken by the sight of Dr No that the following morning the person who had hosted the party in the Treasury had to call the MP into his office to explain the difficult situation that the MP had put the host in. He said to him, "I am sorry to inform you but I'm afraid that you have deeply offended a party donor; the man is terribly upset that you would even consider bringing Dr No into my office."'

They passed each other a knowing glance.

'Dr No was a bad-tempered, frightening man who has always operated in the shadows. He gives the impression that he has something over everyone, secrets over people in powerful positions, related to his presence at the sex parties maybe?'

The conversation moved on. They cantered around the dangers of libertarianism.

Bambi: 'Norman [Tebbit] was determined to close them down, you know, but not as determined as they were to survive, and the proof is in the pudding so to speak, as they are all now running No. 10, so I suppose you could say they won.'

Thumper: 'One of the things I've learnt about the Conservative Party over the long years is the importance of sex. I know this sounds a bit odd, and please forgive me, but everyone sleeps with everyone. From the Dougie Smith Fever-branded sex parties back in the day, which you probably have all the details of, to the behaviour of MPs in the Conservative Party today. In a way, it has contributed to the normalisation of bad behaviour, as in, nothing is scandalous any more. I'll give you an example. If I told you that the whips' office have to rescue MPs from many difficult situations on a regular basis, I doubt you would be surprised because there's nothing new in that, but if I told you that one of those situations recently involved an MP having sex with a prostitute on a billiard table while four MPs stood around and watched him, cheering him on, would that surprise you?'

It did.

Bambi: 'Or the fact that they have a video of one of the most popular ministers in government today being given a blow-job by someone who most certainly is not his wife, who everyone thought was loyal to Boris, until suddenly he surprised everyone and wasn't. Who do you think has that video because it certainly isn't anyone on Team Boris? Or how about the MP who kept safe a laptop containing indecent images of children, on behalf of a paedophile relative, and then swore to police he was only keeping it safe? Or the MP who keeps, in his expenses-funded accommodation, a mistress during the week in London, but tootles back to his doting wife every weekend, except those weekends when he's on a taxpayers' funded trip somewhere in the world?'

I gulped my tea and tried to look nonplussed, like this wasn't more than I had bargained to know.

Bambi: 'The lesson must be that the whips' office still works, when – and this is important – when and only when the information remains within the whips' office, but the thing is, it doesn't always. I'll give you an example. One MP who has been one of the worst critics of Boris Johnson, the most unpleasant and vindictive, was one of the worst behaved when he arrived at Westminster; indulged in unusual sexual activities with rent-boys, things you don't want to detail in a book that doesn't carry an age-appropriate warning and I don't want to offend you.'

I wished he would.

Bambi: 'He did turn to the whips' office to save himself when a video appeared, but somehow, someone got their hands on it and has been using it against him ever since; it's blackmail, pure and simple. And that's not a one-off. Add to that on a much simpler level the pillow talk and the general level of promiscuity – much within the party happens on that level – and those in the fifth column, they've always understood that, hence the Fever-branded sex parties. Smith knew what he was doing. You have many of the voters who regard us as the party of business, the economy, wealth creation, the family and, more latterly, the environment. The people you are talking about, they have very different morals to those who vote for us or support us, and actually, from many of us who would profess to be libertarians in the name of freedom and civil liberties. Let me explain this to you: these men, they loathe MPs with what I can only describe as a deep and visceral hatred.

'The group of men you are writing about: Gove, Smith, Cummings and their band of merry men and the odd woman. They have been around the party for so long, creating so many problems, falling out with so many people, doing deals with numerous devils – one day, provided I lived long enough, someone just like you was always going to be sat in front of me asking me questions; it had to be only a matter of time. The fact of the matter is, surely even by their version of success, to take as long as they have to get to the point that they always wanted to be, has it been worth it? Is there any good that they have done? Because their arguments in the days when they were known as 'the movement' were perverse even then, but they did at least have a plan of sorts, there were some worthwhile issues that they were passionate about – mind, their biggest idea was to burn the party down and build one back up without Brexiteers. The EU was at the heart of it all; it was a taboo subject.

'They tried to legislate for some pretty extreme forms of libertarianism, all sorts of sexual stuff, in their early days.'

Thumper's rug slipped from his knee to the floor as he struggled to catch it.

I smiled as the old nurse in me rushed to the surface and I leapt from my seat and lifted the thick and heavy tartan rug from the floor and helped him to place it across his knee.

Bambi winked at me, in the way only much older men do these days, and observed: 'Shakespeare wasn't entirely correct. I still have my eyes and my own teeth.'

He continued. 'No candidate's name is put forward to any association in any seat without it first being scrutinised by Dougie Smith. Now, in my day it was Dame Angela who had that role, and she did an excellent job. Is Dougie doing as good a job? The answer is no, not by a long way, but he is selecting some candidates over whom he has almost total control and I would say that one of those was Rishi.

'He is also in charge of public appointments and has had his person in place in No. 10 overseeing the appointments process during the Johnson administration; he had Simone Finn in complete control of the process.

'Now, today, the person overseeing appointments is the aide who resigned from her appointment in No. 10 over the Jimmy Savile comments along with Munira Miraz: a top kickboxer, and Dougie and Munira's closest friend. She is a good woman, everyone rates and likes her; they just can't understand the criteria by which she chooses her pals. There are a number of peers in the Lords who have been placed there by Dougie, who effectively negotiated and steered their passage through No. 10 and into the House of Lords. Lord Dean Godson, the man who introduced Iain Duncan Smith to Mark MacGregor and Michael Gove, he's just one of them. I can give you a list if you like.

'Look, how do you think Robbie Gibb was appointed to the BBC? And then there's Gibb's brother's partner, Michael Simmonds, put onto an appointments committee. Boris hated appointments because they were a minefield, so he was happy to stick rigidly to the letter of the process. He must have told you, he sees all this as nonsense and a distraction from the main job of governing. By the way, they will remove old Sharpie very soon. Who do you think leaked the information about his approaching Simon Case about how to make a loan to Boris from a family member in the right and proper way?'

I had had my suspicions, but no proof.

'Why will Sharp go?' I asked.

'He will. Since the moment that story was leaked, about him seeing Case to facilitate the loan. Because he hasn't done what they wanted him to do. Robbie Gibb is seething. He expected Richard to make him chair of one or other of the complaints committees at the BBC. Sharp didn't do it because Robbie Gibb wasn't the right person to chair the complaints committee. It was wrong. Sharp will have told him, "I can't." If Sharpie was doing his job as chair of the BBC in the right and proper way, he would have said, "You are far too political; it flies in the face of everything we want to achieve in the BBC in terms of impartiality. It will stink of bias." From that moment on, from the moment Robbie didn't get the job he wanted, they were going to get Sharpie out and someone they could control into the BBC.'

As I have pointed out earlier, by the time I write this interview up, Sharp has gone and the Heppinstall Report into the affair has been published. It reads, 'As noted above, this inquiry has not considered the Prime Minister's private financial affairs, but in so far as is relevant I am happy to record that I have seen no evidence of Mr Sharp having any role in those matters save for the attempted introduction mentioned above.' Richard Sharp was not reinstated.

Bambi: 'Simon Case appeared to have selective memory over the Sharp affair, and a letter he wrote to William Wragg, chair of the PACAC committee,* was leaked. Another letter written by Case leaked to the Remain media which had whipped up whatever they were being told into a frenzy, but the bottom line was, it is incredibly expensive in this country to be a prime minister. It is not a job for someone who is not a wealthy man or woman, as Liz Truss, who received a bill for £12,000 from Chequers after having stayed for a few weekends, will attest.

'It's all just a jigsaw puzzle, isn't it? If there is something leaked in the media about anyone associated with the party, reputations being destroyed, MPs, Cabinet ministers, anyone, you will see the pieces on the board being moved. Always necessary to take someone down before a reshuffle so the public understand why it may have happened. They claim to be determined to do all they can to prevent a socialist government, and you have to ask, why and how? They are controlling a prime minister who is, day by day, destroying the Conservative Party. What is their purpose? What has it been for the past four decades?

'These men, they get to decide who is prime minister, you've seen that in action yourself, and they decide what is policy. They decide which MPs make it onto the candidates' list and to

* The Public Administration and Constitutional Affairs Committee.

the Cabinet table, and which don't, and even those in their favour, they like to damage their careers along the way to keep them vulnerable and needy of their help and support. Doesn't do to have one of their chosen flock do too well; they may get ideas above their station and think that they are in charge or free of their control. Look what happened to Oliver Dowden when he sent out a tweet they didn't approve of supporting a trans MP. He was quickly given the hairdryer treatment and brought back into line. Every now and then, they need to reel them in with a little bit of leaking, a minor scandal, bad publicity. They get to decide who sits in the Lords and on the committees of powerful organisations and they socialise on the yachts of billionaires.

'Boris was one of the few people to push back against them and I don't even think he even knew why he was pushing back; I think it felt instinctive and wrong for him. I don't think he had a clue how organised and deep the network ran beneath him or how little power he had. But he fought back against the fists that rained down on him from the shadows; they simply couldn't control him and so he had to go. You see, the point is ministers have to abide by the ministerial code, they have rules they have to follow. That isn't true of advisers and in the case of "Dr No", on the one hand there he is supposedly tripping on and off the yachts of billionaires and on the other he doesn't even have any terms and conditions in his contract of employment with the party. Not even anything about disclosing sensitive information. I know at least one party chairman who tried to raise this and was told in no uncertain terms not to rock the boat. Rishi Sunak doesn't make the decisions without consulting these men. I mean, Dowden, he's a wreck when Dougie shouts at him. He is running the Cabinet office now, isn't he?'

They were asking me so many questions, I was wondering who was interviewing whom. It was all so mind-blowingly corrupt, I was actually struggling to respond.

Thumper: 'How do you think it is that all trace of Dougie Smith has been wiped from the internet, apart from the odd piece the *Mail* has dared to write? There is absolutely nothing about Dr No either. His entire footprint, wiped clean.'

I shook my head. It was a mystery.

Thumper: 'You have to ask yourself this.'

He gave up asking me questions and was now suggesting I questioned myself. They were both animated as Bambi shuffled to the edge of his seat and stared at me, watching my reaction. They were enjoying themselves.

Thumper: 'Dougie Smith has no interest in any policy area, other than the woke agenda and control of areas in which people become puppets, and that includes the Prime Minister. Back to my earlier point, and the dominance of sexual relations in the party. It is extraordinary how much happened going right back to the days of Portillo. How many people lived together, slept together and did business together. The gay network has always been strong throughout the party and as I was obviously a big supporter of gay marriage, I am not passing judgement in any way. But because it was a network thrown together by the necessity for secrecy, away from the prying eyes of journalists and cameras, that network certainly functioned behind closed doors, and it was unhealthy and dominant. The promiscuity was legendary and the sex parties, well you know about them. Emma Sayle, who I think took them over from Dougie, said they were just orgies with lots of people squirming on beds. I can tell you, every one of them was one of us, a Tory. Decisions about the Conservative Party were not even taken at dinner parties, but in beds and in relationship networks.

'The fact is that most of the people who support the Conservative Party, who work for it, who vote for it, who pound the streets delivering leaflets for it, they would be horrified if they knew what the behaviour, the morals, the principles and values of many of the people who governed them were. This is why being a party of membership is so important and we need to get back to that. Ask yourself this: why, when Michael Gove admitted to taking cocaine, did not one journalist ask him the single most obvious question, which was, when was the last time you took cocaine? Did that not strike you as odd? Imagine if Boris or Liz had admitted to taking cocaine, they would have had the life grilled out of them. How much? When? Who with? Where? With Michael, not a single really pointed question was asked. I mean, that was extraordinary, don't you think?'

My very literal mind had now realised, he was not looking to me for answers, he just spoke in questions.

Thumper: 'Look, it doesn't matter what policies or ideas the party has, but if we remain an immoral, dysfunctional party, we are bound to crash and burn, and as sleaze got us last time, it will get us again. The public may not be as concerned today as they were years ago about extramarital affairs, but the low level of behaviour among so many MPs and unelected individuals with their hands firmly gripped on the levers of power would, I am sure, have a huge impact on the public if they knew about it. Add to that, the manipulation, the corruption and the game-playing behaviour of certain individuals, and you can see where we are heading. There is a vacuum in No. 10 and in government which these people created by a process of controlling candidates and who will be MPs, therefore isolating the leadership from academia, from professionals, from high-calibre candidates who always played an active role in the past, who reached high office or a significant back room role, by refusing them entry to the candidates' list. That shocks me more than anything, frankly. High-quality candidates are pushed aside because they don't want intelligent, knowledgeable, enquiring minds to be MPs. They control the appointments of substance, the Spad network itself, from within the heart of government. They employ kids. Twenty-something-year-olds. And they control people using fear.

'We are in a place whereby the entire party, the government, is in the hands of a small group of men who think it is all a game and are there to serve self. They will continue to run things, they live and breathe politics. They think of nothing else. If I were a religious man, I'd say there was something about the devil in No. 10 right now. At any one time, there are around thirty MPs getting into serious trouble that they need help with, and that is an extraordinary number, and nothing is done. They behave in the most shocking way and, quite often, those MPs will go on to be promoted. Not straightaway – the misdemeanours are held over them, and if I'm honest, there isn't anything new about that; it's how the whips' office has always worked. The only difference is, this isn't the whips doing it in a whips' way to secure party unity. These men, they despise MPs and, of course, whips are MPs. MPs behaving badly back in my day was a much rarer event than it is today. You might get a tricky situation once a week to deal with. Today we are close to giving Sodom and Gomorrah a run for their money.'

As he talked, a feeling like he was foretelling the end of days filled the room.

Thumper: 'Until we have MPs who are more interested in politics than self-promotion and the media, and Twitter and all of that social media nonsense where they kid themselves they are reaching the voters in a modern world when all they are really doing is indulging their own narcissism, then we will continue to decline. These men in No. 10 – their path to the level of power they have reached today was greased by Theresa May, a hung Parliament, Brexit, the General Election, and a resultant lack of stability due to all the turmoil that the May years brought about when, just like Major, she almost lost us our majority. And who was responsible for Theresa May? It was Michael Gove. Who worked with him? Cummings. Where was Cain? Placed in the Foreign Office close to Boris. Who held one of the key positions in No. 10? Robbie Gibb. Who worked there throughout? Dougie Smith. Who is the man who was everywhere, pulling all the levers? Dr No. All roads lead back to Gove.'

My fingers were greasy from the butter in the shortbread and I was struggling to hold a pencil.

Thumper: 'The absence of good people in the executive has reached a critical level and, as I say, the vacuum has been filled by a small number of individuals who are totally in control of a weak party using dark arts to ensure that their writ goes a lot further than it otherwise would have done during more peaceful times.

'These men, they are brilliant at what they do. And they keep on winning. Many years ago, Mark MacGregor and Dominic Cummings were a bit of a team – I'm going way back now. MacGregor and Cummings were so close they finished each other's sentences, seriously. If both men weren't married and straight, you would have thought they were lovers, and I think they were in a way: lovers in harmony with the idea of disruption and domination. When Iain was leader, they were both working for him and utterly contemptuous of Iain and all MPs; I mean, they quite literally hated them. And then the penny dropped one day: they were actually contemptuous of every single person they met and spoke of, other than themselves. You know, it is my belief that Mark MacGregor has been involved all along and is still involved today; it is almost delusional to entertain the idea that he isn't.'

Bambi picked up his tea and heaped two spoons of sugar in as Thumper put his down and took up the mantle. He reminisced along the same theme, but he was still hard-wired into the party via other means. He was slightly younger, but not by much, and they both shared the heydays of Thatcher and were still dining out on it, with each other. They were an old married couple, and they themselves spoke in harmony.

'Your intake was quite a good one, you know: 2005,' Thumper said.

I instantly felt smug and proud.

I asked the question, 'What do you both think about the role of Michael Gove. Is he the Svengali in all of this, or is he being used? Is he their puppet or a puppeteer?'

They glanced at each other as if seeking approval to speak.

Thumper: 'You know Gove is still good friends with Osborne and Osborne has far more influence than most people realise? You are aware of Osborne going aboard Nat Rothschild's boat to meet Peter Mandelson?'

I was, and that was some time ago now.

'Well, it tells you a lot about that network now and the billion-aires who those running No. 10 meet with today. What hasn't been reported are the yachts Dr No took trips on on and off. But, going back to Gove, he is actually out of favour at the moment, and he's very frustrated on three fronts. They fall out a lot these guys, but this time, Gove is very upset. There has been a shift from Gove because, quite frankly, they just don't need him anymore. Rishi has always been dubious about him; like every-one else, he doesn't trust him. Rishi was right there in 2016 when the plot to stab Boris was executed. He probably formed his opinion of Gove back then, but that was when Gove was useful to him. He's surplus to requirements now.'

'On what pretext have they fallen out?' I asked.

'So, on the first front he's been doing what he always does, and when Rishi's coronation took place he tried to make his department bigger, and he did all the usual departmental turf grabbing, to increase his exposure and relevance. The past six months he has spent trying to get large parts of the Home Office and Justice into his department, which is levelling up and a department which will see no progress. Levelling up – that was Boris's big idea, and they want Boris, politically speaking, dead. Gove wanted the whole Home Office Prevent strategy, the whole Shawcross Report, terrorism, extremism, all of that. He wanted to build levelling up into a proper department to give himself status, because he knew his department was a ghost ship. There were a few small changes in one department, not his; he got absolutely nothing, and that put him in a deep sulk.

'He's been a big part of the plan to nuke Boris forever, and here he was in no way benefiting from all of his plotting and meddling. He's also been building up Kemi Badenoch as the next leader of the Conservative Party, because that was part of the plan and it still is. He's been mentoring Kemi for a long time, possibly, originally, at Dougie's behest. She was helped onto the candidates' list and into her seat, just like Rishi, and became a minister in Gove's department as a part of the strategy, and despite her being a central player in their game plan, the mentee has now flown his nest and is nestled down in Dougie's, and he is very, very unhappy about that. She is distancing herself from Gove, whether she is being advised to – and I use that word reservedly – or she has realised the dangers of being seen to be too close to him. She's second only to Ben Wallace in the opinion polls. The trajectory Kemi is on, she must think to herself, *I don't need Gove any more*. She loathes Penny Mordaunt, regards her as a toxic force in the party, but sadly, Kemi has a way with people which will one day get her into trouble. She is far too brusque and snappy, and she can be very caustic and cutting too.

'So for Gove, his protégée has abandoned him. Kemi's more popular than him and rising higher than he is; she's closer to the new inner circle than him, and patently views him as yesterday's man. She's being pushed up the greasy pole by Dougie Smith to be leader, and by the demeanour of Gove, who has always hung on to the coat-tails of others to keep him near the centre of power, it's a blow to find himself on the outside. It looks like she may not be returning his calls, and who knows whether that is on the advice of Kemi's good friend, Dougie Smith, as maybe now that they are all right in the centre of power, they have decided they don't need Gove to fight for them to keep them in their jobs any longer or, in Kemi's case, to push her up the ladder. They don't need Gove to pick up the phone to make sure Cummings isn't sacked, and that Smith keeps on earning his £100k pay-packet from CCHQ when a party treasurer tries to sack him, and retains his pass and full access to No. 10. They just don't need Gove to do that any longer, because they are unelected and further up the greasy pole than he is. It's just a matter of time before you begin to read a negative briefing about Ben Wallace in the press; they will want him out of the way to make room for one of Rishi's ringleaders, probably Claire Coutinho who organised all the MPs parties for him and dropped the Boris poison into their ears. When that negative briefing hits *The Times*, which is where it will pop up of course, Ben will be off.'

The two men looked tired and I suspected it was a sugar slump after the shortbread, or maybe it was time for an afternoon nap.

'Can you tell me why you think they do this?' I asked. 'Outside of the personality defects. Do you think there could be a bigger reason at play?'

I noticed with a slight shock that veteran Bambi was actually asleep. I looked twice to check he was still breathing.

Thumper smiled at him indulgently. 'Don't worry about him; he's done it every day of his adult life. That's an interesting question. With Gove I think it is the game. The intellectual, Machiavellian, high-stake, risk-taking, the addictive poker player he was for many years using a different outlet in politics for a greater thrill factor. One of the things that occurs to me is, if you look at the G8, Biden, Macron, Trudeau. These men are our world leaders. Sunak is the only one who is in a centre-right party, the rest are in centre-left parties, and yet you couldn't put a credit card between any of them. They are indistinguishable. There is nothing to separate any of them; it's all follow-my-leader on economic and social policy, and yet the people of this country didn't elect a centre-left party, they elected a right-of-centre party, or so they thought, because that is where the heart of the country lies. We are the mother of all parliaments, we have the BBC, the greatest academic institutions in the world. We have the greatest financial centre in the world. We are a magnificent country, punching well above our size and weight, and we've been doing that for centuries. And that's why I loved Boris as leader.

'He is a man of huge historic knowledge and a bigger intellect. He knew this, he had a vision and plans to do great things for this great country. Liz, she doesn't have charm or personality, she struggles with that but she is clever. Rishi, he has charm in bucketloads, but most people in Cabinet are as smart as Rishi. Boris, he had it all, the personality and the academic brilliance. And now, on social and economic policy, we are playing follow-my-leader, as we are indistinguishable from these identikit politicians and centre-left parties around the world, and that intrigues me. Sometimes I worry, *Am I going a bit mad?* Like a crazed conspiracy theorist. But all I present to you now are the facts. I think,

How have we got to the situation where we had Reagan, Delors, Thatcher, you had these political titans, but all slightly different, and like a family of the West, we could all sit around and be not too disagreeable. Are you old enough to remember "Up yours, Delors"?'

He began to titter and Bambi wakens from his slumber and looks around the room.

'But now they are vanilla, bland and boring, so I worry that there is something else happening. Remember Lenin had his useful idiots? Well, they have theirs, like Dowden, and they don't have a clue what's going on. Living in a democracy: that's a joke today.

'I mean, what is happening to the West? Is it about the total annihilation of the West? The disposing of Boris's levelling-up agenda means we will have an increasingly divided society.'

'Why Sunak though?' I asked.

'Because he's an empty suit in a boy band which is on auto-tune. He is politically talentless but he's polished and can be moulded and shaped, wound up like a clockwork toy and placed on a stage. He is a puppet. Feels nothing and he knows even less. They saw that and picked it up many years ago, but they knew they would need the media to project him as the perfect leader, hence the connection with Mas Siddiqui on the NewsCorp board and *The Times* being the only newspaper which is constantly showcasing Rishi. He can be wound up and pointed in the right direction, and he's reasonably good-looking and photogenic. Yes, Rishi was the guy: he ticked all the boxes. He's not your white middle-class, middle-aged heterosexual male. He's not Bullingdon Club; he has enough about him to set him apart. And Dougie, he saw this because that is what he does, he grooms MPs into seats, and he knew he could groom Rishi into No. 10; Rishi and Dougie have been close friends for many years. There are two components to power: money and politics. Liz, now she was taken down by the mobilisation of big money. Boris, he was taken down by politics. Rishi is the first British prime minister ever who is the axis of both.'

The room fell silent as I finished making notes and, as I looked up, they were both fast asleep.

My chaperone smiled at me. 'Time to go?' he said.

I closed the book on this interview but felt like I was opening one on a whole new chapter. I tiptoed to the side of Thumper's chair and lifted his slipped rug back into place. We left them both, chins to chest, gently snoring.

I was silent for most of the journey back to London, the only sound inside the car being the repetitive swish of the wipers clearing away the rain that had come upon us as we were sat indoors. My mind was troubled. How many stones do I want to upturn? How far do I go? At what point do I stop speaking to people, because everywhere I turn someone picks at a new loose thread in the knot. But of course, I knew the answer to that question before the goodbyes to the housekeeper were said and the car turned out of the pea-shingle driveway, the oak doors slipping behind a dry-stone wall and out of view.

The light was fading fast as my chaperone handed me a Werther's Original and spoke.

'I know you will want to focus on all of that now and the behaviour of the MPs who helped to bring down Boris. A billiard table: Jesus! My suggestion is that you retrace your steps a little first and go back to the night of the EU referendum and the hours that immediately followed Gove stabbing Boris in the back in 2016: the smashing up of the Vote Leave office by the people who worked for Cummings at Cummings' behest, and the removal of a certain computer and why it was removed.'

'Smashing up of the Vote Leave office? Where did that come from? Is the story of the MP having sex on a billiard table with a prostitute, while MPs watched on, true?' I asked him.

My question was met with silence.

'I take it that's a yes.'

'It's pretty bad,' he said.

'You know shit like this could bring the party down, don't you?' his eyes narrowed.

'I do. Do you think a party with MPs that have behaved like ours deserves to remain in power? A party run by a small cabal of men, is that who volunteers are working on behalf of? Is that the party people are voting for?'

Again, silence. He was battling now with his allegiance to the whips' code, but not for long.

'The public think MPs just get drunk all night on cheap booze in subsidised bars. How easy the whips' job would be if that were all we had to deal with. It's all broken. Like all the parameters that kept things in place, respect, values, public service, it's all gone. I feel like these guys are trying to rot the party from within. When you were talking in there, it dawned on me, this party today, this isn't what I signed up to.'

'Is the sex on the billiard table as bad as it gets?' I was on the slip road pulling onto the motorway. The traffic, as always, matched the rain, heavy.

'Sadly, no. Look, the thing that disturbed me more than anything was a serious rape that was reported and no action was taken by the party. An MP gave a young female a date-rape drug; the next thing she knew was she woke in a country hotel the following morning. He wanted her out of the room because, he told her, he had visitors coming for breakfast. She staggered for miles before she could find a taxi and help. She was a long way from home. She was very young.

'She was encouraged to go to the police, but she didn't, I think because she was scared of him and scared of it coming out, embarrassed that she had found herself in that position. She came to us. No action was taken by the party against the MP. He wasn't even reprimanded by anyone, his whip removed or the complaint reported further up the line. It never reached Boris's ears. That MP then went on to repeatedly sexually assault and rape, and even though the party knew about him, he retained his whip and remained undisciplined. He was also quite a nasty piece of work in the chamber and in Westminster in general, always attacking the government. He even went to see Boris in No. 10 to ask for a promotion, or maybe it was a knighthood or something. Still Boris wasn't told about his behaviour. When he left the room, I was told Boris said, "What a little creep." The MP got nothing. Boris sensed he was a bad egg, and yet, still, no one told him.

'MPs were always going to see Boris and ask him for favours, but he just refused to be blackmailed. He would rather take the bullets than reward someone who was attempting to blackmail him. He's quite instinctive on these things and, unusually for a prime minister, he has a high level of emotional intelligence.

'Anyway, it was later discovered that someone in the party secretly sent out regular cheques to the Priory Clinic to pay for the treatment of one of this man's later victims, and still nobody spoke out.'

'How much were the cheques for?' I asked through a tight throat.

'I can't remember, but many thousands; I think around £35k a pop. If anyone in authority asked what the payments related to, they were told that a member of the Westminster Conservative family needed help with a mental health issue and the subject was closed down under the pretence of privacy and sensitivity. If action had been taken when that first rape was reported, those other women would have been saved from their life trauma. You could say the men who get into fixes with prostitutes and rent-boys and other behaviour, they do so of their own free will. They have agency and choice. But those poor women … And sadly, he isn't the only one who preys on vulnerable women and has sex with them. It does tend to be vulnerable women they target. I have a list if you like, which includes one MP who took advantage of a young woman on the night before his wife gave birth to their child. The next day, he was showing people the delivery photographs on his phone.

'Do Labour MPs behave like this?' I asked him.

'They do, of course. I think *Panorama* are making a documentary about it and most of the sting is Labour MPs because they are the only cases they know about. The thing is, it's never been good in Westminster, but it's never before been as bad as it is right now.'

CHAPTER 19

NOBODY DOES
IT BETTER

Almost everyone I have interviewed has included the next person on their list of people I should talk to. I asked a Cabinet minister why this was the case.

'Because he's been around for years, he was a friend of Dr No. He's been on the periphery, watching, listening, talking – he's known Dougie Smith since he appeared on the scene.'

We met at the Wolseley. I was nervous about meeting him and about having lunch at the Wolseley. It was my first time. Would I let myself down and not know something I should? Would I be able to understand the menu? It was only as I made my way to the table and felt the draught that I realised the side zip on my dress was undone. I waved my hand to him in the distance as he sat at the table waiting and made a dash for the Ladies to zip up. The Wolseley was noisy and packed, and I was noticed. We were noticed.

Nerves settled. Once the food arrived I got straight to the point. I asked him about the men in the shadows.

'Dr No's behaviour is extreme,' he told me, 'because he's been so successful at it, in growing this power based on the people he controls. You have to understand how long he has been doing this. He's quite an old man now, you know.'

I put down my fork and wondered, *Do I need a glass of wine?*

'You know, there was some sort of dispute between him and a party donor. I don't want to speak ill of the dead, but the donor was a pretty weird guy. Lived in this over-the-top house with a pretty exaggerated country-style grandeur. Very full of himself and pompous and incredibly flamboyant. Smoked cigars as big as your arm. Played the role of the rich country gentleman, but he was totally over the top. Sent helicopters to ferry Cabinet ministers around.

'I remember Oliver Letwin being transported in one. I had refused to accompany him. There was no shortage of willing bodies in CCHQ to take my place. The donor was worth about a £100 million back then, and they set up a think tank and I think Dr No moved into his house but, you know, it came to nothing and questions regarding the misappropriation of funds became an issue. Dr No then lived off-grid which was his great strength. He always wanted power in his hands, but uniquely, unlike almost anyone I've ever met in this game, he was never trapped by the celebrity of power or the publicity; he never wanted that. He just wanted influence and power, and he mixes with and knows a lot of very wealthy people. He is attracted to them, turns on the whole long charm and grooming offensive, and slowly, like an octopus, wraps his tentacles around them, one by one. He makes himself a fixer to the rich. If you're not going to be elected in the world of politics, and he never was, we both know there are plenty of unelected people in the political world, and they all become distracted by the money and the cha cha cha. His pursuit was solely one of power, and one assumes money because that was what turned him on. A deep and complex man, never wanted to be an MP, but has more power than any MP ever has had. Here's a thing, if you walked into any building with Dr No, he wouldn't sit down until he had checked out where all the exit points were. He was always nervous, always gave the impression that someone was after him without actually saying so. Attended Dougie's sex parties, but never wanted to take part, just wandered around watching others, taking names. Found his niche by being super helpful and useful to the mega rich and doing practical things that they couldn't do themselves, and for that, they would give him patronage and he would stroll from one smart drawing room to another across London. Has a police record.

'What is he doing fraternising with Labour Party-supporting millionaires and sitting at the centre of No. 10? He is the person who is actually running the country and no one ever talks about it.'

'And, what about Dougie Smith?'

'He works for Dr No, who is the real power behind Dougie's throne. Dougie, a submarine in a suit, who has been around the centre of the party for at least twenty-five or thirty years, Dr No never comes up in conversation, hardly any MPs have a clue who either of them are. When Dougie was running sex parties as a business, Francis Maude defended them in the media at the time and he defended Dougie's running of them, I think that's where he and Dr No met. Maude had a point: if it was legal and consenting, what was the harm? Well, the harm was this: we are a party of membership and our members have no idea who this man is who exerts such influence at the centre of the party and has done so for so long.

After I had this conversation, I decided that if I was going to find out more about Dougie Smith and Dr No I was going to need to call in an expert. They were astonished at the degree to which Dougie, or someone on his behalf, has gone to obscure the facts about himself. Everything from where he was educated, widely reported to be Strathclyde where he is supposed to have failed his second-year exams and been asked to leave – they have no record for him.

There is even no official record of the one fact that is ubiquitously reported about him: his connection to the Fever-branded parties. The expert was amazed that someone so high profile and who operated in a world where there were so many photographs taken appeared to have only one photograph of himself appear on the internet – he eventually found another. In the expert's view, that is the sort of thing that is only possible with extreme effort – Google certainly do not make it easy to remove data and it's impossible not to wonder why someone so close to the heart of our democracy should make such efforts to live in the shadows. As for Dr No, his profile is even more enigmatic. There is simply no trace of him that my expert could find, not even a photograph or references to his activities.

'Oliver Dowden has been made Deputy Prime Minister,' I added.

'Well, that's no surprise,' my companion said. 'He's Dougie's eyes and ears. Cabinet is an odd place right now; everyone is subdued, fearful, can't really get a handle on where we are going or what is going on; like, with Boris, there was no doubt what the big vision was. One thing is for sure though: I'd put my mortgage on when we lose the General Election, Gove puts himself up again to run as leader, which is why I think Kemi is heading for trouble and why there's trouble in the camp. If both Gove and Kemi go for it, which of his friends is Dougie going to back? My guess would be Kemi. If it's Gove, you will know as soon as the first hostile news report about Kemi appears in *The Times*.'

I'm incredulous. 'No, you are kidding. Surely not. I thought Kemi was the plan; everyone does.'

He laughed. 'They think Gove will give up on that dream. Never. You see, James Forsyth, Rishi's Political Secretary, he's a very odd man. He does that thing when you talk to him, he stays silent so you keep talking. He speaks very slowly and is noncommittal. James will not be pulled into their dark world with ease, and so the fractures with Rishi will appear if James ever pushes back, and then, of course, they will revert to Gove.

'I am a hundred per cent sure of that and, you see, Gove has been seriously sulking. They weren't backing him, they were backing Kemi, and that must have hurt him a lot. He thought backing Kemi was all part of the game; then Kemi became the queen, he was a pawn, and she's knocked him off the board. She dumped him, got too big for her boots. That can only go one way, because these guys, they have so much on each other, they can only eat rat. They can't live without each other because if either one decided to spill the beans, it would be over for every one of them. It's a toxic circle of dependency and when others get sucked in, they find it difficult to escape.'

He pushed his plate away.

'But look, there's little point in looking too far ahead, the ground is always shifting. The really telling moment, the big crisis for them, came the night after Michael had stabbed Boris in the back. Once it became apparent that Michael's bid to be leader was toast and that all the plotting and conniving had been for nothing and May was going to win, Dom and his crowd of young male acolytes went out and got drunk. You can tell he was upset, because Dom almost never drinks. It's the early hours now and Dom goes off to Boris's house and starts banging on the door, shouting, "Boris, you have to believe me, I had nothing to do with what Michael did!" – he was frantic. He had lost every road into the centre of power and all he could see was everyone being on the outside. Robbie Gibb got back in, he got on the inside of No. 10 with Theresa May, and I think that was a relief to them; horses for courses so to speak – he was much more May's type than the others, who have always been thug like. When Boris didn't answer, Dom scribbled a note and put it through the door, saying he had nothing to do with what Michael had done.'

I have checked this with Boris.

'The fact is that he had everything to do with it,' he continues. 'The phone call Cummings made to the former whip at 2 a.m. in the morning seven hours before Gove announced that he was no longer backing Boris, the morning of his famous Brutus act, is just one piece of evidence which confirms this.

'But what is even more interesting is that when Dom went off to Boris's house, he sent his little gang to, ahem, tidy up the paper trail and bring out a certain laptop from the Vote Leave office. There is CCTV footage of this event. [I have had this confirmed and have seen stills from the footage.] They were so furious that everything had all backfired and gone so horribly wrong, they smashed up the Vote Leave office. Desktop hard drives destroyed, the monitors pushed off desks and smashed onto the floor. It was like they had no homes to go to, and they were mad. Gove and his backstabbing had left them all high and dry, and they were left sat like a bunch of losers in the pub with their dicks in their hands with their project to get onto the inside of No. 10 and run the country in tatters, and of course they knew – because these people, they are strategists and planners – that the only way now this could ever happen was one day with Boris. Gove had listened to Osborne and his influence was greater than theirs. I think in the pub that night Cummings realised, it will be Boris one day or nothing for us, and so that was why they went to hide the evidence that Vote Leave had always been about just about losing, it had never been about winning, and that was why he so desperately had to plead with Boris, albeit at 2 a.m. in the morning. Boris was their only hope. The only person left to deceive. It was the most precarious time they had faced in thirty years, and in order to survive, Cummings was very happy to throw Gove overboard.'

'What was on the computers? What did they have to hide?' I asked him.

'Well, they had to get the laptop out because on that laptop was the speech Dom had spent the evening writing, apologising that they hadn't quite managed to get Leave over the line, apologising for why they hadn't won. If it wasn't for Matthew Elliott [CEO of Vote Leave], Vote Leave would probably have lost, but that was what we think they were actually up to. I can give you the list of all of Cummings' little gang members; he always called them his social media ninjas and they were a joke. He was constantly going on about his data and his polling, and every time he brought his magic data to meetings, when people asked for it, it was exactly the same as it had been the time before, and people started asking questions and getting suspicious. Dom said they could work out who was doing what all over the UK, and it was bollocks.

'People were paying a lot of money for something which, to my mind, was just fake. No one ever saw any work. On the night the vote result came in, Dom kept himself away from everyone and he did not look happy. He kept looking at the results but his face was like thunder. Someone asked one of his crew, "What's Dom doing?" and they replied, "Oh, he's communicating with his ninjas." I can only say, it was all a very surreal and odd environment. When it was clear Leave had won, Dan Hannan [Tory MEP] jumps onto the table and gives a rousing speech, and then Dom is called up to give a speech, and he says, "We've won" – but it was so lame, so lacking in enthusiasm. He punched a tile above his head and it fell off the ceiling and onto his head.

'The truth of the matter is, it was Matthew Elliott who held the whole thing together. Dom wanted him out. It was also apparent that Cummings was working hard to make sure Gove was seen as the MP leading Vote Leave, but the public only really wanted to hear from Boris, and he was always coming out with arguments which, when analysed, would actually have damaged us and lost huge support, and it was often confusing. They made announcements without clearing them with Boris, about immigration, and he was furious.

'On the Sunday, after the win, Boris went to play cricket. Cameron resigns. The leadership election is on and then, we all know, Gove stabs Boris in the back at the eleventh hour. Cummings tells people, he wasn't even in town when Michael pulled his stunt. He was up in Durham. He wasn't, he was in London with someone who said he was constantly checking his phone; a huge grin suddenly slid onto his face as Gove pulled his Brutus act and the news broke. He had also been at a meeting with Gove and Boris on the Tuesday, despite Boris having told Michael not to bring Cummings, but that's the thing: it's like Michael can't function without Cummings by his side, so he still must be there in the background somewhere now. It is inconceivable that Cummings has just disappeared, if Gove is still breathing air in a government building Cummings is around. It just isn't possible. When the moment comes and Cummings starts to publicly attack Rishi on one of his blogs, you can be sure there will be a plan behind it and that plan will likely have something to do with Michael and leadership.'

I spoke later to someone who worked on the Vote Leave campaign to confirm some of what I've been told.

'Most of the conversations I was involved in were about how we managed losing,' he said. 'I got the impression that this wasn't actually managing expectations; it came to feel like it was the strategy, and this went on until the end. The day Boris came on board, it was like a shot of adrenaline to the campaign, and we would never have won without him, but I'm not sure that was what they wanted to happen. Remember when the Sunderland result came in?* You would think that the Vote Leave HQ would erupt with excitement, but it was subdued and Dom was the most subdued. He was saying to his tech guys, "This is wrong, we are not supposed to be winning." Jon Moynihan and his wife came in with champagne and bacon sandwiches, they were sent home, the champagne unopened. There was an air, and the only way I could describe it, was of malevolence. The atmosphere was like violence might erupt at any moment. We went home; I didn't wait for the final result and I never went back. Throughout the campaign, priority was always given to Michael, never Boris, and one day I overheard a conversation and it was about Cameron. I can't recall it exactly, but I was left with the impression it was all about getting Gove ready to take over the party; in what capacity – as Cameron was still there – I have no idea. It was like they knew he was going to stand down. You just got the sense, nothing was right, it's the only word I can use, it felt like a crazy cult, not a campaign, and the night Dom's people went in and smashed up the office and took the laptop and other stuff out, you kind of knew then it was all a bit dark, but that's who Cummings was, the Dark Lord. If you wonder how involved Rishi was in all of this, I'll tell you this little story which may help you to get the measure of the man.

'It was New Year's Day, 2022. Rishi was on his own in the UK, as Akshata and the children were in California. Rishi had gone with them and had fully expected to not have to return for three weeks.'

* Sunderland was one of the first constituencies to declare on the night of the referendum, with a bigger-than-expected vote for Brexit.

I knew this to be true. Rishi had actually told me himself the day before he left, with a longing sigh, that he was looking forward to getting away and three weeks of Californian sunshine.

'Dan Rosenfield, Boris's Chief of Staff, was pleading with Rishi before he went not to go for the three-week holiday. We knew Omicron was sailing in and Boris had banged his fist on the desk at one meeting and roared, "We are not locking down again," and everyone was struck dumb, because raising his voice is just not Boris's style. Rosenfield could see there was going to be the mother of all battles, because if we knew anything by now it was that at any minute, Gove, with Cummings in his earpiece (because he was out of No. 10 by now), would arrive pushing Whitty, Vallance and a pile of SPI-M-O graphs in through the door before piling on the pressure to lock down.

'Rosenfield lost the plot. He was begging Rishi: "Please don't go. You cannot fucking go and leave Boris to face the whole fucking machine." Like he can't take on Gove, Whitty, the NHS, the entire British media, Steve Baker and his coalition of anti-lockdown Conservative backbenchers, Starmer, Labour, the unions, Hunt and all of these crazy people on his own. Dan was making the argument privately to him, "We need you in the fucking room, Rishi. You know, you can make a good persuasive argument and you're just leaving it to Boris on his own." Rishi still went on his holiday. He had no interest; he was just California dreaming and took off. And then the only reason he came back is it was leaked to the papers that he was on holiday, not on a work meeting. Rishi had a panic attack and got the next plane home, on the Thursday night I think. Business leaders were demanding that he got a rescue package together, only he was already in the Speedos lying next to the pool when the call came through. Throughout the leadership hustings with him and Liz Truss, Rishi made the point over and over: "I flew back from a work meeting in the

States to prevent the country from locking down." That was the most audacious lie he told on that campaign, and it always amazed me how, even though journalists knew he had actually been on holiday, no one challenged him. The reason it amazed me was it was a fact already in the public domain. The *Telegraph* had run with the headline that he had dropped his holiday, but eight months later, everyone let him run away with the Walter Mitty act that he was in the USA for work meetings. Bull.

'Anyway, Akshata and the children don't return, they stay by the pool, and no one told Boris the truth about where Rishi had been and what he had been doing. And because Rishi was on his own over Christmas, Boris felt sorry for him and asked him round to lunch at Chequers on New Year's Day. Boris saw it as an opportunity. He seemed to think that if he could get Rishi in a more relaxed atmosphere, he could get him to willingly move on to the tax-cutting page. Truth be known, Boris was in despair over the rise in corporation tax, it didn't make a scrap of sense to him, and talking to Rishi about it in No. 10 was as close to having a conversation with a robot as you could get.

'So Rishi arrives. He brings a gift for Wilf and a piggy bank for Romy – cue the banter about him being Chancellor and all that. And the only thing I can say is that he was over-the-top nice. Like, sweet and sickly nice. He was on the floor playing with the children. This is what Rishi does, he's so clever. It's like he knows that the way to impress caring parents is to be especially nice to their children.

'And it was, like, he and Boris were getting on really well, to be fair, and you could see Boris really liked him. And Boris's sister, Rachel, has she told you about how Rishi had been so nice to their mother, Charlotte, and had pushed her wheelchair, and Boris had been really touched by that? Boris loved his mother and I can see, looking back, if you want to cast a spell on Boris, you just had to be nice to the people he loves, and it worked. Boris spent a lot of time talking about the country and Covid recovery, and Rishi spent a lot of time talking about his diet and how he fasted on Mondays, and that was all a bit weird in a fifteen-year-old-girl kind of way, but on the face of it all, he was very warm and chummy with Boris and, I don't know, looking back now it's a little bit uncomfortable. You know, the way he was sitting there, opposite the table from Boris, like he was his best friend, and it's hard to get your head around it when you think of the mix of family, politics, loyalties and ambition, and all the time, he was just playing Boris. He's spoken so much about honesty and integrity in politics, and there he was, agreeing with Boris on the big political ideas. Giving the impression that he was one of Boris's best buddies, that they would achieve great things for the country together. There was a palpable excitement in the air, as Boris, you could see, was trying to use the lunch to develop that team ethos.

'Rishi never challenged anything; he didn't disagree, although he did refuse to engage on the conversation around corporation tax, which I knew was disappointing for Boris. Despite that, I think he was definitely trying to give the impression that he had Boris's back and was there for him and was up for … you know, they were going to build a better country together. At no time did he say, "Well, actually, I don't agree. I don't think you are the right person to lead the country." There was no hint of that. He sat there as though he was a brother to Boris as he broke bread with him around his table, laughed with him. You'd have thought he was very fond of Boris and they were close.'

Nine days earlier, he had registered the Ready for Rishi campaign website.

BORIS: THE SEQUEL?

My first interview with Boris was on the day the Queen died, and today, the morning after the Coronation, it is my last. The Coronation has kept the disastrous local election results out of the media, but there is definitely a hint of discontent in the air. Sue Gray area is no longer, as her nickname suggests, but has left the civil service and her application to become Starmer's Chief of Staff is being considered by the appointments committee. Her son is a Labour activist and has been seen out canvassing with Starmer. Gray has refused to cooperate with a Cabinet Office inquiry. She said that she is unhappy with the process and didn't think she had been given enough assurances as to how evidence would be treated, obviously referring to concerns regarding leaks and guarantees of confidentiality. Which some might say is a bit rich given that she was the author of the Partygate report and once head of ethics and propriety, but given that Simon Case is the Cabinet Secretary, I can see where her concerns may lie. She also knows the ropes, and if anyone knows how to avoid being stitched up, it will be Sue Gray.

My phone has been buzzing. Some of those who were the most active foot-soldiers among MPs in removing Boris are sat in the most plum seats in the Abbey for the Coronation service, which, given that some reports say that Queen Camilla only had twenty family members and friends in attendance, jars somewhat. I am told that the pressure from No. 10 on Buckingham Palace to release more seats for MPs was intense. I would use the word corrupt. The sight of Steve Baker sat in a prime seat raised many eyebrows. The former cheerleader for the Brexiteers, who had been out on the television championing the Windsor Framework agreement,* who has publicly declared that he has spent his entire parliamentary career plotting to remove prime ministers, led some to comment at the Coronation that he hadn't backed the agreement at all, he had just done so as part of a deal with No. 10 in exchange for a plum seat at the Coronation. I'm guessing he bartered for far more than that as a reward, but only time will tell. Sadly, this sort of talk among MPs has become the order of the day and is no longer surprising. Pieces of silver are being hawked around the MPs' tearoom daily.

There are many whispers around the privileges committee hearings and the investigation into Boris Johnson, and there is a fear that the rule of law in both the party and Westminster appears to be breaking down. If this is true, what comes next?

We met at 9 a.m. on Sunday morning at the Cotswolds house that was in the process of being cleared, its contents packed up, ready for the house move. He greeted me at the gate dressed in a navy T-shirt and in a Sunday-morning state of disarray, as I pulled up at the front of the house, and he told me I was late, which made me laugh, as I was, by ten minutes.

'I've not shaved,' he said, as he hugged me.

'That's okay, neither have I,' I replied.

'Douwe Egberts, Nads?' he asked as we moved into the now familiar kitchen, which, like the rest of the house, was half

---

* The Windsor Framework: a post-Brexit legal agreement between the UK and the EU, announced in 2023.

cleared. He boiled the kettle, I took down the mugs from a shelf over the worktop, we both measured out our own coffee, and I poured in the milk.

'Golly, milk first?' he said, surprised.

'Milk first in coffee, last in tea,' I said as we carried our drinks through into the sitting room.

'Carrie waited, but she's taken the children for a walk to the farm so we can talk in peace,' he said, and I noted to myself how different he was now, how happy and relaxed he was compared to the first time I had spoken to him when I embarked on this project.

We settled down on a sofa in front of the beautiful Georgian French doors that looked out onto a valley of lush green grass and a field of cows grazing in the distance.

'What did you think of the local election results?' I asked him as, taking in the view, we both chatted about his children, my granddaughter and life in general.

'What a nightmare,' he exclaimed. 'You know, it's just so sad, it makes me so desperately sad. Look, in Sunderland and all these areas where we were kind of taking off and going in one direction, we are now going backwards, even in Darlington where we actually have an incredible story to tell with all the investment and all the changes which have happened.'

'Don't you think Rishi should have been up there banging the drum?' I asked him. 'Where was he?'

Rishi was nowhere. He visited one constituency that bordered his own constituency of Richmond, but he hadn't actually travelled very far from his country home to do that.

Boris was correct about Darlington. It was a part of the country that Labour had taken for granted for so long, assuming working-class voters would always vote Labour, and we had turned that around, and investment that created jobs had been pumped into the area. Boris had thrown his weight behind Darlington; now he was gone, the voters had deserted us.

'The thing they have wanted to do is develop a narrative which hangs Rishi's failure at the local elections around you and Liz,' I said, 'which is the most preposterous strategy. I mean, really, eight months later, to say it's all your fault when Rishi didn't even go out and campaign?'

'Are they?' He sounds surprised. 'Is that really what they are saying?'

The narrative is flying around, repeated to me at the coronation a number of times. Team Rishi damage-limitation whispers were in full flow. The spin and the narrative out of the door before the final results had even landed.

We talked through my book for a while and he commented, 'I heard that Cummings has said he started to plot to get rid of me in January 2020.'

'From what I've been told, I don't think that's true,' I said. 'It was long before that.'

'I know, I can see it now. The plot was always to get Rishi in. I just couldn't see it at the time. It's like this Manchurian candidate, their stooge.'

I looked quizzical.

'You remember, the film …' He laughed. I tried to look as though I knew what he was talking about.

We both laughed. I didn't actually know what I was laughing at. He was in a very happy frame of mind.

I told him that they had all been working together and, for the first time, he really looked like he gets it.

'I've been right about Gove all along you know,' I said. 'There's just too much of it all that points to him.'

I told him about press office parties, the things which had taken place. The impropriety and accusations which I cannot bring myself to include in the book because isn't there enough to disappoint? I showed him my phone and a series of WhatsApp threads I had received about Lee Cain.

'Did you know about that? Did you have any idea what was going on in the press office on Friday nights?' I asked him.

He shook his head and rubbed his chin, pushing himself into the back of the chair.

One of the messages referred to an incident after lockdowns were over, and Boris coming down very, very early one morning from the flat in No.10 and finding Lee Cain so out of it in a chair, he could barely move. I was told Boris went back up to the flat for something he had forgotten and got into the lift, and Cain staggered into the lift after him and started lunging at him and manhandling him in a possessive way, and that he was absolutely blotto.

'Were you suspicious then?' I asked him.

'It was the first time I had seen anything like that. I thought it was a one-off and I never saw anything remotely like it again. I thought he was troubled, maybe something personal.'

I turned to face Boris on the sofa and shared with him some of the information I had been given. Much of what I know will never see the light of day due to the 'legals'.

'I think the party has got to the fifth labour of Hercules part of its history,' I say. 'Clearing up, it's not going to be easy.'

A spark flickered in his eye. He always came back to the question he posed to me – 'But why?' – and he did it now.

'But, why, why, why would they do this? We were running the country. Why? Was it just to show that they were in charge? That they could get me out?'

'Dougie told you on that phone call, didn't he? If you don't resign, we will remove you, and they did. If that isn't power, having the ability to engineer events and manipulate circumstances in order to achieve their goal and decide who is the prime minister of our great nation, what is? What is the point of anyone ever voting Conservative again? It's a sham. The people who went out and voted for you in 2019 were actually voting for Smith, Gove, Cummings, Cain ...' I counted them off on my fingers.

'But why? We had just won a huge eighty-seat majority?'

'Because they are addicts? Addicted to this particular game, one of power and control and intrigue. It's what turns them on. As to why Rishi, son-in-law of a billionaire, in particular, well, that is a much bigger question.

'They have been in control before and they are again, truly in control with Rishi in No. 10. They know how the machine works. When a Dougie-supporting member of staff left No. 10 at the same time as Munira, she was put onto the payroll of one of Rishi's close billionaire friends, along with Munira. They are using Rishi's political ignorance to run rings around him. They are only being exposed now because they couldn't control you, they went too far with you, they got carried away, and they are probably kicking themselves right now because they may suspect that they are about to be blown up.'

I could see him mulling something over and so I stopped talking and waited for him to speak.

'Do you remember that funny business? It was at the start of the 2019 party conference. My first one as PM, when we were riding high and pulling away from Corbyn in the polls, and then this very weird story appeared?'

I did. 'It was from Robert Peston's partner, Charlotte Edwardes. That you had groped her at some lunch and had simultaneously groped her female neighbour on your other side.'

'It was totally untrue,' he said.

326

'Boris, I know.'

I have commented that he has loved well and not always wisely, and it is true, but he's not a groper. He's not that man, the underhand, bullying type; that's just not him.

I remembered him being just sort of totally flabbergasted by this, and it did blow up his first conference as Prime Minister in his own right and almost ruined it.

'I thought, *Why? Why is this happening? Why would they say that? It is so untrue. Why make it up and why are they saying it now, at the start of the conference?*'

'But, you know, the same thing happened to IDS, the same trick was pulled on him on the eve of the 2002 conference when he was leader,' I said. 'Robbie Gibb was going to run some appallingly untrue *Newsnight* story about Iain misappropriating funds; he had to take out an injunction to prevent it. He only found out just in the nick of time. That was twenty years ago, the same people playing the same game.'

He shook his head as though still in disbelief.

The groping story about Boris came out on the eve of the party conference. The story ran for the first twenty-four hours, and it was toxic and threatening to derail everything. It became a sort of a 'me too' moment; the narrative they had so expertly managed to get out there. He's untrustworthy, he gropes women, it was all just so tacky. He came out and issued a very flat statement calling it out as wrong, because it was. Looking back, it's clear, I think, what they were doing was because we were building up such a head of steam, it being our first conference before an election where we still won a stonking majority, the biggest for forty years, such a long time, the story was engineered to take the air out of his tyres, to deflate him a little; it's possible, because they could. But then it got out of control and Cummings panicked and went into reverse.

This was reminiscent of how Partygate became a story. It was first leaked to the media by Cummings, who was not fully aware that most of the parties and the appalling behaviour were happening in the press office on Friday nights. That was a story that became out of control and he couldn't rein it in. However, even to this day, utilising their network, those people were and are still protected.

The second woman in the groping story came out and denied being the second woman, which is what all the rumours were saying. She said it wasn't true and so the story was killed stone dead.

Left with only one source, the second source having discredited the first, the media could not legitimately continue to run the story. It was a vicious and manipulative attempt both to damage Boris and to derail our party conference.

The hand of Cummings was all over it.

Cummings manufactured mischief but then he could never hold the tiger by the tail. That applied whether he was leaking stories about parties or about fictitious groping.

The other problem Boris had was the huge number of people he had to battle; it wasn't just Cummings. It was like so many parts of the media actively wanted him dead.

I said to Boris, 'You know, someone close to you was sat next to Roula Khalaf, the editor of the *Financial Times* at a dinner, and she didn't know that the person she was sitting next to was a close friend of yours, and he asked her, "So what are you up to? What's your mission in life?" And she replied, "My mission in life is to bring down Boris Johnson." So, you know, the hostile crap, the constant stream of negative briefings from Remainers, constant from the Remainers. They were never going to forgive you for Brexit; they were never going to back down. You were really up against it.'

He wasn't fazed or surprised.

'You know, Nads, when we started this, I was very much focused on all the things we had done and achieved, and I was proud of them and remain very proud. I think we did a lot at huge speed and we have a lot to be thankful for that we got done. But the greater the gap, the more time passes, the more I worry. You know we just aren't doing enough to fix our energy supply problems, we aren't doing enough to build nuclear reactors. HS2 has become a total joke. Levelling up has been all but forgotten. What's happening to gigabit broadband? I don't hear and don't know what's happening to all the infrastructure stuff. We hear nothing on skills. The whole social care reform has been junked and so much work went into that. Leave Brexit to one side, there was a massive agenda we had as a government to transform the country, and it doesn't seem to be happening in any form of articulated way. I'm particularly concerned that there's no grand economic strategy for growth. Why? Where is the vision for the country?

'If you can have a post-Brexit Britain, why the hell are we putting up corporation tax in this way? Why not cut corporation tax to 10 per cent? You know, why don't we just do what the Irish do? Why not just outbid the Irish? We don't have to obey international norms on corporation tax. It's absolutely mad. And the UK, look at what the head of Revolut said. People are starting to mark the UK down as the tech capital of Europe and yes, we still are, but it is in the balance now. And I think the whole thing needs a massive kick in the pants; I think it's all drifting. I really, really think that unless we grip it, the results of the local elections will be repeated at a General Election, and Starmer will be a complete disaster. How can we? You know, I feel a massive, massive sense of frustration that we had an eighty-seat majority. We had a fantastic agenda. We could have kept the whole thing going if these people had not prevailed upon Rishi to do something that was not fundamentally in his interest or in the best interest of the country.'

'I don't think he's happy doing what he's doing, do you?' I asked him.

'He doesn't strike me as a prime minister who absolutely loves his job and who gets out of bed every day with a song on his lips ... Does he come across like that to you?'

It's a pertinent question as reports seep out of No. 10 that Rishi is frequently bad-tempered and tetchy, demanding to know why it has all gone wrong. That pearly white smile, too rigid to be real, too ready too often and too unnatural.

Mentioning a song on the lips, Boris diverts to the Coronation.

'By the way, didn't you think that anthem was fantastic yesterday?'

He bursts into song, '*Oh make a joyful noise, Oh make a joyful noise, de de de dum, Oh, make a joyful noise* ... It was great, wasn't it? That guy, Lloyd Webber, he can really knock out a tune. The nicest piece of music. I didn't like the one they played at the end, which was at the '53 Coronation. Too discordant. It was a great day. Anyway, you ask where I am. I'm frustrated. I'm seething. I'm a caged beast. I'm a coiled mamba. I'm a ... you know ... I just can't see. We're drifting; we are losing the plot.'

He made me laugh as I knew he was joking. I had been told that Rishi was avoiding him: wouldn't speak to him, not picking up his calls and it had been a wall of silence from No. 10.

'Is that true?' I asked him.

He sat up. 'It is and it's extraordinary because there are things we need to discuss.'

This is spectacularly rude and unprecedented as far as I am aware. There is an unspoken protocol that holders of office have always spoken to their predecessors. A respect that one prime minister will always show to another. It is, after all, the smallest club.

I mentioned this point and, as always, the almost-too-forgiving side of Boris reared its head.

'I understand his point. He's thinking that the public maybe had too much of me and my vision and the great things we wanted to achieve, and he thinks the public are fed up with that and they want something different. But you've got to have a positive agenda for change in the country. You know, people still feel hacked off. They voted for change in 2019 and they are drifting back to Labour in those Brexit seats because they're not seeing a changed government. Nothing to rally behind, nothing; we are just drifting into defeat.'

I'm puzzled by the wall of silence from No. 10. I've learnt enough to know, they are up to something. His resignation honours list has been submitted. There will be a reason behind why they won't talk to him.

Carrie and the children returned from their walk, and Wilf ran into the room and launched himself into his father's arms. I felt a surge of affection towards Carrie as I got to my feet and we embraced. Always there, by his side, never wavering through the worst of days that would have sent most women running for the door. Always his rock.

I bought a present, an outdoor game for Wilf's birthday, and Boris and I take Wilf into the garden to assemble it. Carrie takes Romy to the bedroom for her nap and we begin to play.

'What's the game called, Daddy?' Wilf shouts.

'Give a toss,' Boris replies as he competes with his son to launch beanbags into the right holes, and laughter fills the air.

As we hugged our goodbyes I said to him, 'You know the question I am asked every single day is, will he ever be back? We are nearer twenty-four points behind now, heading for a cata-strophic defeat.'

He shakes his head; he's resolute.

He knows, the party, the MPs, they would rather risk losing under Rishi, because to take him back would mean admitting they were wrong to have removed him, and they will never do that.

I head off to meet my family for lunch in a pub nearby. Boris and Carrie are about to entertain a visiting member of an over-seas royal family who was here for the Coronation.

As I pull away, I see a happy man in the rear-view mirror, loading up a Toyota truck with boxes to transport to his new home and his new life.

At the end of the drive I looked up the meaning of Manchurian candidate: *'a person, especially a politician, being used as a puppet by an enemy power'*. I slip the car into gear as I remember his words from one of the many conversations we had, one sentence that comes back to haunt me over and over.

'I rather naively thought that in this country power flowed from the people into Westminster when electing a prime minis-ter.'

It seems we were all wrong.

AFTERWORD

COTSWOLDS, 20 SEPTEMBER 2023

Conservative ideals of freedom, equality of opportunity, small state, big people, aspiration and home ownership are my political core. I have been a member of the Conservative family for more than thirty years and like all families, it is preferable if more embarrassing issues are kept private. Writing this book has been a difficult process. There is much I have learnt which I have not wanted to include and some have warned me not to.

This story has been recounted to me by so many, so often, almost all of whom were too afraid to speak out publicly that I hope it can at least be understood that I felt I had no choice but to write this. Given the gravity of the revelations, I have had to anonymise some of my sources at their own request or through legal advice, in order that their voices can be heard in full. They do need to be heard, just as I felt compelled to speak out.

What is true is that many of the predictions made during the year-long course of writing this book, have come to pass.

It was a minute-long segment of an interview by Laura Kuenssberg of Dominic Cummings – and the comments he made on a BBC News Special on 20 July 2021 which went astonishingly unchallenged and unremarked – that shine the brightest light into the darkness of the events the book describes (the italics are mine):

LK: But, you've just said that within months of the Prime Minister winning the biggest Conservative majority in decades, you and a *few* others from the Vote Leave campaign were discussing the possibility of getting rid of him (Boris Johnson).

DC: Days, not months.

LK: [Incredulous] Within days not months, you were discussing getting rid of him.

DC: Yes ... *We* only got him in there because *we* had to sort a certain problem, not because *we* thought he should be Prime Minister ...

ACKNOWLEDGEMENTS

First and foremost has to be my agent, Piers Blofeld, who has been by my side every step of the way, and for almost a year the only person I could trust and talk to and discuss a story which unravelled as each interview took place. I could not have written this book without his unwavering support, encouragement and his always clear, solid and sometimes inspired advice. He guided this book through the legal challenges, which were many, and finally brought it over the line. It has been pure teamwork.

Boris, for his willingness to contribute. When we discussed this in the rose garden at Chequers, I told him I could only do it if his voice was a golden thread throughout. He obliged and I hope that as a result of reading this book, people may see the side of Boris those who love him know: a kind, loyal, visionary man. It is a travesty that he was removed, but maybe social media, which has brought into Westminster the first generation of MPs addicted to likes on Twitter and Facebook and the dopamine hits they bring, has altered the political landscape, forever.

HarperCollins, for taking this project on. The book turned out to be nothing like any of us expected at the beginning. Thanks to Adam, Ajda, Charlie, Arthur, the barristers and everyone who worked so hard to make it happen.

To everyone who trusted me. I could never thank you enough and you all know who you are.

To my family, as always, but mostly to my late husband, Paul. Over the long years we knew each other from our early days in Liverpool, your deep understanding of how politics did and should work, your keen sense of injustice, your passion for democracy, your buying me a book on our unwritten constitution by Ferdinand Mount when I first became an MP so that I would understand the principles of democracy and their importance – it was all there with me throughout and I could almost feel you in the room with me as I wrote. As with anything worthwhile I will ever do or write in my future, this is for you.